Choir
Gareth Malone

Also by Gareth Malone:

Music for the People

Choir
Gareth Malone

Collins

First published in 2012 by Collins

HarperCollins*Publishers*
77–85 Fulham Palace Road
London W6 8JB

www.harpercollins.co.uk

1 3 5 7 9 10 8 6 4 2

A catalogue record for this book is
available from the British Library

ISBN: 978-0-00-748800-1 (hardback)
ISBN: 978-0-00-748801-8 (paperback)
ISBN: 978-0-00-748802-5 (ebook)

Printed and bound in Great Britain by
Clays Ltd, St Ives plc.

MIX
Paper from
responsible sources
FSC www.fsc.org **FSC C007454**

FSC™ is a non-profit international organisation established to promote
the responsible management of the world's forests. Products carrying the
FSC label are independently certified to assure consumers that they come
from forests that are managed to meet the social, economic and
ecological needs of present and future generations,
and other controlled sources.

Find out more about HarperCollins and the environment at
www.harpercollins.co.uk/green

For my grandmother Patricia –
wherever you are

Contents

Acknowledgements

First and foremost, thank you to everybody who has let me into their lives and offered their voices for what has been an incredible experience for me.

TV is a collaborative art form and I've worked with some of this country's very best. I'd like to thank the many people who have helped make *The Choir* over the past seven years. Just in case you thought I did it on my own, out in the field were:

The Choir series 1: Ludo Graham, Annabel Borthwick, Sam Grace, Dave Wickham, Richard Farish and Katie Nicholson.

The Choir series 2: Claire Whalley, Harry Beney, Rob McCabe, Vicky Mitchell, Sarah Keenan, Ben Richards and Neil Kent.

The Choir series 3: Dollan Cannell, Vicky Mitchell, Freddie Foss Smith, Howard Mills and Dave Harcombe.

Gareth Goes to Glyndebourne crew: Cesca Eaton, Nina Lowes (and Harry Beney again!).

From the Glyndebourne team: Katie Tearle MBE, David Pickard, Gus Christie, Nick Collon, John Fulljames, Graham Ross, Karen Gillingham, Julian Philips, Nicky Singer and Sarah Cant.

The Choir: Military Wives team: Stephen Finnigan, Vikki Rogers, Peter Lown.

Sing While You Work: Colm Martin, Stuart Froude, Leah Caffrey, Pete Cooksley, Charlotte Bridger, Steve Jones, Sophie Mohamed, Charlotte Sinden, Morgana Pugh, Paul 'Titanium' Taylor, Callum Howell and Zach Newby.

A huge team of pianists: Vicky Savage, Liz Burley, Elspeth Wyllie, Michael Higgins, Anna Tilbrook, Elfyn Jones and many more.

Back at the Twenty Twenty offices: Kirsty Adams, Caroline Patton, Holly Johnson, Claire Sweeney, Sophie James, Katy Mclachlan, Zoe Valmas, Morgana Pugh, Katen Paxton and Helen Alsop.

The executive team: Tim Carter, Ana DeMoraes, Lucy Hillman, Jamie Isaacs, Sam Whittaker, Alannah Richardson, Kate Humphreys, Hana Canter, Helen Soden and Julian Alexander.

At the BBC: Roly Keating, Charlotte Moore, Emma Willis, Ben Gale, Jan Younghusband, Janice Hadlow, Richard Klein, Emma Fox and Adam Barker.

A veritable army of editors: Drew Hill (*The Choir* series 1 and update, series 2 and update), John McNamee (*The Choir* series 2 and update), Richard Guard (*The Choir* series 3 and 4), Tim Bridges (*The Choir* series 3 and 4 update), Frank Burgess (*Gareth Goes to Glyndebourne*), Martin Cooper (*Gareth Goes to Glyndebourne*), Derek Wilson (*The Choir* series 4 and *Sing While You Work*), Paddy Lynas (*The Choir* series 4), Finlay Milne (*Sing While You Work*), Dermot O'Brien (*Sing While You Work*), Brad Manning (*Sing While You Work*) and Wesley Thomas (*Sing While You Work*).

In post production: Dan Jones, who has been dubbing mixer across all the series, and Pete Neil, who has put the finishing touches to the programmes before broadcast.

The indefatigable Sam Mathewson, who has been sound supervisor on all of the projects mentioned above and has arms of steel.

Those who have helped me with the running of the choirs: Chris Modi, Paul Craven, Helen Collins, Simon Lubkowski, Pam Wise, Christine Wyard, Russ Clancy, Terry Petit and everybody on the SOC Committee and at Ascend South Oxhey, and Simon Wookie.

The music team who helped mould the choirs on *Sing While You Work:* Dan Ludford-Thomas and Peter Mitchell (London), David Ogden and Paul Woolley (Bristol), Lucy Griffiths and Rob Challenor (Midlands) and Ian Chesworth and Ben Smith (Manchester).

Special thanks to those involved with the *The Choir: Military Wives* series: The Chivenor Military Wives Choir, The Plymouth Military Wives Choir, Nicky Clarke, Caroline Jopp, Lieutenant Colonel Leigh Tingey and Kerry Tingey, Commando Logistics Regiment and 24 Commando at Chivenor, 42 and 29 Commando in Plymouth and many others who made it all possible; Paul Mealor, Jon Cohen, Chris Evans, Gratian Dimech, James Heath, Athol Hendry and everyone at SSAFA, Russell Thompson, Sue Freeth and the team at the Royal British Legion, Tim Marshall, Gary Barlow OBE, Lord Andrew Lloyd Webber and Eliot Kennedy.

At Decca records: Dickon Stainer, Tom Lewis, Louise Ringrose, Molly Ladbrook-Hutt, Gavin Bayliss and Rebecca Allen.

At Curtis Brown: Jacquie Drewe, Gordon Wise, Hannah Clarke and Fran Linke.

At HarperCollins: Hannah MacDonald, Craig Adams, Laura 'Book Lady' Lees née Summers and their talented team.

Special thanks to Philip Dodd for invaluable assistance with this book and for helping me to make sense of a morass of memories.

My assistants Gill Allis and Nina Swann.

My parents, for listening to all the woes of the various productions late at night on the phone from the back of a taxi.

My wife Becky, who has approved every song choice, every idea, every outfit, every haircut, everything. She is the under-sung *sine qua non* of the entire operation. Thank you.

Just as the Sun Was Rising

January 2012. Heathrow Airport

Ping. It's my phone. My mother is texting: 'Get a copy of the *Mail*'. I'm about to board a flight to America to shoot a pilot for USA Network, which is strange enough, really. But what I read in a free copy of the *Daily Mail* while I'm waiting by the gate at Terminal 5 makes me aware of just how far I have come since my days selling ice cream on Bournemouth beach.

It's now the New Year. The Military Wives have their victory – their single was Christmas Number One – and I'm busy jotting down ideas for an album on the back of my boarding pass. The whole extraordinary news furore that surrounded the release of 'Wherever You Are' has gone as cold as the weather outside and yet out of the blue one man breathes life back into the story.

In black and white, one of the most famous men in the world is quoted describing me (a tweedy choirmaster with a penchant for the music of Schubert and a love of country rambles) as follows: 'He is like a stealth missile, he has sort of crept up on everyone. He would be good for us. I wasn't furious about the Army Wives single beating us, I had two copies of it on pre-order.' This is Simon Cowell speaking, no less, and I realise that my life has been irrevocably changed.

••••

Mr Cowell was not the first Simon to change my life.

In November 2005 I had a party for my thirtieth birthday. Having moved to London four years earlier – like everyone else, trying to make it in the big city – I had got together with Becky, who is now my wife, and it was a chance for us both to celebrate with all of our friends.

I felt good that night: not only did I actually have the £200 I needed to put behind the bar (a revolutionary moment after living a student's life for two years), but when people asked me, 'What are you doing next?' I was able to say, 'Oh, I'm making a series for BBC Two.' It was an exhilarating time. In fact, the very first day of filming on the first series of The Choir was on my actual birthday: 9 November 2005. Now that's how to turn thirty.

A few months earlier, I had just finished a massive London Symphony Orchestra project assisting American conductor Marin Alsop with the chorus on a project she was doing with the London Symphony Orchestra. This job had been a significant step-up for me as only weeks before I'd finished studying. Sat there in our slightly shabby West Hampstead box-cum-flat on my first morning off, I dithered over my next move while drinking a third cup of viciously strong coffee. I was exhausted, so I'd decided to relax, take the Monday really easy and have a lazy duvet day where I could sit and watch *This Morning* and not think about classical music at all.

But first I elected to have a long shower. Returning to my desk an hour later I found a message on my mobile from Simon Wales, a colleague of mine at LSO St Luke's, the London Symphony Orchestra's education centre.

The message was short and to the point. 'We've had a call from someone from a TV company called Twenty Twenty. Would you be interested in being on a television programme?' Forget the duvet day; I was intrigued and spurred into action.

The first thing I did was go to the Twenty Twenty website and check out the programmes that they had already produced. What caught my eye was that they had made *Brat Camp*. A couple of years earlier I had been quite ill one Christmas so I had been lying in bed watching television when the 'Where Are They Now?' update version of the show came on. The one-hour special revisited the whole journey and interviewed the kids who had participated in it (and their parents), allowing them to reflect on the impact the experience had made on their lives. I don't mind admitting that it reduced me to floods of tears (a running theme in this book).

Years later I worked with the directors of that original series of *Brat Camp* and discovered that they had filmed the programme the hard way: that they'd lived in the Arizona desert and stayed with those kids for months and months to capture the amazing transformation in their lives.

As a rule I didn't take anybody to the desert for therapy sessions, but I had been working in music education, which I'd found to be powerfully life-changing for many people. I imagined that something with a similar structure to *Brat Camp* could be done with music education. This was how I approached the project, thinking I could do the job I had been doing all over London to bring music into different schools and communities. I've always been zealous in wanting to encourage others to make music.

Music is part of my life: I have always sung. I remember my mother singing proper lullabies to me at bedtime. The sound of her voice was a very soothing presence when I was a young child. She would often sing an English folk song called 'Early One Morning', or 'I Knew an Old Woman Who Swallowed a Fly'; simple songs for us adults but so absorbing when you are a child. I would join in on songs like 'Incy Wincy Spider', and become very involved in the story, visualising the spider clambering up the drainpipe. It's lovely to sing these songs to my own daughter, rather like passing on the baton.

Even now whenever I hear the music and the words: 'Early one morning, just as the sun was rising, I heard a young maid sing in the valley below', I can see a house, a house that isn't actually mentioned in the lyric, and a garden I invented for the maid to be singing in. Songs, and music generally, have always been very visual for me. I find music massively stimulating: I am sure that if you took a scan of my brain when I am conducting, singing or playing there would be a large amount of blood flowing towards my visual cortex. This is why I hate pubs and restaurants with background music. I can't type, talk or concentrate when there is music on because I become absorbed in the sound.

Nowadays I start to see the way that a person is breathing or a violinist is bowing, but as a child it was much more about images and feelings. So those early songs were very powerful influences on me. I think that folk songs form the basis of your knowledge of harmony and your sense of what singing is for; ultimately, for me, it's about communicating emotion

There was also one very particular moment when I was six or seven. I heard a Christmas carol which I remembered from the year before, and I felt a warm glow of recognition I had not experienced before. With hindsight I can see how powerful that was.

This was the beginning of an on-going connection with music, from stress-inducing competitions and piano exams to the excitement of duet lessons with a fellow pupil called Helen (with whom I was deeply in love when I was nine).

At ten years old I had my first taste of professional music-making. My school music teacher, David Naylor, came into the school orchestra rehearsal full of excitement to tell us that Andrew Lloyd Webber was seeking children to be part of the touring production of *Evita*. I was determined to get into the show. Andrew Lloyd Webber was sending someone to *our school* to run the auditions.

Michael Stuckey was the man he sent to find some stage-ready kids. Michael was to have the biggest influence on my life of anyone I ever met. He dazzled me with a combination of keyboard mastery and an easy manner with young people. He did not patronise me; he expected the very best. I met him for all of 20 minutes but they were 20 minutes I have never forgotten. I got into the choir and was sent a cassette with Michael's voice teaching me the part. I had it on loop for a month. And I can still sing every note: 'Please gentle Eva, will you bless a little child?

For I love you ...'. I fell in love with the stage during 16 wonderful performances of what I consider to be a very fine musical. Should the call come, I'm ready to play any of the parts. From memory. (Just in case you're reading this, Andrew.)

Years passed, and when I came to work with young people I realised that I wanted to do it just like Michael Stuckey. I wanted to change people's lives in the same way he had changed mine. I sought him out in 1999 through a new and exciting website called Google, and was sorry to hear that he had died unexpectedly years before. No doubt he's whipped the celestial children's choir into shape by now.

After that pivotal experience I began performing whenever and wherever possible. If there was a musical opportunity I was there: singing Christmas carol concerts, playing in the orchestra, learning percussion, piano lessons, doing music theory. At home I made up songs based around what was happening in my life. I wrote my first publicly performed piece of music (which, now that I think of it, was heavily derivative of the ITV *Miss Marple* music) for a school play in the first year of secondary school.

In my teens I started several rock/pop combos, the first of which was called Silence Is Purple. A later band was Little Nicola; we played a few gigs around the Bournemouth area in which I screeched my way with far too much vocal effort through some self-penned songs influenced by the Beatles, Led Zeppelin and Pink Floyd – all very retro. Choirs. Orchestras. Jazz bands. It didn't matter what the music was, I wanted to be involved.

All of this experience gave me a conviction that I could use music as a tool for self-discovery and that I could get any young person interested, given the right chance. A TV programme could be just that opportunity.

I arranged to meet up with Ana DeMoraes, now the head of development at Twenty Twenty, but then a more lowly member of the development department. It was Ana who had had the original idea to do something with choirs. Ana is a fascinating and unusual product of Brazilian and Japanese parentage, but since she has lived in the UK for over ten years she is also a passionate Anglophile. She is quiet and thoughtful, with an impeccable sense of what is fashionable in footwear. She's also the most creative person I've ever met.

I later found out how Ana had tracked me down. At that time if you Googled the words 'community choir', mine was the first name to come up, because there was a brief CV and a photo of me on the London Symphony Orchestra's website and the LSO had a high Google rating. Ana had looked at that and thought, 'Oh, he might be half-presentable.' There was a short clip of me singing a song with some kids and talking about what I was doing with the community choir, so Ana realised that I could string a couple of sentences together. Simultaneously she had contacted the LSO and asked them for some recommendations, and they'd said, 'Oh yes, we've got the perfect person, Gareth Malone,' so – thank you, LSO – they had put her straight on to me.

Ana's voice is chirpy and she delivers her body blows in a silk glove. Her first audacious idea sounded almost impossible: 'Could you go into a community and get it singing? In about nine weeks?' 'I could,' I said, 'but, to be honest, to make it a *real* and lasting project, you would need an enormous amount of time because it is very difficult to get a whole community onside.'

I had first-hand experience of this because I had been doing precisely that for the London Symphony Orchestra, working with local people just north of the Barbican. It is a very mixed area, with a strong Turkish enclave and a white working-class community, but there are also plenty of affluent people who live in the Barbican flats.

For a couple of years I had been trying to create a community choir by bringing all the different groups in the neighbourhood together: there was a little old lady who lived over the road from the church, one guy from down at the Barbican Centre and some kids from the local school. At that stage I had about 35 singers in the choir, but I was finding it really hard to get a sense of the choir as representing that whole community. Ana DeMoraes was suggesting repeating the experience in a matter of weeks. It *was* impossible.

I hastily warned Ana off that particular idea for the time being (although it would re-emerge three years later as *Unsung Town*), and suggested that we should try to create a choir in a school instead. I had also done a lot of work in schools and knew that the experience would be much more contained and controllable. It would give me the opportunity to work with a small group every single week, which is far more manageable.

Ana was intrigued and came down to one of the children's choir rehearsals at St Luke's, a beautiful Hawksmoor church where the LSO has been based since 2003. She says that the first thing she thought when she met me was, 'He looks like one of the kids!' But although in her eyes I looked so young: 'The minute the rehearsal started, you were in control. I could tell the kids absolutely adored you. They wanted to please you. It reminded me of what I was like with my favourite teachers at school. And that had to be a good thing.' She also thought that the warm-up exercises I started the rehearsal with 'would make good telly'.

Apparently happy with what she had seen, Ana went away to do some more work on the concept. At that point the idea for the series was one of a social experiment. What would happen if we sent a genteel choirmaster into the lions' den of a secondary school? Would he be ripped apart? Would it be gladiatorial? Would there be blood? I'm sure that someone at the BBC relished the prospect of a few chunks being taken out of me. Ana certainly saw some potential. 'It seemed like the perfect combination: a posh, baby-faced choirmaster who nobody would think could win a bunch of rough kids over, with the passion and the skills to actually do it.'

So it was that, armed with a little Sony PD150 camera, a girl called Dee from Twenty Twenty who knew how to focus the thing came over to St Luke's and did some filming of a rehearsal of my children's choir. I gave it my all. Things went quiet again for a while. I had an agonising wait for any news about the series over that summer. Even though I was thrilled by the prospect, I didn't want to alert too many people by telling them that I had been approached to be in the series, just in case it all came to nothing.

Life went on. I graduated from my post-graduate course in vocal studies at the Royal Academy of Music in June. Afterwards, at lunch with my parents in Getti's Italian restaurant on Marylebone High Street, with me wearing all my finery and clutching my certificate from the Academy, I told them: 'Oh, I've had a phone call about this possible television project, but it probably won't amount to anything because I don't think they've got a broadcaster involved. It is all very early days.'

To my parents it didn't seem that improbable that the TV job might happen. They had become used to the idea of me working, not just for the LSO but also with English National Opera, Glyndebourne and the Royal Opera House on various education projects. However, I had begun other projects that had then fallen through, so in a very British way we were all quite reserved about the idea. But secretly I was really bloody excited.

It was important to me that my parents knew, because they had always been supportive of my musical ventures. My mother was, and is, a very good singer, who had studied as a child. She has a very pretty soprano voice, and loves opera. In fact, she had first met my father at the Gilbert & Sullivan Society in Tooting.

My father is also very musical, with wide-ranging tastes. His is a completely amateur enthusiasm, but he knows a huge amount about music, has an encyclopaedic memory for the Great American Songbook or anything twentieth-century, and rock and pop music up to circa 1972.

My maternal grandmother came from Mountain Ash in the valleys of South Wales, hence me being called Gareth. My grandfather was part of a theatrical family full of musical comedians, actors and actresses, so there was a huge amount of performance on my mother's side of the family. I definitely think the humour and the clowning I often resort to comes directly from this – there is music and performance in my veins.

Over that summer of 2005 nothing much happened. I think it was heading towards the end of September when I got a call from Twenty Twenty, who had been busy pulling the series pitch together. At the end of an insane afternoon's session for English National Opera, in a children's centre working with about fifty toddlers, I was just leaving when my phone rang. It was Ana. She very simply said, 'Yeah, we've got it, it's been commissioned.' I asked, 'What does that mean?' 'It means you are making a television programme.'

Click. It was one of those life-defining moments where I thought, 'This *could* change absolutely everything but then again it could change absolutely *nothing*.' At that stage I had the feeling that the series might just get put on at 11.30pm and ten of my parents' friends would watch it. I worried that it would be like so many TV programmes: utterly forgettable.

But I did consider what might happen if people liked the series. One night in our flat in West Hampstead I had a seminal conversation with Becky. It was getting late and as we got up from the sofa to go to bed, I said, 'If we say yes to this series, it could completely change our lives. We have got to consider that. What if it goes to five or six series?' That seemed like a total pipe dream at the time, but when you are signing up for something like this, you just don't know. It's like being at the top of a rollercoaster waiting for it to begin – sickening but thrilling.

My gut told me that this could be a good thing, that it would use all my skills to good effect. That gave me confidence about it. But I didn't want to dither about whether I was going to take the plunge or not. That evening Becky and I both agreed, 'Yep, we're prepared. Let's do this.' To be honest we had no idea what we were getting into. We were two students. What did we know?

What I did know was that I enjoyed talking, and that was going to come in handy if I was featuring in a television programme. I am an only child so I have never wanted for attention. As a boy I had had loads of adult company. I was always spoken to as an adult, and talked, a lot, at a very early age. I always say I could talk for England.

One way and another I was confident that I could perform on television, but I did not realise the size of the challenge that Ana had dreamt up for me: 'Do you think you could take a group of children who've never sung before and get them ready for the World Choir Games in China?' 'I don't know.' I sucked in some air. 'I'll give it a try.'

The prospect of taking a school choir to the World Choir Games in China the following summer sounded like a good focus for the whole adventure. How naïve I was. I had no idea of the difficulty involved. But for time being I put fear and dread aside, sipped the first of too many pints of London Pride and got on with my thirtieth birthday party.

If They Only Learn

My first taste of this new reality was walking into Northolt High School. Northolt had been chosen for the first series of *The Choir* because it was in an area of 'relative deprivation' as the head-master put it: that was the phrase everyone bandied about. The TV company weren't going to send me to Eton after all – they wanted a place that screamed, 'There is no choir here.' That suited me fine.

Northolt wasn't a place I knew much about, other than its location off the A40 heading west out of London and that it had a tube station somewhere along the far reaches of the Central Line. I discovered as I arrived in Northolt that it had a nice little duck pond in an almost villagey centre. And there was also this huge and forbidding school.

When I saw the buildings they immediately reminded me of the school I had been to in Bournemouth. 'Oh, it's one of those schools,' I said, on camera. I was thinking about the period of architecture, but that brief remark got me into a bit of trouble.

What I'd really meant but failed to get across was, 'It's one of those schools from that particular era of architecture, built in a hurry just after the war,' exactly like some of my school's prefab buildings. What rather a lot of people imagined I meant was, 'Oh, it's one of *those* schools,' as if I'd been educated up the road in Harrow on the Hill. Quite a few people got really upset, and I had several letters of complaint (another running theme in this book). In fact, when the programme went out, I had a text from my cousin Keith immediately after that comment was aired saying, 'You've just lost a million viewers.' A little too late I realised that everything I said might be taken out of context. There was a lot for me to learn.

Northolt had 1,300 pupils and, like all large schools, there was constant activity and noise, with kids and staff swirling around on a typical morning. Spotting me arriving, one smart alec shouted, 'It's Harry Potter!' out of the window when he should have been concentrating on maths. This led to me having the nickname among the production staff of 'Gary Potter'. Thanks very much to that young gentleman.

I suspected the BBC thought I might not survive but that it would make jolly good telly. However, I felt fairly robust going in there and not unduly daunted. I'd spent years working in places like Hackney, Lambeth and Tower Hamlets in some pretty hot situations. I knew how to handle myself – oh yes – or I thought I did. On the day I'd started with the London Symphony Orchestra in 2001 I had found myself in a classroom full of 30 decidedly sweaty teenage boys in Hackney, left alone in charge of them with just a double bass player for moral support, as the teacher seemed to have disappeared.

Now that definitely *was* intimidating. Surely Northolt would be a walk in the park?

What I didn't feel all right about was being filmed; that was much more stomach-churning. Shortly before filming I'd sat down with the director of the series, Ludo Graham, in the Black Lion pub in Kilburn for a 'getting to know you' pint. Ludo, who is married to Kate Humble from *Springwatch*, was very experienced in this kind of television. Previously he had made *Paddington Green*, a documentary series in which he had followed characters from a small corner of London for a year or so. Over some London Pride and before I had fully signed up to the project, Ludo attempted to reassure me that making a TV programme would not finish my career *if* I trusted him.

Ludo spoke a little bit about Kate's presenting career, and what he had observed about her experience of that. 'Gareth,' he told me, 'I want you just to do your job, and for me to be there filming everything. When it goes well, I want to be right there knowing straight afterwards that it went well. Equally when it is bad, I want to see you pissed off at the end of the day and irritated. I want you to tell me that and believe that I will edit it fairly. Sometimes you might go too far, you'll say something because you are emotional and tired, but you've got to trust me. It will be fair and balanced.'

His argument was that everyone lets off steam: you come home from a bad day at work and badmouth your boss to your wife, husband or whoever is around, and then you have a glass of wine and a sit-down and everything's OK again. It's part of the process of getting it out of your system. That was exactly what Ludo wanted. Ludo has a winning charm and I began to believe that it would be all right.

For a programme about music this was something of a leap of faith, because up until then in most documentaries about the arts that I had seen, everyone was on their best behaviour: 'Well, when I worked with Sir so-and-so we got on very well, lovely chap, etc.' You didn't tend to see the rawness of the preparation and the ups and downs of the journey to get there. This was a chance to show the reality of struggling through difficulties to reach the final performance.

Perhaps because I had watched *Brat Camp*, I had seen how engagingly human that emotionally frank style of TV could turn out to be, and that it was important to have those peaks and troughs. The chat with Ludo had a big influence on me: it set me up for the way I approached the making of *The Choir*, which has been very, dare I say, organic, very much about following me setting up each of the choirs, on the good days and the bad: I am doing my job, making the decisions, dealing with the challenges, all under constant scrutiny. It's been seven years now, so I have learnt to adjust to the pressure, but back in 2005 it was a very different story.

I was apprehensive about handing my life over to that degree. What made me feel a little more comfortable was that I was not handing my personal life over. This wasn't going to be like *The Osbournes*. But I was handing my professional life over. And I didn't even feel like it was the part of my professional life at which I was best. At the time I felt I was just getting good at singing. I was having lessons at a high level. That side of my life was going well, so what on earth was I doing trying to tackle a bunch of teenage kids and persuade them to start singing for me? I didn't even consider myself to be a conductor.

One plus point was that I wasn't living too far away from Northolt. Becky and I were renting a flat just off West End Lane in West Hampstead. During the series Ludo used an exterior shot of the outside of the building, which was a typical London town house. The building had four floors, was semi-detached and looked as though Gwyneth Paltrow or Nigella Lawson might live inside it.

In reality, the space had been carved up into small flats. We were living in two tiny rooms with the kitchen squeezed into one corner. We had all of our stuff crammed in. My office, the dining room, the living room, the kitchen and my rehearsal room were basically all the same space. On television it appeared as if we owned the whole house and people assumed I was this highfalutin choral director, which was a very long way from the truth. Every week I would catch the bus to Northolt. Heady days.

On that first day at Northolt High School what became clear to me was that music was not at the heart of the school's activities. It was a foundation school that specialised in technology: indeed, I was given a tour round the brand-new information technology block. We weren't actually going to be filming in there, but I could see that the head teacher, Chris Modi, was really proud of the new building. So we dutifully walked round, admiring the advanced network capabilities and smelling the new paint. I had a feeling at the time that this might not make it into the final documentary.

What I really wanted to know was what musical opportunities there were within the school. Because of the strong focus on technology, music just wasn't a central part of the school ethos at the time. As Chris Modi himself put it, this was 'fertile but unploughed ground'. This is not uncommon in schools where the head teacher is not particularly interested in music. It's not that they are failing in their obligations to teach music, but there is a sense that they aren't going the extra mile.

Against this background I needed to find some secret element of alchemy that would allow me to locate undiscovered talent and convert that, in an environment where singing was not really on the agenda, into a choir the whole school could support and be proud of. No mean feat. Without a large existing pool of singers to draw on there was nothing for it: I needed to get stuck into the auditioning process.

From early on, staff at the school had issues with the whole idea of auditioning: they hated the fact that we were going to be auditioning children on TV. They were terribly worried about it turning into something like *The X Factor*, and that we would humiliate the kids who weren't good at singing. It was a fair concern. That was absolutely not what I wanted to do, but I did have to select the singers who would have the aptitude and commitment for this huge task. Creating a choir that could be selected for the World Choir Games in China was going to be a serious business. And besides, there were only 25 places on the plane.

Bournemouth School, where I was educated, was a selective grammar school. Everyone who was there had won a place by passing an exam. Whatever the rights and wrongs of the system, it had got me used to the idea of selection. Being auditioned seemed a perfectly normal thing to me: I'd been going to auditions since I was ten. I'd learnt early on that sometimes you didn't get the part, that there was always the possibility of being rejected. At school I had missed out on being Romeo in *Romeo and Juliet* – a boy in the year below me got it. OK, that still rankles. But in general the idea of rejection was fine for me because I've got the resilience to bounce back and try again.

My school also had an atmosphere where achievement was really valued by the students and striving was cool. If you had the best result in the test, you got respect for it. You wanted to do well. I wanted to achieve. My school had both offered possibilities and fostered ambition: they encouraged you to go off and start your own projects and do whatever you wanted. It gave me a level of self-belief that has stayed with me ever since.

From many of the kids who auditioned I detected much less overt ambition. Like most teenagers they were content with the styles of music they knew and certainly would have seen little personal benefit in attempting to tackle the choral classics. Choral singing was not exactly the prevailing musical interest at Northolt High School when I turned up in 2005. Choir was not cool.

An audition process for me seemed the only way to tell who was serious and who just fancied being on TV. About 160 kids turned up. Something about the chance to go to China and to be on television caught their imagination and for some it kick-started a determination to succeed. Aiming high is so important in life. Why aim for the middle? I wanted to show these kids that you could do something truly adventurous.

Rhonda Pownall was one of the singers whose voice I liked a lot. She says that she was shocked by some of the kids who turned up to the auditions. She had thought it would be 'the same faces who did singing. Asking people at high school to go and sing in front of a camera that was going to be broadcast nationwide was like asking them to perform star jumps in their vests in assembly.'

The auditioning took two full, very long days, with me sitting at the upright piano and the kids walking in one after another. I didn't have long to assess their singing, but over the years I have become quite good at recognising who has potential. I usually know about three notes in. So I asked each of them to sing me a song, cold and unaccompanied, which told me masses. If they were singing something where I could discern a tune, even if was a song I didn't know, that was always a very good sign.

Sometimes, however, it was hard to tell. A lot of the kids sang their own version of R&B songs with what appeared to be no discernable note, merely a collection of groans and squeaks. My brain was genuinely struggling to recognise the contours of what they were singing. If I couldn't recognise a tune I'd say, 'Right, sing me "Twinkle Twinkle, Little Star",' because pretty much everyone in every culture knows that song. It's also a good tune for testing singers: there's a tricky interval, a fifth, in the melody, and if somebody couldn't manage that, then I knew that they would struggle in the choir.

I had my bellyful of Mariah Carey-style R&B singing. That style of singing uses a tone that I have worked hard to avoid both in my own singing and when working with young people. I feel it is all too often the facsimile of emotion, a sham, effectively saying, 'Listen to me, everybody, look how emotional I'm feeling.' Ghastly. From a vocal point of view the auditionees were using their noses as a kind of resonator and had a collection of vocal tics and burps that were carried off with considerably more panache by Whitney Houston (RIP). This style works for Mariah Carey because when it comes to the big notes, she can deliver; there is muscular support there, there's an actual *sound*. But when it is adopted by 13- and 14-year olds, it can sound like foxes mating.

I followed that up with an ear test, playing them a few notes for them to sing back to me. This instantly sorted the wheat from the chaff. Unsurprisingly, some of the students found this to be impossible. I managed to contain my exasperation as many of them valiantly, but ultimately unsuccessfully, tackled some tricky intervals. I gave each of them a score out of ten, and if they were below a seven, there was no way I could have them in the choir. Full stop. It came down to ability.

Sometimes it was a small difference, a dab of performance skill, that helped. Rhonda did a little dance while she sang 'Tainted Love' and that made her stand out for me when I was looking back through the 160 faces as 'the girl who did the dance'. She remembers the audition as nerve-wracking. 'I was terrified. I was shaking. You were laughing a bit, you did the note test, and then I went outside and had a quick panic attack.'

When I came out of the auditions I was worried about the boys, many of whom were struggling with the trauma of their voices changing (I much prefer 'changing' to 'breaking – they don't break, they just *grow*), and the fact that I didn't have a single sixth-former out of a fairly reasonably-sized sixth form: not one. I don't know whether that was my fault or their fault, but we struggled to reach that age group. On the other hand I was very confident about the quality of the girls' voices. There was some real talent there. Clarion-voiced Lisa was a real turn-up and in a superb example of nominative determinism(had her parents had an inkling?), Melody Chege turned out to have a lovely melodic voice. Even so, in my selected 30 for the choir of 25 plus 5 reserves, I only had 19 definites and 11 maybes.

Quite soon after gathering the choir together to start work (it was my *Fame* moment: 'This is where the real audition begins!'), I hit a problem. I wanted to include a girl called Chelsea Campbell in the choir, but she was in the middle of what they call in educational circles a 'managed move', which meant she was being relocated to another school. Nobody would say why but I assume she'd been in trouble of some kind. Although I had not spent more than five minutes with her, the moment when the head told me she couldn't be in the choir was included in the documentary.

After the programme aired I received a bunch of letters stating that it was unfair and that I should have fought harder with Chris Modi for her inclusion, but it wasn't as if I was pre-warned, 'Go in there and fight for Chelsea' – Chris said no and I had to respect his decision. The letters all said 'how wrong the school was', but in fact as far as the school was concerned it was quite a minor administrative decision: she doesn't go to this school any more, so she can't be in the choir. Although it might have appeared unjust, that was the reality. Chelsea had a rough couple of years at Northolt and it was time for her to move on. Goodness knows what running the choir would have been like if she had stayed, because she was very feisty; she had it written all over her face. At least I had a choir. I can't say I was leaping about with joy. I had some great singers and some concerns, but although the choir was imperfect, I could start rehearsals with them.

We began with a bump. From the very first scales I could hear some distinctly unpleasant noises akin to a vacuum cleaner being started up or the braying of a clearly unwell donkey. Nevertheless I was resolutely chirpy: I would make this group sing if it killed me.

In order to enter the World Choir Games each choir has to submit a recording as well as the repertoire for the final performance. I was taking a risk since the choir had been together for only a few weeks. Normally I would not have submitted a repertoire until I knew what they sounded like – how can you tell what an imaginary choir will be able to achieve? I certainly didn't know what sound I would ultimately be able to draw from the Northolt High School choir. I hoped it wouldn't be the sick donkey one. Also, I would never generally make a recording until the choir had been properly rehearsed, so we were ridiculously unprepared for what came next.

After only a few sessions with the choir, I took them down to a local recording studio in Chiswick to make a CD. We had a limited amount of time, about an hour or so, to record 'Can You Feel the Love Tonight' from The Lion King. It was one of my first times in a recording studio, so I was learning the ins and outs of the technique while the kids thought they'd hit the big time and were buzzing about finding themselves in a studio.

Early in our development though this was, we didn't have a choice because the submission had to go in around the Christmas holidays. I was spooked by this and so was really determined to make the recording as good as we possibly could despite time being against us. However, I couldn't work miracles. Some of the singers hadn't yet learnt the notes.

For me a particular low point was when I asked Raul, one of the less confident singers, not to sing on one of the takes. I was caught between wanting to create a recording that would get us into the World Choir Games and appearing heavy-handed and insensitive to a boy who was doubtless trying his best. The fact was that Raul was brilliantly keen and had positioned himself right in front of the microphone. He was bellowing. And it wasn't sounding great. I knew it, the choir knew it and the recording engineer told me that it was obliterating the sound of the rest of the basses and tenors. I tried moving him back a little. That didn't work (I could still hear him). I made a snap decision, which I regretted later: I asked him not to sing.

I learnt a valuable lesson from this moment. There is a balance to be struck between artistic ideals and educational motivation. I got it wrong that day. That is, of course, what I feared: that my mistakes would be highlighted on BBC Two and as I watched myself back months later I cursed the decision and hoped that the public and Raul would forgive me.

Would I do the same today? I hope I would have found a better way to ask him, perhaps more sensitively suggesting that he sing more quietly because his 'powerful voice' was cutting through or some other way of sugaring the pill. So do I regret asking Raul to pipe down? Yes.

To his immeasurable credit Raul bowed out of the take and we got something down that was passably in tune. In retrospect, most of the singers were shouting, but they had very little experience of singing, a lack which was matched only by my own inexperience of the situation.

This was a moment that I reflected on for months and which I believe gave rise to my working method for series two: *Boys Don't Sing* ... but I'm getting ahead of myself.

After we had finished singing, we went into the control booth to listen to the playback. This is always an amazing moment. Ashley, one of the younger girls who had a feisty attitude and a neat turn of phrase, turned to me with a look of shock on her face and said, 'You can hear *everything* ...'. She was horrified because she had thought, as many people do, that there was 'studio magic' that would suddenly make them sound good.

It was their first experience of hearing themselves singing. They were quite shocked that all the sections that were rough around the edges could be heard. They had had enough rehearsals to know the music and wanted to get it right, so they were alarmed when it didn't sound absolutely perfect.

I don't think they were all that impressed with the CD (I know I wasn't), although Rhonda played it to her mum, who cried buckets when she heard it. Bless her for that. For Rhonda the recording studio was the moment that changed things. 'We hadn't really bonded with anyone else in the group. We knew people, but it was still, "Oh, hi." But at the studio we had a chance to go, "This is actually serious. Let's do it and enjoy it", and we started talking.'

The choir members might have been starting to bond more, but I was really only just getting to know them. Because the Northolt High School badge had a phoenix emblazoned on it we

28

had by now decided to call ourselves the Phoenix Choir. We were hoping to set the competition on fire or something like that. Or at least that's what we said at the time. Fighting talk.

The truth was that it was very early days. By Christmas I had merely done a few warm-up rehearsals with the choir and just about got them through learning one song. I certainly hadn't taught them to sing at that point. We had a seriously long way to go. I had the triple pressure of pleasing the school, creating a choir for the World Choir Games and making something worthy of BBC Two. And so the sleepless nights began.

I'll Sing You a Song

I am not good with heights. I don't like them at all. So when I found myself teetering rather precariously on the top of a pole at some dizzying height above the ground, I really started questioning the wisdom of agreeing that a high-ropes session would be a wonderful way to do some team-building with the Phoenix Choir. It had seemed like a necessary step, though, since the choir was coming apart.

Slammed doors, cross words and lost time in rehearsals were threatening to derail the choir. I needed to take action. It was only when I was strapped into a harness and craned my neck to see where I was meant to climb that the fear kicked in.

I struggled to get up that pole. I was genuinely frightened. There was no doubt that, for me, this was a major challenge, but despite the terror, I relished the chance to lead by example. I wanted the kids to see me conquer my fear of heights and really push myself, because that was exactly what I was asking for from them. On the high ropes the big issue is learning to trust your harness, to know that if you lose your footing your harness will save you from falling. In the same way the kids in the choir had to learn to trust me, and trust each other.

Our team-building exercise came towards the end of the year and after I'd pushed myself up that pole we all realised that we'd come a long way together, not just literally, but as people. There was a lot of laughter and it was lovely not to be struggling with harmonies in rehearsal for once.

At the end of the day, we pitched a few tents in the field and got a campfire going. I'd brought along my trusty guitar, which has been a loyal companion since my teens, and in the dusk we all sang the Beatles' 'With a Little Help from My Friends'. It was a lovely moment where I think they felt a growing sense that singing was now a part of their lives and not something weird. They were all completely happy to sit around and sing a song with absolutely no fear, in front of a load of cameras and, more importantly, in front of each other. That was rather nice. It wasn't pressured: it was just a normal thing to do.

There had been one moment that day when a couple of the kids joined me at the top of my pole and the three of us stood up there together, literally clinging on to each other, before jumping off. Very weird: you don't normally expect to do that with your choristers.

In that whole team-building day, Chloe Sullivan (one of the students who climbed up the pole to join me), was the biggest surprise. I suddenly began to understand her. Chloe had been having a hard time: her dad had died when she was in her first year at Northolt. 'It happened when I just started at high school and my mum re-married the same year. It threw everything up

33

in the air.' Up until then she had apparently been an outgoing, sparky kid – just like her mum, Fiona – but she had evidently lost quite a lot of the sparkle. At school she was very withdrawn, not enjoying the experience at all.

Yet, in what for me was an incredibly challenging situation, Chloe was taking the team-building day totally in her stride. She had done gymnastics when she was younger, so she was running along these poles with absolutely no fear. I found that really impressive, which gave me a new insight into her character. I had a renewed interest in her as a member of the choir, and a sense of, 'OK, this experience *is* doing you good. Even if it's something that it seems I am forcing you to do.'

I remember an extraordinary change in Chloe during the last few months of the choir. She was making friends within the choir; she was chatty and outgoing. 'I remember thinking they were quite neeky at first,' says Chloe down a crackly mobile line from west London. I'm not sure I've caught the word correctly. A neek? It's a mixture of a nerd and a geek. 'They wasn't like my type of people. Not part of my social group.' At first she had made no effort to become part of their group. Before she got to know Chloe better, Rhonda Pownall thought of her as someone who 'never joined in. Seeing the people she hung around with she was someone I would not associate with. She was intimidated by that as well.'

'It changed,' says Chloe. 'I was more open to different types of people.' Ultimately it was this that she counts as the highlight of our year: 'That feeling of togetherness. I hadn't experienced it before at home or at school. I didn't have very many close people around me.'

I'd called Chloe to ask her how she felt about the experience now that six years had elapsed since the Phoenix Choir's trip to China. To my considerable surprise I caught her in the middle of writing an essay about plate tectonics for her BSc in International Studies. She was hoping to go on to find a job in sustainable development. Chloe has changed.

But I couldn't understand what it was that had persuaded this reluctant scholar to audition in the first place. 'It was quite a spur of the moment decision to go in for the choir because I wasn't really involved with stuff that happened at school.' Chloe is good at understatement; she was often entirely absent. 'It was quite out of character for me to audition, but I thought on the last afternoon of the audition, "Right, I'm gonna do it."'

When I agreed to be in the first series I'd thought I was going to be making a programme about choral singing. Having been working in music education introducing young people to classical music, that was my mindset: using popular songs as a way to draw them into the world of choirs. But the programme turned out to be about confidence, and the transformation of Chloe was the essence of that story. From a starting point of having very little self-belief she got to a point where she could stand on a stage and sing a solo.

The first time I had noticed some potential in Chloe Sullivan was quite early on when I took the choir to the Barbican Centre and asked for volunteers to stand up and sing a solo. Slightly to my surprise, Chloe had gone up and had a go, which took more nerve than I thought she had. As I listened to her, I thought, 'Actually she's got something, there is a voice there.' I had a feeling that she would be able to handle a larger role, not just stand in the back of the choir.

That was quite a small decision for me among all the other decisions I was taking to shape the choir, but the effect of that on Chloe's life was huge: as a teacher you don't know how a decision you make will affect another person. You never can quite tell who is going to be transformed or how. But I had a sense that there was more to Chloe than she was letting on.

She now tells me that it was crucial for her that I refused to give up on her. 'It helped that you were persistent instead of ruling me out.' To be honest, I nearly did. She would have tried the patience of Job. But I could see that Chloe was on the fringes, never quite a part of the group, and I wanted her to be drawn into the choir.

Chloe was at a point in her life where she needed somebody to place their confidence in her. She had gone off the rails, dabbling in areas of life that weren't helping her. The choir was the beginning of her turning this around. She came across as sullen, shy, reluctant. But I sensed that within Chloe there was something there to encourage, something to draw out. If the feisty Chelsea had stayed at the school and been in the choir, my job with her would have been all about containing her energy; with Chloe the task was to encourage her to let some energy out.

At the auditions, she had not shone particularly brightly. I marked her as 'borderline', just over a seven out of ten, my cut-off mark. When I asked her what song she was going to sing to me, she'd mumbled, almost incomprehensibly due to shyness, what sounded like, 'I doan know ve name of it.' And who sings it? 'I doan know dat eeva.' At Northolt most of the kids had this very particular and inexplicable accent – part Estuary, part Asian, part Jamaican, part Ali G. It was a really strange mix to my ears. Perhaps I'm just getting old.

What had Chloe made of me in those early days? 'I thought that you were very posh. *Strange*. I'd never met somebody like you before.' It seems we both had plenty to learn. It was a culture clash.

As far as the song went, I wasn't sure about Chloe's ear, her ability to sing in tune, which is odd in retrospect as she ended up being a soloist, but these were snap decisions based on short auditions. I was also put off because she had chosen an R&B song with lyrics that seemed really inappropriate and sexual – it was one of those awkward moments where a teenager is sing-ing you a song and the basic message of the lyric is, 'I love you, I want to do intimate stuff with you.' That had happened a lot during the auditions: teenagers standing there singing all sorts of words to me as if that was normal and me not knowing quite where to look. 'Thanks. That was … very interesting,' I'd stutter. Despite Chloe's uncertain, nervous audition, she had a pleasant voice and way of singing.

I'm amazed how far I was able to get her to progress, espe-cially since she was very, very often a no-show at rehearsals. Chris Modi, the head teacher, had been concerned about her reliability and whether she would be able to commit. I'd phone her to try to track her down … but 'answer came there none'. Often it turned out she was in detention – or earning another one. And when she did come along she'd be at the back, giving me 'the face'.

This, of course, was frustrating for the other kids in the choir who turned up to every rehearsal. I am always fond of the good students, the ones who try hard all the time and who really deserve the reward.

One of the star sopranos at Northolt was Mariza De Souza: she was smart, she worked hard, she aimed high, she was at every rehearsal and brought the right sheet music along. Although in the end she did get a small solo when we performed in China, it seemed less prominent in the TV show because the change in her was less obvious, but no less dramatic. She had started off from a high point and continued to get better, but there was not that obvious degree of turnaround that someone like Chloe demonstrated. I didn't even raise an eyebrow when I heard recently that Mariza is studying physics at Imperial College London. Watch out Brian Cox.

So all those others, like Mariza, deserve their moment of recognition. You cannot help but have those that you prefer, musically speaking, the ones within a choir or a class who are on time, do their homework, have learnt their notes. And then there are those who don't make an effort. Of course I do not and *will not* give up on those other ones and always strive to turn them round, not always succeeding. But it is such a joy to have somebody like Mariza who not only worked hard but remembered to say, 'Thank you!'

Rhonda Pownall was also really impressive, from day one. I dubbed her 'Agincourt Girl' because of the stirring speech she gave to the rest of the choir before the final performance. Yet even before the auditions, she had said she was going to go for it, even though she was sceptical at first: 'The film crew swanned in with you. It felt a little bit like a low-budget *X Factor*.'

Not only was Rhonda always positive in rehearsal, but she was understanding and helpful to me. She had a lot of maturity and was great about coming to tell me if they were having any problems as a choir, and then reporting back my reaction to the rest of them and helping massage that through. Alongside Mariza and Rhonda there were many of these hard-working kids in the Phoenix Choir, like Lacey and Sophie. I spent a lot of time working with Keecia Ellis because she was a fantastic singer and had a great work ethic. Boys like Enock and Etienne, Marcus and Jerry did their very best and that's really all you can ask for.

After the first round of auditions failed to turn up any decent basses I went out on a hunt for talent. Somewhere between the vending machine and the grimy sofas of the sixth form common room the gruff voice of Jason Grizzle entered my life. He was extremely unassuming and had a shock of wild Afro hair. Jason showed little early promise, but managed to get through a quick audition.

After the first rehearsal Jason remarked, 'That is possibly the gayest thing I have ever done in my life.' There was a bit of kerfuffle at the BBC about whether he was allowed to say that on air or not, because Chris Moyles had recently got into trouble for something similar on his radio show – which is entirely right, but then that was the phrase school kids were using in 2005. So it went in.

Of course, apart from an unpleasant twisting of the word 'gay' to mean 'a bit crap', this revealed what boys generally made of singing and summed it up rather pithily. Boys fear that singing will make you 'gay' or, to put it another way, they fear the feminising force of singing. It's not really appropriate to ask boys to sing, is it? Shouldn't they be out on the sports fields hurting each in shorts? This insight into the twenty-first-century 'boy' and his singing voice would set me up well for the second series of *The Choir*.

But enigmatic Jason Grizzle was to turn out to be a real surprise: this kid could really sing. He was one of the people who make me feel, 'Hang on a minute. Here we have a really good singer.' He had a great voice. He could remember pitch like no one else in the choir, even though he didn't play an instrument and had never done any music at all, he had a good head on him and he had ability. And what shocked me was that nobody in the school knew this about him. How could this be the case for somebody in the sixth form?

When I met Jason I asked him whether he could sing: 'Uh, I don't know, I'll try.' He didn't *know* because he had never done any singing, and had never been given the opportunity. Jason's mate Shaheen encouraged him to come along to a rehearsal, and he turned out to be the absolute rock of the choir. He took the bass line, went home, learnt it and anchored the whole thing. Jason was extremely modest about this achievement.

This really made me question how someone could go through their school education and not have sung a single note from Year 7 to Year 13; it was only when some choirmaster came in and told him he had a good voice that he realised he might be able to sing. Up to that point Jason had had absolutely no idea. He genuinely did have a useful choral voice and it upset me at that time to think how much untapped potential there must be within schools.

I must be careful to acknowledge the pressure that teachers are under and the kind of difficulties they face. My wife is a secondary school teacher and I have seen at first hand the demands of the curriculum. I've also spent a fair amount of time over the last fifteen years in classrooms working with teachers. They are under constant scrutiny and assessment. This doesn't always leave time for the niceties of extra-curricular music.

That said, I hadn't been greatly impressed with what I'd seen of what Northolt were doing, musically speaking. In the term I arrived there the school play was a staff-written version of Roald Dahl's *Charlie and the Chocolate Factory*, and this was for a school of teenagers up to the age of eighteen. I know that the staff weren't pushing them in the direction that I wanted to go with the choir. Consequently there was a certain tension between me and the music staff there.

From what I could glean, in recent years there had been quite a high turnover of staff in the music department. To me that was a sign of where – at that time – music sat on the overall agenda of the school. The head of the music department was fairly newly qualified, and certainly had not been in her post for very long. I don't think she was as old as I was, and I'd only just turned thirty. There was also one teacher in the middle of his qualifying period.

Enter Gareth Malone swanning about declaring experience with the London Symphony Orchestra and the English National Opera, blah, blah. They could be forgiven for being really quite irritated. Neither of them had had much chance to get to know the capabilities of the kids outside those who they taught. Neither did they have the resources and allure of a TV company and the time to invest in individuals. So although I tried very hard not to ride roughshod over what the music department was trying to do with limited resources, they would have been perfectly justified in resenting my presence in the school. I'm sure I would have felt the same if I'd been in their shoes.

The head of music wasn't sure that I'd find anyone who could sing, though it wasn't her job to look for them. Her contract was simply to get the first three years of the school through the music curriculum and then concentrate on those who'd elected to study music at GSCE and beyond. But she didn't realise the lengths I was prepared to go to. Part of my sales pitch to the boys was, 'We have some nice girls ... We might be going to China ... We also have biscuits.' I can be extremely persuasive.

Even with Jason Grizzle and a few of the other sixth-formers on board, however, the lower end of the voices was still very fragile. I had plenty of good sopranos – Mariza, Lacey and Keecia in particular – and altos, including Marcus, Gemma and Laura, but the foundations beneath them were as rocky as the pole I had climbed up on that team-building day. And I was now starting to push them harder with far more demanding classical works.

Around Easter time I decided that we should do a performance in a school assembly to get the choir ready for China. As we entered the fray it was like a bear pit, the smell of aggression was ripe in the air and feral Year 11s circled like a pack of wolves waiting for the kill. The piece I had chosen for us to sing was Vivaldi's *Gloria*.

We survived the day to moderate applause. The truth was that the tenors and basses had started to sing the tune rather than their harmony line. Afterwards one of the girls who had been listening, said, so sweetly, 'Oh yes, they should win. They sound like a professional choir.' I doubt she'd heard many professional choirs ...

In the back of my mind I knew that as part of the choral programme I was planning for the choir to sing in China there was a piece by Fauré, 'Cantique de Jean Racine', that was not only in French, but significantly harder to sing than any of the other pieces. The next few months were not going to be easy. Time was seriously running out.

Nonetheless the choir was starting to make an impact in the school and Rhonda, the choir's motivational centre of gravity, recalls that a few students who hadn't auditioned started to regret it: 'I think a lot of people were very jealous. There were a few snide comments.'

By now the choir had become an all-consuming project. It was dominating my every waking hour, because although I did have other work to do during the nine months I was working with the choir at Northolt, I put nearly all of it on hold to make sure that I had time for the choir. I was spending any days off doing preparation work for my visits to Northolt and thinking about what I was going to do and how I was going to overcome the challenge of getting this still pretty much scratch choir ready to appear in the world's biggest international choir competition.

Emotionally it was intensive. I would build myself up to a main rehearsal each Thursday, which was intended to be the

43

high point of the week, but which often turned out to be a low point because of the problems it threw up. Each week I would start out thinking to myself, 'I have got to get this right, we must learn this much music this week or else we are not going to be in good shape for China, always assuming we're selected.'

Then in rehearsal I'd find that something always got in the way, that one of my key tenors hadn't turned up for rehearsal or that everyone had gone down with the lurgy. Another week went by with the choir no closer to learning the pieces; I was feeling pressured. With hindsight, I think I could have cut myself a little bit of slack: it wasn't an easy task I'd been set.

I felt very much on my own. It was alarming. I didn't really have anyone to talk to about what I was doing. The only confidantes I had were the camera, and the director. And Becky, of course. She lived and breathed the whole experience with me despite having pneumonia during the filming (thanks, Becky – it was a tough year).

The day was drawing closer when we would board the plane to China. Shortly before we were due to travel, we gave a performance of the pieces to the school and the parents. Becky came to watch and was fairly silent afterwards, which I took to be a bad sign. On the train heading back home she turned to me and said quietly, 'They're not good.' I was absolutely gutted. I had been working on the project for nine months by then and I knew what they had sounded like back at the beginning of the process. But in fact it was a real help that Becky had been so frank; it gave me the kick I needed. I went back to the remaining few rehearsals and drilled the choir harder than ever, and the standard of their singing went up considerably.

In June 2006 I felt a weight of expectation to get through the first round of the Choir Games in China. I needed to prove myself, and at that stage it was going to be about musical achievement, not about what it would mean to the kids. In subsequent series working with the other choirs, I changed my tack – not least because of the experience in Northolt – towards how singing in a choir can change your life, how it could change attitudes. I set myself more nuanced ambitions, whereas working with the Phoenix Choir was at times entirely about musical achievement. We rehearsed those songs until we were almost sick of them

My focus was to get the choir, by hook or by crook, to as high a standard as they could reach. I had asked each of those kids to trust me that I would make them sound good. It was time to deliver on my promise.

When You're Weary

I am not ashamed to admit that on the night after the Northolt Phoenix Choir performed at the World Choir Games in China, I ended up crying my eyes out. I'm a crier, don't get me wrong, but this was different. I blubbed. Sobbed. All the pressure, all the tension, all the responsibility I had been carrying for nine months flooded out of me like a dam bursting.

We had done our competition performance early that morning. Bearing in mind that there was eight hours' time difference, I don't think any of us even knew what day it was. The results of the first round were due out later that evening. I had spent a lot of the intervening time marching up and down a huge flight of steps in front of the Xiamen People's Hall for some shots that the film crew needed, so I was feeling physically exhausted.

I hadn't had any dinner, and, believe me, I'm not good when I haven't eaten any dinner. By the time the results came out it was a quarter to ten. It came up on a plasma screen inside this edifice to communism. I shrugged and thought about my stomach.

We hadn't got through. I felt quite sanguine about it; I didn't think we deserved it. We weren't as good as the others, but the choir had genuinely given it their very best shot and I loved them for that, because so many of them had worked harder on this than anything else in their lives. I know I had.

I went back to the hotel where all the kids were waiting to hear whether we had made it through to the second round. I didn't beat about the bush: I let them know as simply and straightforwardly as I could that we were out of the competition and going home with a certificate. They were also totally fine about it: I had prepared them well for the possibility. And then a few of the kids, Rhonda, Laura and Jerry, came up to me and said, 'We don't want you to go. We want you to stay.'

And those few words did it. I was absolutely broken by them. I started to cry. And once I started, I couldn't stop. I wasn't crying because we hadn't made it through. It was because of a whole collection of different emotions.

I had grown fond of the choir and I knew that this was a finite project. Even though I had arranged for the school's choir to continue, I felt like I was leaving them and that was something I was really ambivalent about. On top of all that was a major dose of jetlag, as well as the release of all the tension, and sheer relief at having got to the end of this journey with the pressure of all the scrutiny I had been under, with television cameras observing me close up for nine months.

I was also going to be leaving the TV crew I had got to know so well: Ludo the director, Sam the sound guy, Dave the cameraman; these great guys I had spent so much time with. I had no idea if I would ever shoot another day of TV again.

And I was sobbing because I was thinking, 'Look what these kids achieved, look how much they are transformed by this, look how they feel about being in a choir *now*.' And in that moment I felt angry too. Angry that more young people didn't have this kind of life-changing opportunity. It was a seminal moment that would change the course of my career and my life. There is no word for the emotion I felt that evening: a mixture of pride, relief and loss but above all happiness that it had worked. I was happy for these kids.

As I sat there bawling my eyes out, the indefatigable soundman Sam Mathewson began to mist up, as did the supposed man of iron, the director Ludo Graham. Only the cameraman stayed dry-eyed. Dave Wickham: seen it all, hard as nails ...

It had been a brilliant idea to aim for the Phoenix Choir to compete in the World Choir Games – a very creative and very televisual decision by Ana DeMoraes to set an overly ambitious goal. It was a real game-changer, and it seemed to be perfect timing. You couldn't open a paper in 2006 without reading about China, about the coming Olympics in Beijing, about what an amazing, emerging economy China was and how the country would be the dominant force in the century.

I had sent the application off in early January, crossing my fingers as I dropped it into a post box somewhere near the school after a late rehearsal. I genuinely didn't know if we would be allowed into the competition. As part of the application we had to supply a photo of the choir. A couple of them were embarrassed that it was shot by the basketball courts and we looked quite scruffy, but in fact I felt that sent out a strong message to the Choir Games organisers about who the choir were, that the Phoenix Choir was not a bunch of chorally educated kids, just regular kids who had decided to sing.

The Choir Games rules meant I also had to decide on our repertoire for the competition at the time of the application. There were a number of constraints: there had to be pieces in a foreign language, from before the twentieth century, and only one free choice. The programme I had chosen included Simon and Garfunkel's 'Bridge Over Troubled Water', Fauré's *Cantique de Jean Racine*', 'Fairest Isle' by Purcell, and Stevie Wonder's 'Isn't She Lovely?'. I was creating this for a choir who at the time could not sing in parts very effectively, where I didn't have enough guys for the tenor and bass parts, so it was no mean feat to try and find pieces I thought they might be able to sing six months down the line.

I remember several people who watched the programme thought that it was a forgone conclusion. Surely with the might of the BBC the choir would be a shoo-in? Well if it was, nobody told me and I had a nervous wait with the rest of the choir while our application was processed.

I honestly didn't open the letter which told us the result until I was with the choir. Watching it back now, I can see genuine relief on my face. I shot a glance off-camera to the production team. If they'd known already, they did a bloody good job of keeping it from us. Besides, it wouldn't have been the same if I'd already known and the choir didn't: we had to go through the experience together.

The choir had been accepted and we all felt exhilarated. It was around this time, however, that we realised there was a second round to try and get through to. That was when it got competitive.

Inevitably we had a few bumps along the road to China. One that completely caught me unawares was when Josh and his sister Ashley told me they could sing nothing of a religious nature because they were Jehovah's Witnesses. This was tricky because in the programme I had already submitted, the 'Cantique de Jean Racine' was based on a Matins hymn, and the Purcell piece was about the goddess Venus. I did point out that Venus was from antiquity and that as far as I knew no one worships her any more, that it was a myth, a legend – but they're weren't having any of it. They were being extra-careful. They had suddenly realised that they were about to be singing very publicly indeed and, as Jehovah's Witnesses, wanted to err on the side of caution because they have strict ideas about what is and isn't acceptable singing material.

I spoke to some colleagues who taught singing and asked them what my options were. They all said, there is nothing you can do. In the event, Josh decided to quit long before the China trip, not because of the religious issue but because, as he put it so damningly, it was 'getting a bit long'. However Ashley chose to stay, but not to sing the two religious songs. I was an alto down for my two most difficult pieces, but it wouldn't have been fair to Ashley to force the issue.

Another rocky moment was when we made the decision to re-audition the entire choir. A few of the singers – and it was definitely a minority – seemed to be taking part for the wrong reasons. This manifested itself in their general attitude to the rehearsals: they were not turning up or, if they did, quite frankly not putting in much effort. I remember another chorister called Ashley (this one a boy) saying, 'I am in it for the China ...' Any teacher knows that this attitude can be toxic in a group. I did my *very* best to encourage him to have a more positive attitude but, alas, he floated away from us.

What I had not predicted was the appeal of appearing on television. Not only had it enthused 160 auditionees, but many of those who were in the choir were only there so that they could have their five minutes of fame. But this was not the 'low budget *X-Factor*' they thought it was – this was real, it was hard work. They were learning to become a choir. Some of them didn't care and I knew it.

So it felt morally right to me to make sure, on behalf of the ones who really were pulling their weight, that everyone deserved and justified their place on the plane. I was quite prepared to be flexible about the standard if I felt that the effort was there: Enock Chege, for example, who had originally been one of my five reserves, was not fantastic when he re-auditioned, but I felt I wanted to have him on the trip because he was so enthusiastic and positive about the challenge. At the very first audition he said he was going to give it 'my best voice, my best concentration.' And he did.

The re-auditioning process was a tough sell to the school, who preferred a more broad-access policy. They felt I should have got it right the first time (as did many people who wrote to me afterwards). How could I? How could I have known, based on a five-minute audition, who would prove to have the stamina? I suppose that's the kind of background I'm from: if you don't put the effort in, you don't get the rewards. I had to be ruthless.

Some didn't make it in because musically they had failed to get hold of the notes. Raul, for example, continued to struggle and it was becoming obvious to the rest of the choir that he couldn't sing the parts. These were awful decisions. But this was the situation I found myself in and I was determined to make the best of it.

The contrast between those who were committed and those who had lost interest was most marked between Ahmed and Jack. At the 11th hour and after months of me badgering him Ahmed said he was only doing it for his parents. Jack was understandably as completely gobsmacked as I was. He looked at Ahmed in disbelief. 'I really, really want to go,' he said, and he meant it. I felt Jack's attitude was to be rewarded, whereas to be involved in this fantastic opportunity because you thought you could please your parents seemed to me a completely misguided reason. You can't sing for your parents, you have to sing for yourself. I didn't want a choir full of conscripts. I wanted it to be full of kids who really desperately wanted to be in it. Crucially, because his heart wasn't in it Ahmed hadn't learnt the music. Exit Ahmed.

But some of them really cared. When Kodi Bramble walked out and slammed the door – smashing the glass, by the way – he did so because of simmering tensions in the choir between the different sections: the altos were finding it easy, but the tenors were often a man or two down and finding the parts a challenge. Kodi, however, was highly musical and wanted to get it right. He is now a professional rock drummer, with tattoos to match, but he had a pleasant tenor voice and a damn good ear. I'm not sure how much he appreciated his nickname of 'door slammer Kodi'.

At one rehearsal, as time was running out, I lost it in front of the choir. They were not focusing, they were messing around. 'Excuse me!' I yelled. 'That is the only time you will hear me shout. You are being utterly discourteous. One more time and I will walk out.' It was classic denial behaviour: there was so much at stake and yet they were merrily wasting time. They needed to be reminded of what they'd agreed to. It brought them up sharp.

Rhonda had doubted that I had it in me: 'At our school you needed to be tough with people,' she said to me with a worldly air. 'I didn't know if you would be able to be tough with *anyone*. And maybe it would be a bit of an easy ride.' They underestimated me. I have a touch of steel behind the mild-mannered exterior. Fundamentally I knew what the pressure would be like in China, and from necessity I transferred some of that pressure onto them.

By July we were as ready as we were ever going to be. The kids had designed a uniform: the male outfits were Mandarin-influenced, while the girls had dresses of which even the sartorially picky Chloe approved.

On paper I thought the design looked pretty cool. Jerry had masterminded it and we raised an absolutely astronomical amount of money to pay for these ninja suits to be made by a local seamstress. She happened to be one of the smallest people I've ever met and I still have a vivid image of her valiantly struggling with enough black, shiny material to kit out the terracotta army. Unfortunately the kids had picked a material that was so smooth and shiny that the stitches wouldn't hold, so the poor woman was engaged in a Forth Bridge-style endeavour trying to keep the things together. I swear that I ended up with someone else's jacket. We affectionately referred to the outfits as our pyjamas.

We flew out to China and arrived in Xiamen via Hong Kong. It was everyone's first time there, me included. I got off the plane, so jet-lagged, so tired. I went into my hotel room, lay down on the bed and even then sobbed into my pillow, already feeling the pressure. It was a nightmare.

China is about as alien as it's possible to get without leaving the planet. The signs are incomprehensible even when in English. The 'Chinglish' breakfast menu was a real treat: 'Com of Cream Soup', 'Five Precious Ingredient Gruel', 'Its its juice' and 'Baked Frog' delighted us all. I was thrilled to be welcomed at one venue by a sign declaring, 'Classical comfortable pursue-quatity enjoylife travelledevery where of senda specialty attitude enjoyment joviality'. I knew this was somewhere where the rules were different.

We only had one day to adjust before we found ourselves at the grand opening of the event. This was held in a conference centre that made the O2 arena look like a garden shed. It was absolutely enormous; a vast space with thousands of people and a procession of national flags. Every country in the world seemed to have a choir there. There were only two choirs from Great Britain, us and Farnham Youth Choir. When the Union Jack came out, something cataclysmic happened.

Here I was with all this group of kids from Northolt, many of whom were children of immigrant families (first, second and third generations) who I think had never identified that strongly with being British because of their other cultural links. Suddenly, out there in China, in an alien environment, they were being photographed and feted as representatives of Great Britain. They had a powerful sense of being British. When the Union Jack emerged they screamed as one at the top of their voices. I looked at them all yelling as loud as they could, and thought, 'Oh, no, they're going to wreck their voices for the competition' – we were due to be performing at 8.45 the next morning. I screamed down the line, 'Stop shouting!' They took no notice and continued to blow their gaskets.

The next morning my lead tenor, Kodi Bramble, with whom I had had so many ups and downs, came up to me at breakfast to croak, 'I can't sing, I've got no voice.' This was the day of the competition, so this was not good news, but I told him that he must at least come with us to sing. Who knows? His voice might have come back by then.

Grim-faced, we set out for the venue. As the air-conditioned bus shuddered to a halt, the soupy morning air of the Chinese monsoon season poured in through the open door. The time had arrived. Up sprang Rhonda to deliver her impromptu speech, worthy of Henry V. 'We know our parts perfectly,' she told the others. 'We have gone from nothing to something really, really beautiful. Do it for England, Northolt, Gareth, our families, our friends. But most of all let's do it for ourselves.' The first of many tears that day threatened to break my equilibrium.

Rhonda's pride was clear and she still recalls the performance with affection: 'It was seeing how far we had come from a group of ultimately mismatched personalities, and we were united.' But this was no time for sentiment. There was singing to be done.

Alas, the bravado she stirred in the choir was fragile. Not long afterwards we were standing backstage at the competition venue just about to go on to perform. The choir who were on before us gave this almighty bang with their feet on the floor and let rip a 'hah!' as if they were doing the Haka before singing something very red-blooded and exotic, not at all in the English choral tradition. The kids looked round in absolute horror. I could see them thinking, 'Oh my goodness, what have we got ourselves into? We are hopelessly out of our depth.'

It hit me as well. Back at the beginning of the whole process when I had been asked whether I could create a choir good enough to compete in the World Choir Games I had brazenly said, 'I can try. I don't know exactly what that is going to mean or how far we can get, but I will give it my best shot.' Now, just like the kids, when I heard the quality of the other choir I realised exactly what we had got ourselves into. It was a daunting moment for us all.

Jerry Cleary was the linchpin. He was one of the later influx of sixth-formers who had brought a new maturity to the sound (and the behaviour!) of the choir. Even the spirited Rhonda couldn't bring them together in the face of this fearsome opposition. But she remembers everyone looking to Jerry at this critical moment. 'He took on a very fatherly role, he was geeing people up and saying, "We can do this, it doesn't matter, we'll do it ourselves, we will do it our own way."'

The now voiceless Kodi was an essential part of the difficult Fauré piece, 'Cantique de Jean Racine', so needless to say that particular song was not nearly as good as it had sounded in rehearsal, although he wasn't alone in not being up to par. It is often the case with inexperienced singers that however powerful in emotional terms a final performance is, the moments where they really achieve their best are in rehearsal. Looking back, those are the moments that I cherish. Under the pressure of live performance the technical side can suffer in comparison.

So the competition performance in China was not our best: pressure, time, exhaustion, and a group of very inexperienced performers were all factors. But it was precisely because of all those circumstances that I felt inordinately proud of every single one of the Phoenix Choir. I had thrown them to the lions, I really had, and they had risen to the challenge and performed as well as they possibly could on the day.

Months later I watched the footage back and saw that, unbeknown to me, Jerry had also cried on that final evening. He said this beautiful thing: 'If you have the bottle and the right sort of teacher, you can basically do anything.' I have to report that upon watching it, I broke down in tears again.

Only then did I understand the value of the choir to the kids. Finally, they had realised that I, and everyone else, believed in them enough to say, 'I reckon you could go and do this incredible thing. You might not succeed, you might not win a medal, but you can at least go there and say you did it. You deserve to be pushed as hard as possible and to be made to sing to the best of your ability.' I had an opportunity to challenge them. That was a privilege.

It's an experience that changed us all. Not only do many of them still listen to the *'Cantique de Jean Racine'* on their iPods, they emerged taller and, I believe, richer as people. I've just put the *Cantique* on in my office and it's the first time I've listened to it since 2006. I simply couldn't face it until now. I had to stop typing to listen to it. What a stunning piece of music, and even now it transports me back to a wonderful, brave time in a shabby school hall in Middlesex where a group of secondary school kids overcame the odds and entirely failed to win a medal. I know that this piece is with them forever as it is with me. I hold the experience in my heart.

Having never been part of a television series before I wasn't sure what to expect next. During the months when the editing was under way I had not seen very much, just the bit that is shown at the beginning of each programme where there is a very fast sequence of scenes. When I first watched one of those it was exactly like what they say happens when you drown: your life flashes before you. And every moment that flickered past actually triggered a whole other set of experiences and memories; click, click, click, an incredibly intense feeling of sensory overload.

When the final version of the series was ready I picked up the DVDs early one afternoon, raced home, sat down and watched the entire thing back to back on my own. All I was focused on was whether or not I looked like a complete and utter idiot. That was all I could think. Had I said anything that I was going to regret and were the classical music police going to come round with their sirens wailing, and grab me because I had made a stupid slip and said that Fauré was German rather than French?

What were other choirmasters and conductors going to think? I had just come out of the Royal Academy where the whole ethos is about working as hard as you can to do things to the highest possible level. So if I had made a bum note on national television, I would have felt really bad. There were a couple of tiny moments where I winced. I have learnt that in any series there will always be those few minor moments because over such a long period you simply can't be perfect. And I have also learnt that the only people who really care are me and a couple of angry bloggers.

After watching the series through and deciding I did not, in fact, come across as a complete and utter idiot, I watched it back again with Becky. We went from thinking, 'Well, we could tell our families about this,' to, 'We can probably tell our friends about this,' to, 'We can probably tell everyone we know,' to at the end thinking, 'This is great. Maybe people might like this.'

I had one other realisation. I had begun by thinking we were making a series with someone who works in music education – what we call in the trade an 'animateur' – but as I realised that no one would know what that meant I appeared as 'a conductor'. Some of the newspapers actually said, 'London Symphony Orchestra conductor', which of course was completely untrue. I had worked with the LSO, but the orchestra had a highly regarded, internationally renowned conductor of its own in Sir Colin Davis. Consequently there were a few reactions and rants along the lines of, 'Who is this man, who thinks he is the London Symphony Orchestra conductor? Upstart oik. Put him back in his place!'

The first programme of the series went out in December 2006 – a good five months after all the emotion of that final night in China. It was the weirdest week. Strangers started speaking to me in the street. I was getting emails and phone calls from people I hadn't seen for years. The weekend before the series was shown I had gone on a stag weekend in Spain with a mate of mine called Marcus. While we were out there I had a call telling me that the series had been featured in the TV preview section of *The Times*, which felt very exciting.

I then raced back from the stag do on the Sunday to appear on *BBC Breakfast* the following morning. Even though I had been pacing myself during the festivities, I had not left the bar until four in the morning and rushed to the airport to catch a plane at seven. I was *very* bleary-eyed. I just about got through Sunday, and then I had to wake up early again the next morning to be on *Breakfast* to launch the show. The great thing about live TV is that they slapped enough make-up on me so that no one could tell quite how tired I was – I hope.

As I had wearily got on the plane that Sunday morning to come back from Spain, despite the woolly head, I did have a very clear sense that I might just have enjoyed my final moments of anonymity. I wasn't complaining. I had decided to sign up for this: I would roll with the punches.

How Foolish, Foolish Must You Be

A couple of months after the first series of *The Choir* had gone out on air, I found myself back in yet another school assembly, facing an audience entirely made up of teenage boys and a predominantly male staff. I thought that *en masse* they would be seriously sceptical about the prospect of singing. With only the briefest of warnings I was standing up in front of them to sing, completely unaccompanied, a traditional and to them doubtless unbelievably twee folk song called 'She's Like the Swallow'. To make matters worse, to find my starting note, I had peeped it rather weedily on a descant recorder. I suspected this was not going to appeal to the macho bunch lined up in front of me. I revelled in the incongruity.

Half an hour earlier, sitting around at breakfast in our less than salubrious hotel on the London Road in Leicester, Harry Beney, one of the directors of the new series, had said, 'You've got to go and make an announcement to the school, Gareth. Why don't you sing a song?' 'Yeah,' I thought, 'that's really good. That is exactly what I should do.' This was my music education background coming to the fore: 'Get in there, be unashamed about it, this is what I do. I like to sing, I am going to sing you a song.'

I thought I should choose a song that those particular schoolkids would not normally hear. I am sure most of them that morning had never heard an English folk song before, especially as the school had a high percentage of boys from an Asian background. So it felt absolutely right and proper, although I no doubt looked ridiculous. The headmaster certainly looked seriously bemused.

Yet many of the boys who were there later told me that was a key moment, because I was not afraid to stand up and sing in front of them; I was not afraid to make a fool of myself. Aleister Adamson said he respected me for coming in 'all guns blazing'. I imagine they understood instinctively that I was telling them, 'And neither should you be.' With teenage boys you have to lead by example. I gritted my teeth and dug in.

The fact that I was there in that assembly at Lancaster School, Leicester, one of the biggest all-boy comprehensives in the country, was a direct reaction to what had happened in the wake of the Northolt experience. There had been a divided response to the first series. On the one hand there had been a great outpouring of public enthusiasm about it, which had taken me pleasantly by surprise. But to counteract that, there was a fair amount of criticism about its value as an educational project, and that criticism was the more telling because it raised questions that I had asked myself.

The executive producer for both series was Jamie Isaacs. At the time I was afraid of him, because not only does Jamie have a *basso profundo* voice that shakes the room as he speaks, but he has a single fleck of white hair in his eyebrow, which gives him the aspect of a superhero who might at any time cut you down with a laser coming from his steely glaze. However, Jamie was delighted. The 'numbers' from the first series were fantastic, peaking at around 3.7 million people. As he put it to me, 'That's one person on every single bus in the UK who knows who you are.' Quite an adjustment for me. I've had to remember to be polite to bus drivers.

But not everyone was happy. Jamie was shocked: 'My God, the choral world is really angry with you!' A number of people had publicly said that the series was unrealistic because, as I knew myself, no music teacher would be able to devote that amount of time to working with one group of students. This was at a time when people were feeling the pinch in music education, and here I was spending hours and hours with a small group, funded by the BBC. I think there was an irritation among school music staff, along the lines of 'I've been trying to set up a choir in my school for the last 15 years and not one pupil, especially any boys, wants to join my choir.' Because that's what choirs meant in 2005. As Jason Grizzle had said, it was the 'gayest' thing in the world. It was the thing furthest from their minds.

Before the first series ended I had spent a lot of time talking with Northolt High School about how the choir could carry on after the end of filming, and they had assured me that it was going to continue, as indeed it did. The school's music staff, Clare Hanna and Patrick Golding, did their best to continue the choir. However, the final shot of that first series was of me walking out of the school pulling a suitcase behind me, and turning away down the street into the distance. It was a great shot for television, but it left many people asking, 'How can he leave just when they are getting good?' The reality of it was that half the Phoenix Choir were leaving the school that summer and going on to do other things. The rest were staying and they did have a choirmaster in place, but none of this featured, so I think people's impression was that I had cynically dropped the project and gone, which had not been my intention. I continue to keep in touch with the Phoenix Choir, I catch up with some of them on Facebook from time to time, and I returned to Northolt a year later for a reunion (armed with a BAFTA!).

In the fall-out from the series, there was one blogger in particular, with the pseudonym of Florian Gassmann, who wrote a very insightful, if negative, blog about why it was a really bad series. 'Malone's efforts,' he wrote, 'seem to have failed to establish a choral tradition in the school – most people can manage a successful "one-off", whether the cameras are there or not – and I'm not even sure I would brand this one "successful". Thousands of hard-working music teachers demonstrate much more consummate skills, year in year out, without being able to offer "be on national TV" or "come to China" as incentives.'

Florian G. (the pseudonym of a head of music somewhere since he said he would never employ me in his department) had plenty more to say. 'Real teaching is about establishing enthusiasm, offering continued vibrant experiences and engaging generations of pupils for years to come – all skills that Gareth Malone has failed to show he possesses … I suspect that he will come to regret selling his soul to the devil.' Ouch.

Well that's what you get when you go on TV. You become public property. I must admit that I was furious when I read this. It felt unjust. It hurt. But in some ways I think it spurred me on in the following years to find greater and greater ways of proving this man wrong. So Mr Florian Gassmann, I thank you. This inspired me to fight back.

I *had* made repertoire choices that were wrong, our goal *was* unrealistic and what was going to happen to those kids afterwards? He said it was my responsibility as a practitioner to make sure that I saw that through. I was thinking, 'Really?' I had never been in that role before. In all my previous jobs I had worked for a boss, so someone more senior would take care of any aftermath and more experienced people could think about the wider aspects of any project. Here I was suddenly in the firing line, getting all the flak.

Luckily I could set Florian Gassmann's blog and others like it against an absolute outpouring from people who had loved *The Choir*, a pile of letters saying how moved they were by it, how it had really touched a nerve. But that one particular blog preyed on my mind, because I knew many of the points of criticism to be true and valid. There *were* things we could have done better.

Although I was piqued, the criticism did me an enormous amount of good because I found that I had the resilience for a role at the national level, and I determined to address those issues when I had another opportunity to make a series of *The Choir*. The first series went out in December 2006, just before Christmas – perfect timing. I had the first calls about a second series around that time and we started having planning conversations soon after the New Year break.

As I sat in those meetings, I realised that the word 'unrealis-tic' that had cropped up as a negative had really struck home. I always see the first series as a Disney version of what a choir can be like: the joining, the coming together and the big emotional pay-off at the end, a lovely, simple fairy-tale struc-ture. Now I wanted to aim for a much more organic approach. I got fired up with indignant zeal. 'Right, we are going to damn well make the most ethical programme we possibly can. I am going to think about legacy. I am going to make sure that this goes right out across the school.' I wanted to get the end points right this time and have more involvement in the overall direction.

Ana DeMoraes reminds me that the second series grew out of the first: 'We started thinking what to do next, and it was Jamie Isaacs who suggested we should concentrate on boys, as that had been one of the best aspects of the first series. You felt really strongly about it: boys think singing is "gay", or it's for girls. So it seemed like a logical progression.'

But the first series had been so emotionally demanding, how could we top that? Ana, too, wanted it to feel like a bigger commitment this time, and with a legacy. 'The idea came that you should actually join a boys' school as one of the teachers, and work with the existing music teacher to change the boys' – and the staff's – attitudes to singing.'

Originally we had been looking at the idea of me teaching in another mixed school like Northolt, but at the last moment we opted for a single-sex school. With the production team I was looking at tapes from various possible schools, and it came down to two schools that everyone liked. I watched the video from Lancaster School in Leicester and remarked, 'Boys ... That is really difficult. Yes, that is exactly what I want to do, because that was the big problem on the first series: the boys were impossible. So why not go right into the jaws of the lion with a boys' school where nobody sings and see if we can make them sing?' Of course once I'd said that, it was a no-brainer. So I took on the challenge of getting 1,250 testosterone-charged boys to sing.

Lancaster School in Leicester was grappling across the board with the same problem we had uncovered at Northolt; that singing, especially among boys, was not cool. It felt like a really demanding challenge. I had proved that I could make a choir, but could I make a choir under much more difficult circumstances where there were no girls to help me out?

The whole thing was far more organic, much more experimental. On the first series the possibility of performing in China was already on the cards as we started out. When we went into Lancaster School, we had no idea what we would be able to provide as the big end to the series. We didn't know what we were doing. We had the vague ambition: 'Wouldn't it just be great if the entire school would sing?' while simultaneously thinking, 'Oh my God, how are we ever going to do that? These are sullen, disinterested teenage boys. They are not all going to sing ...'. But that was the goal.

This time round, and it's to Twenty Twenty's credit that they allowed me to do this, I started to become much more of an active participant. I felt empowered to say, 'No, hang on a minute, it doesn't feel right to do that yet. We can't perform here, we can't do that, this is what we need.'

I had also acquired a small amount of authority; only a patina of authority, but authority nonetheless, that allowed me to cold-call people more actively. So I rang the local music service to say, 'I am in the area, what support could you give me? Is there any way we can work together?' When I got in touch with King's College, Cambridge, there was now an under-standing of 'Ah yes, it's that *Choir* programme. That was really popular. Maybe this could allow us to show what we can do, what is possible and what is of quality.' That really shifted things, as doors were that bit easier to open when I was looking for ideas or support. Whenever I picked up the phone to people, they wanted to help and advise.

It felt like it was a fresh start all round. Becky and I had just bought a flat in Kilburn and I had been reunited with my piano, which her parents had kindly been piano-sitting for the best part of three years. (In our rented box in West Hampstead I'd been using a digital keyboard.) I knew I would be playing a lot over the coming months, and felt I ought to brush up my piano skills, so I arranged for it to be craned up and in through the window and its arrival helped to mark the start of a new period, although until you've seen your favourite possession dangling 20 feet in the air on a crane you haven't lived.

And so in spring 2007 I arrived at the school full of eagerness and ready to begin. I soon found out that for many of the pupils, singing was an alien concept. I knew what the problem was and if I hadn't known then I was swiftly reminded by a random boy in the corridors: 'Singing is boring, innit, like church singing … It's gay.' The gay word again. Only this time with a tinge of genuine homophobia: singing *makes* you gay. Nobody at

Lancaster should openly admit to being gay; so nobody should sing. I was up against it here.

If Northolt High School had been my work experience, then going into Lancaster School was my proper apprenticeship. I learnt to teach. I learnt classroom management working alongside the head of music, Helen Collins, who was a hugely inspirational influence for me. I watched her getting things right, I watched her getting things wrong. I got things right, I got things wrong. We tackled the challenge together, over the months of the project. It was a completely different experience.

Helen had a fantastic relationship with the boys. She had most of them right in the palm of her hand. She was a really good person to be dealing with a group of teenage boys as she had previously been working with very demanding and difficult kids in Pupil Referral Units, and she had an air of complete unflappability, which was a huge asset. And she had sung in choirs, which meant she understood the whole purpose and point of what we were trying to achieve.

She had noticed that around the ages of thirteen or fourteen the boys lost interest in singing, unless it was rock or rapping. She remembers now, 'Trying to get them to sing was hard, but even harder was trying to get them to sing in front of others. The boys would do it but only because they'd been heckled into it by me, through detentions and other means: bribery, chocolate, whatever I could throw at them to do it.'

Thank goodness Helen was there to guide me, because when it came to the teaching, I felt ill about the prospect. Yes, I had confronted some of Hackney's most reluctant musicians in a number of school outreach projects, but then I knew I was

there for one day only and that I would be going home at the
end of the workshop and not coming back. At Lancaster School
I was doing it every day, standing up in front of 30 unconvinced
kids and trying to claw my way through a lesson with pretty
minimal training. That was intimidating.

Helen had not been at the school very long, maybe just over
a year, and had made good headway but saw this as an opportunity to shake things up. She had seen the previous series of
The Choir and I think that had given her the belief to persuade
Paul Craven, the headteacher, to let me come into the school.
She says, 'Paul thought it was a good idea, although some of the
staff were a little reticent. They thought it might be a *Panorama*
documentary into inner-city schools.'

Where technology had been at the heart of Northolt High
School, sport was one of the driving forces at Lancaster School.
Lewis Meagor, a floppy-haired cherubic boy with all the promise
of an all-rounder, commented that singing 'wasn't the cool thing
to do. Everything was about football, basketball, rugby, cricket.
Sport, sport, sport.'

The sports department had their own separate building.
Once I'd got out on the sports field, a lot of this department
became the lifeblood of the staff choir, but initially there was
suspicion on both sides. Schools are like marketplaces: each
department has to fight to be heard. The teaching staff are
obliged to concentrate so much on results and making sure that
the basics are covered – that the maths department is functioning, that the English department is covering the curriculum –
that it seems to me that knowledge is in danger of becoming
segregated, which happens less in the real world.

Music, however, is a wonderfully multi-faceted discipline, involving history, technology and science, to name but a few elements; so I believe quite strongly that separating this subject from the others is artificial. When I was at school it was certainly like that. From what I remember, I don't think there was very much love lost between my wonderful and inspiring music teacher, Stephen Carleston, and the head of sports, who also made me feel like the enemy. This project would be about settling some old scores.

So with this in mind, it felt rather predictable to come into this school in Leicester where sport and music were based in different buildings and both sets of staff were trying to timetable things at the same time. It felt as if the music department would never leave the comfort zone of their own classrooms to go over to the sports department – and vice versa – to say, 'Is there any way we could make this work?' None of them had any spare time. They all had so many obligations.

I had a unique opportunity to go in to see the sports guys and say, 'Well, why don't you have Tuesday and I'll have Wednesday?' so that the boys who were good at sports *and* music could do both. In that environment, this way of thinking felt quite unusual, even revolutionary. The same divide goes on in the kids' minds as well: you are either a 'sports' kid or a 'music' kid. My point of view was, 'Why not be both? They are not mutually exclusive.'

However, we all had a lot to learn. When I decided to start up a staff choir, I was amazed at the variety of excuses the staff members came up with not to attend the first rehearsal. My favourite was the joyous individual who, when I accosted him and asked, 'Are you going to come to staff choir?' gave me a point blank, 'No!' 'Why not?' I asked. His answer will stay with me for a long time as the most unexpected I have ever heard. Without missing a beat he said, 'Horses …'.

But the weeks went by and the resistance of the boys was impressive. In some of the lessons I began to get an unpleasant hotness in my ears that reminded me of being told off by the teacher when I was eight years old. The boys knew how to push, push, push until they found a weak spot. I was out on a limb and flailing about. The seemingly insurmountable difficulty of trying to create a choir while implementing singing across the curriculum started to dawn on me. Florian Gassmann's words rang in my ears. Maybe I wasn't cut out for this teaching malarkey after all.

Those Summer Days

Many of the boys were overtly resistant to the idea of singing together but the work in the classroom was beginning to pay dividends. My remaining major headache was how to engage *all* of them, across the school, especially those kids who seemed only interested in rapping. To them, the idea of joining 'the choir' was anathema.

This was a problem I wrestled with throughout my time at Lancaster School and initially with little success. But on this series I had some new and extremely experienced advisors. I had been invited to the House of Lords for tea with Baroness Andrews, who was then the Parliamentary Under Secretary of State at the Department for Communities and Local Government. We had a delicious spread of preposterous teacakes in the very strange, rarefied world of the Lords, during the course of which she said, 'Oh, you must meet Howard Goodall.'

She invited me back to Westminster for tea shortly afterwards to meet Howard, who has written a wide range of choral music alongside all his work in musical theatre and for TV (he will, of course, for ever be remembered as the composer of the theme tunes for *The Vicar of Dibley* and *Blackadder*).

Over yet more preposterous teacakes I told Howard about the specific problem I had, of boys who not only viewed singing as a girlish thing to do, but thought that the choir was essentially not 'street' and therefore not right for the black and Asian boys in the school. Although that was something of a generalisation, it certainly was true for the guys who were heavily into urban music. I wanted to do a PR job on them. 'Why can't we change the notion of what a choir is, but still call it a choir?'

Among a number of terrific ideas, Howard suggested I contact Sense of Sound, an urban vocal collective with a rolling roster of participants, a mixture of professionals and amateurs.

Excited by the possibility, I asked the group to run a one-off workshop with the recalcitrant Imran Siddique and his crew. The group is based in Liverpool, so they had to squeeze into a minivan and travel all the way down to Leicester for the workshop. In only a short space of time, with these difficult-to-convince boys, they worked wonders. The kids who had previously been so reluctant said, 'I want in, this is great.' It was a major revelation to me. It completely changed my approach and made me focus far more on the music that they wanted to do rather than always imposing my musical selections. By that stage I was just happy to hear them sing.

Following the day with Sense of Sound we set up a beatbox group called the Playground MCs. It was a lunchtime club that more often than not would float quite close to, if not across, the boundaries of school rules. The boys at Lancaster School were not allowed mobile phones on the campus, yet this group all had mobiles. They wanted to play me songs on their phones and I'd have to say, 'You must put that away, because it's not allowed,' although obviously I wanted to engage with them musically. We danced around the school rules as best we could.

Organising the Playground MCs was hellish, because I was taking their natural, utterly anarchic playground activity of 'battling' – displaying prowess at how many words they could remember and how quickly they could get them out – and trying to put it inside the framework of the school day, making it a formal school activity. It became fairly fraught at times and, of course, the boys did not want any leadership from me. They wanted it to be like youth work, where I could be allowed to watch, and at certain times maybe offer advice, but only when it was asked for. Anything I came up with was by definition 'rubbish' and anything they came up with was of course cool but totally shambolic.

It was interesting for me because this was the first time I had been in the position of being the uncool teacher. I had done so much work in my previous role with the LSO where I was the one who went in to schools and could be all friendly while the teacher had to be the person who maintained discipline and enforced the rules. That is why the Sense of Sound session worked so well: they came in as total outsiders with a bit of street cred, and they weren't teachers. It was a humbling moment as I saw the power that these outsiders had. I longed to be cool again.

Only one boy in the MCs was also in the choir proper. Matthew Robinson was the first boy to walk in at the initial sign-up and proved invaluable in helping me tread the line between singing and beatboxing. Matthew was talented and had the application that Imran lacked. One of the songs that the boys suggested was Justin Timberlake's 'Cry Me a River', which we worked on in an *a capella* version. This was a turning point and Matthew was crucial in helping to keep the MCs on the right path.

At Lancaster School there were two proper boy trebles, both active choristers, Elliott and Josh, but it took a while for them to make themselves known to me. Of course they were extremely good, but I had had to work hard to persuade them to come to rehearsals. It said so much about the atmosphere around singing at the school that the two most likely candidates were so reluctant.

For my own sanity, and as an antidote to the Playground MCs' activities, I asked the choir to sing Handel's '*Ombra Mai Fu*', an aria from his opera *Serse* about a king surveying his kingdom from the shade of his favourite plane tree. I thought this was rather an appropriate choice; still quite strongly male, but also showing a softer side. It was in direct contrast to many of the lyrics the beatbox boys were used to, what they called 'spitting rhymes', which were often misogynistic, sexist and about drugs and guns; everything you wouldn't want to hear in a school setting.

The Sense of Sound workshop had shown the MCs' group a way of combining rapping and choral music. Afterwards I asked them, 'If the choir could be like this, would you join?' 'Yeah, of course. We don't want to do "choir", but we'd do this.' Fine. I didn't mind how they justified it to themselves; my ultimate aim was to get them to sing. By pitching it like that, I managed to get most of them onside. One or two of them never sang, and only ever beatboxed, but most importantly for me it hooked in the slippery Imran Siddique.

I had originally thought my way in to that group would be through Imran, whom Helen Collins and a couple of the other teachers had pointed out to me early on as someone who could really sing. He was known to them: he had sung in school. But I had been finding it tough to convince Imran that this was something he should be doing, because the rest of his mates were not interested and he was very conscious of his standing among them.

I think I had gone into Lancaster School with a thought in the back of my mind: 'Is there another Chloe Sullivan here? Where is my rough diamond?' Imran, however, was right at the very worst moment of the teenage years, idolising everything that is wrong as far as adults are concerned. I was meeting all of that head on but with a naïve predetermined mind-set of, 'Ah, here's my Chloe Sullivan.' I soon discovered that there couldn't be another Chloe because everyone's different.

As I got to know Imran better I discovered that his father is a singer. His parents were separated, and Imran said to me that his mother, whilst proud of her son, tried to keep his feet on the ground about the notion of a career in music and sometimes discouraged him from being a professional singer. Imran told me a story that the one time he had sung at karaoke with his father, he had been criticised by him for choosing the wrong song, and it had knocked him. These two facts partly explained his reticence about singing so publicly. You could see in Imran a really troubled sense of whether singing was appropriate for him; was it masculine? Here he was, a boy whose voice had not changed yet and who was capable of singing incredibly high notes, but you would never have caught him singing those notes in a choral sense. If he was singing a Prince or a Michael Jackson song, then it would all right, but it was only all right under a very specific set of circumstances, the rules of which I was not allowed to know.

Imran and I had a volatile relationship that seemed to start off well whenever we had our one-on-one singing lessons, but as soon as he was in front of his peer group, he would become difficult and confrontational.

As the song goes, 'many years have passed since those summer days' – in fact five years as I write – and Helen Collins is now sanguine about Imran's involvement. 'I think it was quite difficult for Imran. He was torn. He knew he could sing and he knew this was going to be a great opportunity for him, but he just couldn't help but act the bad boy to keep that image up.'

At the time I found it hard to be quite so understanding. There were other boys who needed attention and I felt that I was wasting my efforts. It seemed to pain Imran to be praised for doing the right thing. Why would he act up in class and yet be as good as gold in his singing lessons with me? Why this contradiction?

Helen says, 'It seemed to be impossible to do the two. A lot of teachers came up informally and said, "What are you doing? All that attention is making him worse."' She is right. The glare of the spotlight made Imran very difficult to deal with. If I was teaching him with the rest of his class he had to demonstrate that he was 'the man' in that situation. He was in control. I understood it – we have all messed around at the back of a class – but it was very hard to teach.

At one point, in a very difficult situation, when I had been obliged to give him a detention for wearing a coat in class, not something I wanted to do, I lost my temper and after the boys had long left the class I slammed the desk and lashed out with an F-word in frustration: frustration with the situation, with Imran, with myself. I had reached the point where I was so pressured trying to get the actual task in front of me done that I couldn't worry about losing my rag. You can't teach and always be an ocean of calm.

I had several letters about that swear word, one which included a stamped addressed envelope, presumably for an apology. Needless to say I didn't respond: the pressure of the situation was immense and whatever people feel about expletives, I defy anyone to teach Year 9 music in the summer term to boys who don't want to be there *without* losing their cool. The more immediate problem for me was that because I had been told to give Imran the detention, he didn't speak to me for months. The whole idea of involving all parts of the school in the choir looked like it was going to be permanently derailed. I spent the summer break wrestling with how to deal with the Imran situation. It was my 'How do you solve a problem like Maria?' moment. Luckily Howard Goodall came up with the solution in Sense of Sound.

Once Imran was talking to me again, I knew I wanted him to sing with the choir, and I had this idea that he should be the soloist in the final performance because not only was he one of the most talented boys, he was also one of the most influential. He was one of those boys who made me feel, 'If he falls into line, they will all fall like ninepins.' That proved to be right. He was what I think of as a 'mood-maker', so when he decided that being involved was acceptable, he took us one step nearer to everyone being in the choir. I never quite got Imran to the choir rehearsals proper, but at least he sang in the Royal Albert Hall.

At tea at the House of Lords, Howard Goodall also pointed me in the direction of Guildford County School, where Caroline Gale had put together a choir of 200 boys and got them singing. I took a day off from my teaching duties and caught the train to Guildford.

Guildford is not Leicester but nevertheless it had a school full of boys and somehow Caroline had managed to draw them into her choir. I was desperate for some inspiration. Caroline isn't a world-class conductor or a magician: she's a teacher who is totally committed to her students and who has made some very smart choices. She taught me the importance of repertoire. She went absolutely unashamedly to the songs that the kids already knew and recognised, and then pushed them onwards and upwards from there. She also allowed the boys to sing in any octave, not being too chorally strict about it.

I took notice, because it was clearly working. The sound she achieved was rough around the edges, yet spirited. I saw a huge choir of unauditioned boys giving their all to a few pop hits. I knew I could do the same at Lancaster School. I went back to the piles of sheet music I had carted from London to Leicester and looked for some new songs for the choir.

I picked Sting's 'Fields of Gold' for the choir to sing at a school concert. There are certain subjects that I find really universal. Walking hand in hand with somebody you love, even if you haven't done it, is a slightly idealised version of love that I thought would work for teenage boys, and they brought a sort of innocence to it, which I thought was quite charming. It is a song I really responded to, which is my first rule of thumb with a song: does it provoke an emotional reaction in me? The second decision is whether or not I can hear the choir's voices singing it.

Lewis Meagor sang the solo in 'Fields of Gold', which happened to be his mum's and nan's favourite song. He had never done anything like that before, but he was a good little performer, really charming. In the solo audition he had thought carefully about how he wanted to put the song across with quaint actions and gestures. It was the complete opposite of the 'cathedral-style' choristers in the choir who were used to standing very still to sing. At the time Lewis was particularly into sport, but after the experience of the choir he decided he wanted to pursue a more creative pathway and become an actor. 'Being in the choir propelled me into that artistic side. I'm fully determined to be an actor.'

When Lewis sang that solo in the school concert, it was such a simple, heart-warming moment: Lewis singing to his mum. That's just a human moment. Naturally, his mum was on the verge of tears. It reminded me of singing 'I'd do anything for you, dear, anything' from *Oliver* with Lucy Harris (with whom I was, of course, deeply in love) in my final year of primary school. We couldn't look each other in the eye because it was so embarrassing, and gave one of the most unimpressive performances of that song ever, I am sure. But my parents and grandparents were there, and that was what counted. These are profound moments in your life.

As I continued to grapple with the challenges facing me at Lancaster School, I remembered some wise words of advice from Ralph Allwood MBE, then the Precentor and head of music at Eton. He told me that early on in his career he had been teaching in a school where it was an effort to get the boys to sing, so he had spoken to them all and said, 'I am here to persuade you that singing is a good thing for you.' I took note of that central word 'persuade' and used it to set the tone for everything I was trying to do.

Many of the issues that cropped up during *Boys Don't Sing* I had been through at my grammar school in Bournemouth. Stephen Carleston, the great music teacher at that school, arrived there a term of so after me, and proceeded to set up a school choir. For half a term my mother badgered me to join it. I kept saying, 'Yes, yes, I will,' but I was too busy learning how to deal with the routine of this new school, getting my homework diary organised, sorting out the textbooks and the sports bag. Finally I thought, 'OK, I'll go and join,' and then I sang every single day for my entire school career.

I did get a bit of stick about joining the choir, but the great thing was that being in the school choir got you out of morning assembly. Even on those days when I had forgotten to do my homework and I was really stressed knowing that the maths teacher was going to murder me when he saw me, I had a moment where I could start the day well, with song.

I remembered that when we tried holding afternoon rehearsals at Lancaster School, it turned out to be impossible because many of the boys kept missing rehearsals to go to rugby fixtures. In the end I said, 'Why don't we do the rehearsals before school?' We broke the budget and bought a toaster and some bread, and that did the trick. A good way to motivate any teenage boy is through food. They would all turn up, have a slice of toast and sing before school. It worked. We had some of our best rehearsals in the morning because they were all fresh and alert, and yet not *too* awake – slightly dazed and therefore agreeably compliant.

Many of the boys were dealing with the trauma of their voices breaking. I remember the ambivalence you feel: happy to be growing up, but also aware that your days of singing the tune are over. As a treble in the school choir I had been able to sing glorious top As without any effort whatsoever. At 13 or 14 I was on a car journey with my mum when I told her, 'Of course I can't sing the high notes like I used to be able to.' She laughed and said, 'There is absolutely no sign of your voice breaking.' I remember being slightly disappointed, because at that age a part of you so desperately *wants* your voice to break to prove your manliness.

Finally I did get the longed-for but also slightly feared wobbly voice. There were a few weeks where I stopped going to choir, but it wasn't for very long. Stephen Carleston gave me some good advice: 'Just sing through it, keep going and sing whatever feels comfortable.' Within a very short space of time I was singing tenor. Then I was incredibly disappointed because I wanted to be a bass.

It gave me an understanding of what the boys at Lancaster School were going through, struggling because they had gone from having a clear vocal identity to a period of difficulty and then suddenly not really knowing where their voice was. Many boys never recover, never emerge from that hinterland of vocal development. It is a very difficult phase. Lewis Meagor remembers, 'Everyone was quite narrow-minded towards singing. At Lanky everyone cared what they looked like and what their reputation was.' Lewis was prepared to take the risk: 'I started to enjoy myself and didn't care what people thought – but I was in the minority.'

To encourage the boys not to lose their confidence and to see singing as a manly thing to do, I needed to bring the teachers into the choir, particularly the sports department and the head of year Alex Foreman. Alex and I had an ongoing banter about how I was going to get him in the choir. 'I'd rather have a beer with my mates down the boozer,' he retorted to my initial suggestion. In the end he absolutely understood the value of it and although he hated the idea, he realised it was simply about getting the message across to the boys, 'Look, all your favourite teachers are doing it, get involved.'

One day with one of my more difficult classes I burst into a class that Alex was giving and we sang a song that the boys had written in 15 minutes, the opening words of which were, 'You're big, you're bold'. The boys had actually wanted to sing, 'You're big, you're *bald*,' but somebody misspelt 'bald' and I said 'bold' was better – and far more diplomatic. Alex was a good sport about it. He enjoyed all that because there was a nod and a wink to it. I got the impression that he would come around eventually, but he was resisting it to the last minute. On another occasion I gatecrashed his office with a keyboard and gave him a singing lesson. I can remember watching that moment back with a group of friends and them guffawing with laughter as I told Alex, 'You have a really big powerful instrument.' I don't know what all the fuss was about.

After months of playing cat and mouse, in the end I managed to persuade him *and* the rest of the sports teachers to take part in a staff choir performance at the school's sports day.

We rehearsed in secret after the boys had gone home. I soon learnt that there is nothing more difficult than controlling a roomful of teachers, because they all sit at the back and talk – they have to deal with those naughty kids all day and this is their chance for revenge. We had a few rehearsals all crammed into the music room, and it felt exciting to have a clear aim. There *was* a very macho environment in that school and some of the female teachers struggled with that and how to soften the boys a bit, so to sing together seemed to everyone to be a good thing.

Helen seemed incredibly nervous that day. I suppose if it had gone wrong it would have undermined our efforts. 'I could say my nerves were almost equal walking out onto the Saffron Lane athletics track as walking out onto the Royal Albert Hall podium,' she remembers. Thinking back, it was the only time we gathered the entire school for a performance.

As it was, we won the day. When the staff choir stood up and belted out 'World in Union', there was a significant shift in the boys' respect for their teachers and in their attitude to singing generally. My original pitch to the staff had been 'it doesn't matter if you think you are crap. I'm an expert with crap people!' They certainly weren't crap that day and it was a first chink in the armour of the boys' defence against singing.

The other big sea change took place when we went to King's College, Cambridge. I had met Nicholas Robinson, the head-teacher at King's College School, quite by chance at a concert. He was enthusiastic about the importance of sharing skills and showing our boys what was possible with hard work, so gave us an open invitation to King's. When the boys rolled into town he welcomed us with open arms and an excellent lunch. Amazingly, in the entire history of the building there had never been a filmed rehearsal in the King's College chapel. This was an extraordinary moment.

I really enjoyed watching Stephen Cleobury, the conductor of the choir at King's College, dealing with the Lancaster School kids. Of course they were completely on their best behaviour because they knew exactly what they were there for. Richard McNicol, who had been my mentor at the LSO, once said to me, 'If you trust young people they will never let you down.' Before we went in I said to these boys, 'We are in the seat of choral singing in this country. It doesn't get better than this. I need you to sing your best, I need you to behave impeccably. I need you to be better than you have ever been before.' They were massively intimidated by the older teenagers and young men in the King's College choir, and on top of that they had Paul Craven, their Lancaster School headteacher, and most of the senior staff staring them down like military snipers.

Naturally they exceeded my expectations. It was magical to hear the two choirs combine and fill that wonderful acoustic with song – truly unforgettable. The choir was inspired. They learned an enormous amount about confidence and the level of commitment needed to sing. It was good for them to see how a professional choir was run, how Stephen Cleobury could say, 'Let's just do that again and go from bar 15,' and it just happened without any fuss. They could sense that that was the way that rehearsals should run. The boys were also blown away by the fact that the King's choir sang one piece, 'The Twelve' by William Walton, which they had only rehearsed for the first time a week before.

The day at King's was an eye-opener in another way. These Lancaster School boys had only been at it for a very short space of time, and the choir had been completely un-auditioned. Yet I could see one or two of them looking out of the corner of their eyes, listening to these other boy trebles and thinking, 'I could do that, I can get halfway there.' Maybe they couldn't read music to the same degree as the King's choristers, and maybe their voices might not be quite as strong or as beautiful, but the feeling that they held their own gave them an enormous boost of confidence. It was a good stepping stone.

I could also see Paul Craven and the other staff members realising that this project was working and had the potential to reflect extremely well on Lancaster School, that music could present a really positive public face. One of the most sceptical sports teachers had also come along and he told me afterwards that he could not believe that these boys he taught on the sports field were standing here shoulder to shoulder with a choir of such excellence. For him, and for Paul, this was a revelatory moment, and from then on there was a growing sense of pride throughout the school.

The Night Has Come

I was now ready to start bringing together the different elements of Lancaster School: the staff choir, the Playground MCs and the main boys' choir. I'd split the choir into two different groups for rehearsals, upper voices and lower voices. I was doing so many rehearsals a week that I was waking up in the middle of the night singing the songs.

We had a definite target, performing as part of the Schools Prom at the Royal Albert Hall. Looking back, to start at 'Lanky Boys' without a specific end point in mind had been pretty brave – not just for me but for the BBC too. However, for the premise to work we had to find out what it was we were dealing with before we created the ending. Perhaps because of all the discussion that the first series stirred up, I wanted a British national showcase for our achievements. The experience of China, which was so inspirational to everyone involved, made me seek out something on the same scale. If I had a pound for every boy at that school who asked me, 'Are we going to China?' ...

When I was at school I went to a Schools Prom at the Royal Albert Hall and I was both dazzled by the building and impressed by the experience. With this in mind I went to see Larry Westland CBE, then the chief executive of Music for Youth, a national organisation dedicated to offering musical opportunities to young people. We met at the Royal College of Music, a building lovingly referred to by former students as 'Colditz', because of its architecture and its reputation as a hothouse for young talent: once you're in, you don't get out! I climbed the front steps with a degree of trepidation.

Larry Westland cut an imposing presence and had the air of someone who would not easily be flannelled. He took some persuading. Larry saw a possible PR benefit in being featured on the TV programme but he was seriously concerned about being fair to all the young people who had fought their way through competitive rounds to win a place at the Royal Albert Hall, and we also wanted to include the staff choir in the performance, which complicated things still further. After some jousting, a compromise was hit upon. We would be there as 'inspirational guests' – there was a precedent for this, they'd had them before. For me this only added to the pressure because now the performance *had* to be inspiring. There was only one solution, we needed a *lot* of boys. We would be speaking to the nation. I had to prove that boys *do* sing. 'You need a lot of people, otherwise the sound will simply get swallowed up in the Hall,' said Larry with impossible gravitas. He was envisaging a choir of a hundred or more. At the time I was barely achieving twenty regular members. It became a numbers game.

However, that was now in the past. The months of toil were behind us and I had managed to build up the choir to the necessary hundred singers. The work had paid off. Preparations were hotting up.

The final rehearsal before the Royal Albert Hall was in the school hall at Lancaster Boys. School halls all smell the same. Although highly polished, the parquet flooring had grime embedded in the wood from generations of sweaty teenagers. It's the sort of smell that whisks you back to the lost teenage years you'd rather forget. The hall at Lancaster School was barely large enough for my newly formed 'super choir' and we were bursting at the seams.

The moment arrived to finally put it all together. It was days before we were due to perform at the Albert Hall. I'd come straight from the end of another long day of teaching, having fought my way through a lesson with one particularly recalcitrant group of Year 8s. This mega-rehearsal was a treat, the first time each of the component parts would hear each other singing, and the first time I'd heard the whole ensemble. It would prove whether the arrangement I had knitted together during stolen moments would actually work in practice.

We started off with the junior section of the boys' choir, which we called the upper voices, and then brought in the lower voices, the tenors and basses. Remembering what I had learnt from Caroline Gale at Guildford County School, I had allowed the boys to go with whichever group felt comfortable, although sometimes I gave them a subtle nudge in the right direction. The two parts of the choir used to rehearse on different days, so bringing them into the same rehearsal was also a first. The harmony worked but we still did not have all the pieces in place

After about half an hour of fine polishing the teachers arrived. I could hear them singing as they walked all the way down the corridor to the main hall. They were joining in with the boys even before they got there because they knew the arrangement. They burst through the doors all together because they had just been released from a staff meeting. The rehearsal was gathering a head of steam.

Lastly I brought in Imran and his cohort. With their now familiar swagger and an air of musical entitlement they sauntered in to assume pole position. I was creating a chimera. I had asked them to come a little later so that I could have everything ready. 'Right, everyone let's go for it,' I suggested and we leapt into our first run. At first the beatbox choir maintained their cool but as their part began they were joined by the sound of 140 people backing them up. They broke into boyish grins. It was like the first day of spring after a very long winter.

As I cajoled the choir into life I could see out of the corner of my eye that the MCs were really getting into it. They couldn't contain their excitement; they were bubbling over physically. At the end of the first time through there was this wonderful, wonderful moment where Imran exploded in rapture. It was amazing, electric. You dream of a moment like that. Everyone who was there realised in the same instant that this combination of voices was going to work. We only ran through the piece a couple of times more, said, 'That's it, that's fine' and went home on a high, thinking, 'This is going to be good.'

I was so pleased for Imran. He suddenly went from being a slightly peripheral figure within the school establishment to being the main soloist with a backing choir of 140 staff and kids. That would be quite a moment for anybody, and for him that was exciting. Crucially it still felt cool because his friends were beatboxing with him. I'd won the day.

It did feel like a victory at the time. I had been slogging away for months and this was the first moment where I felt large numbers of boys had decided, 'This is a good thing to be involved in,' not, 'It's Mr Malone banging on about singing again.'

It also justified my choice of songs. I had been trying to find one that would work for all the different sections of the choir. I had shipped virtually every song book I owned up to Leicester and spent hours flicking through them trying to find the combination of a song that would highlight the strengths and diversity of the choir, but not be beyond their capabilities.

'Stand by Me' was a song I remembered from the Rob Reiner film with River Phoenix. It was a movie I loved and it had meant a lot to me when it came out in the 1980s, just as I was about to enter my own teens. The theme of the film was about boys all working together, going on a journey of discovery. It seemed the perfect song given what we were trying to achieve at Lancaster School, but for some reason I couldn't seem to convince anyone else of this.

During that hot summer of 2007 I was decorating the living room with a dark olive paint that was getting in my hair and eyes. The painting job was turning into nearly as daunting a task as putting the choir together. I had the radio on all day, but as a particularly turgid afternoon drama began on Radio 4, I started flicking through the stations. As I reached Radio 1, on came this song. That's 'Stand by Me', I thought, but it wasn't; it turned out to be a track by Sean Kingston called 'Beautiful Girls'. Since the two songs had a similar feel, I had the idea of combining them. Weeks later, back at school, I pitched the idea to Imran and the Playground MCs. 'We can have a mash-up, the choir singing one bit, you singing another part and then it will all come together.' Because they knew 'Beautiful Girls', they cottoned on, and once I had sold the idea to them, everyone else signed up for it. More or less.

I wrote the combined version of the two songs during lunch hours, sitting in restaurants in the evenings, jotting down an arrangement on napkins, 16 bars of this song and then a bit of the other one, testing out different variations. I spent a few days agonising over whether or not to include the word 'suicide' from the 'Beautiful Girls' lyrics. Once I had managed to work every-thing out, I rehearsed each of the elements separately, so no one had heard the complete version, and in any case it wasn't sounding that good because there was no orchestra: I would be playing the piano with one hand and trying to conduct with the other. This was why it was such a joyous moment for us all when it worked so well the first time we put it together.

We had persuaded ourselves that we were ready, but first we had had to convince a far tougher audience in the shape of Leonora Davies MBE, the extremely well-respected music advi-sor representing Larry Westland at Music for Youth. I had met Leonora before in my early music education days working in Tower Hamlets and I knew she took no prisoners. Not for her the fluffy, 'Hey kids, let's bang a few tambourines together and call it music. Didn't we all do well?' approach. She was interested in learning tangible skills where proper educational objectives were clear, structured and measurable.

I was intimidated by the idea of Leonora coming to evaluate us. Don't forget that at this point I was still feeling that this was not my job. I was winging it very publicly and I thought I was about to be found out. A respected senior colleague, much more experienced than me, was coming to judge the boys, but I felt that I might just end up as collateral damage.

Leonora first came to see the choir at a huge singing confer-ence called Singposium in Birmingham. She listened to the choir and made a number of valid criticisms but in a measured, posi-tive way. As a professional educator she knew it would have done the choir a disservice to say, 'Yes, you are ready, it's fine,' when we obviously had months of work to do. Leonora was canny and set us targets – improving the pitch and thinking about the phrasing – that she wanted us to achieve by the time she came to listen again. She had made exactly the right call, because come October, when she came back and said, 'That is much much better, you have worked really hard,' the boys were elated. They respected her because she hadn't blown it too early. Relieved, I had an extra glass of red wine with dinner that night.

Now they were ready to prepare for the Albert Hall. At the beginning of the autumn term I had stood up in an assembly and announced, 'We are going to the Royal Albert Hall!' I took the murmur from the boys as a buzz of excitement, but coming out of the hall one of the other teachers, Ben Ratcliffe, said, 'You got that really badly wrong, Gareth. They have absolutely no idea what the Royal Albert Hall is.' He was right: the boys admitted they didn't know where it was, had never heard of it. The buzz had been one of confusion – and disappointment. They all knew the Phoenix Choir had gone to sing in China.

So, chastened, I went back another morning to show them photos. This time I was more convincing: 'It's in London, it's a 5,000-seater venue, it's of national and historic significance – and boys, it's a day off maths.' Hurrah! The day-off bit did it. Suddenly they were all up for it.

I knew that the sound of the boys' voices alone would not be enough. We needed help. We arranged to play with the local county-level youth orchestra from Leicestershire Music Service, who were based just round the corner. The youth orchestra did a sterling job, bringing in all their best string players and, in particular, a fantastic trumpeter. What I didn't tell anyone at the time was that it was the first orchestra I'd conducted. I think I got away with it.

To find another soloist to counterbalance Imran in the finale, I decided that we should hold auditions, and this time consciously made an attempt to create an *X Factor* feel because the boys all understood exactly how that worked. I argued that it *had* to feel nerve-wracking, so when they walked in, they'd experience that lurch in the stomach that all performers know so well. It makes you sick and you think, 'Oh, I don't want to do this any more.' But contrast an audition in your school with stepping out at the Royal Albert Hall. I knew what it would be like on that stage, utterly terrifying. Whoever we chose would need nerves of steel. I was joined on the panel by Helen, and the head, Paul Craven. Paul really got into his role. I think he thought he was Simon Cowell.

Although initially sceptical about the project earlier in the summer, Paul had been particularly kind to me when I was struggling to drum up support. My grandmother, who I was very close to, had had to go into hospital during the last days of the summer holidays. I missed the first couple of days of shooting in the new term. As a result I rushed back to catch up and didn't feel as if I had got my head straight after the endless hours sitting by her hospital bed. Added to my cloudy head there was a general lack of momentum as the boys had grown about four inches over the long break: 'Oh, *choir*, that is what I *used* to do last year, when I was young. Now I am mature, in Year 8 and I play rugby.'

Autumn term at the Lancaster School meant rugby, football, going outside and extreme muddiness, which of course they loved. Even the most musical boys were missing rehearsals to go off and play rugby. I was becoming increasingly vexed. So first thing one morning I went in to see Paul in his office. When I laid out the situation for him he was hugely surprised at the lack of numbers. 'Right, come on, let's go, there's a year assembly right now. Let's go in and speak to them.' Suddenly I was in front of all these kids, with nothing prepared, having to advertise the Royal Albert Hall project. That was the time Ben Ratcliffe told me afterwards that I completely fluffed my presentation, and Ben also said, quite rightly, 'Paul saved you,' because he had rushed in to my defence.

Six months before, Paul might have let me fail, but by that point the sports day with the staff choir had been a massive hit, a high-profile moment for the school with singing right at the heart of it, there had been a successful school summer concert and the Singposium event. He was starting to get the impression that, 'This could be a good thing, and if we are going to go onto a national stage, I am not going to have my school let down.' Once you have got the head onside like that it is so much easier, because when you ask if the choir can get out of school a bit earlier to rehearse, all the usual reasons why it is not possible magically evaporate.

At the end of the audition process for the soloist the choice came down to Tojan and Wahchi. I thought long and hard about the decision. Tojan would have been the easy choice: he was a really nice kid, had a lovely big smile (Leonora Davies said, 'Hearts melt when Tojan smiles'), a beautiful singing voice and a completely easy relationship with singing. But for me it was imperative that we had a boy with a changed voice. The whole point of the exercise had been about what happens to boys when they go to secondary school: their voices change – they don't 'break', they grow – and so they find it harder to stand up and sing any more. Although Wahchi was less musically experienced than Tojan, he spoke to me of 'every boy'. He had never thought about singing in a choir before; his parents were immigrants who didn't speak much English but who sang at home. He really loved singing. I thought that was absolutely right.

As I celebrated this moment of apparent triumph, the gods of music chose to taunt me: Wahchi's voice disappeared to a croak. He just couldn't sing and we were only days away from the Albert Hall. It was a sweaty moment.

Wahchi felt a huge sense of responsibility. We took him all the way to an ear, nose and throat specialist in Nottingham so they could feed a camera probe up his nose and down his throat – which can't have been much fun for Wahchi – and have a good look at his vocal cords. There wasn't much they could do. The specialist gave him some antibiotics and said, 'Drink a lot of water.' Wahchi was just about all right by the day of the concert. He said that though he was 'acting a cool guy' on the outside, he was surprisingly nervous and scared on the inside. But he did a great job, though his voice wasn't as fresh on the night as I would have liked. There's nothing you can do about that sort of thing. And despite the frog in his throat, his performance has attracted over four million hits on YouTube.

With over 600 hours of footage for the series, the editors had a huge task on their hands in making the final cut. Harry Beney, one of the two directors, worked tirelessly through long week-ends sifting through the footage, trying to tell the story of what had happened during those extraordinary months.

Looking back, one of the things I most remember, but which perhaps wasn't shown, was everything I learnt about being a classroom music teacher. Helen Collins put me through my paces, and by the end we both felt we'd got closer to integrating singing into the class teaching.

Helen talks about all the lessons we gave throughout the summer. 'We found some great success there, books and books and books of repertoire. I remember singing "Joseph and the Amazing Technicolor Dreamcoat" and one particular class going absolutely mad about it. It was a shame that none of that was shown, because you were starting to become an educational practitioner. That was my only disappointment, that the series didn't show enough of what we achieved in the classroom. It focused more on how difficult it was rather than the outcome we achieved.'

Helen and I were inseparable that year and I wanted to make a public statement that showed how grateful I was for her trust and support. So I asked her to conduct *'Ombra Mai Fu'* at the Prom. She hadn't done very much conducting, if any, before and not surprisingly was daunted by the prospect of her first public outing as a conductor being in front of a packed Royal Albert Hall. I had re-arranged the piece to suit the choir and produced some sheet music with a fairly slow tempo marking, but when we tried it out, the boys simply couldn't handle the breathing as the phrases were too long. So I kept saying to Helen, 'Speed it up, speed it up, they are going to go purple and die ...'.

However, I think she felt the presence of the music police looking over her shoulder and saying, 'Helen, no, you are going too fast.' I was encouraging her not to worry about it, but when we started the piece on the night she took it at an absolute snail's pace. I felt her nerves, could sense that she didn't absolutely love that moment, and could hear the boys struggling. Poor Helen. What a thing to have asked her to do, and what a trial by fire for her! (I'm very glad to say it didn't put Helen off conducting for life, as she subsequently took some courses, really got into it and now runs a very successful special needs choir, which is winning plaudits.)

So when I walked out onto the stage afterwards to conduct the full choir and orchestra on the 'Stand by Me/Beautiful Girls' piece, it was like wading through a soup made out of terror. It was down to me to pick them up by the bootstraps and communicate somehow through my facial expression, 'Come on, we have only got one more song, and we have got to pick this up. Let's fight for singing. Let's smash it.'

At the end I clenched my fist, as if in triumph. It was partly because we ended 'Stand by Me' with the trademark 'dum dum, da da, dum dum' and the choir had this awful tendency to do one 'dum dum' too many, or one boy would forget and launch a lone 'da da' into the silence. I had told them all to watch me like a hawk. I was counting down in my head, 4, 3, 2, 1, now! That was the fist-clench. I wanted no one in that room to be in any doubt that this was the end of the song, and there was an element of trying to give the choir gestures that felt determined and masculine. Since then, and maybe a little more self-consciously, I have done a fair number of fist-clenching endings.

As I watched back the series I was delighted to see Imran singing along with the choir. It had been a beautiful and anarchic success. It almost didn't work, but somehow I had made it happen by sheer doggedness. My time at Lancaster Boys introduced me to a new level of hard work. The icing on the cake, though, was when Imran delivered the most succinct review of the whole event: 'Wicked, man.'

Stand Up and Face the World

The next time I clenched my fists was in the interests of self-defence when I engaged in a little light sparring with Matty Leonard, a former boxer and leading light of the South Oxhey community. I had agreed to go one round with him in the ring at the boxing club he ran there.

It may surprise you, but I had never been in a boxing ring before. Lurking outside the ropes was a group of youths baying for blood, quite possibly mine. Matty climbed in the ring like a paler, smaller version of De Niro in *Raging Bull*. 'Let's go, singer man,' he quipped in his distinctive cockney drawl.

I'm probably an idiot but I suddenly wanted to prove myself. I thought I was relatively fit – I'd been doing a lot of cycling round South Oxhey – but I was not at all prepared for how exhausting a boxing session was: even before I got in the ring they had made me pummel some practice pads. It is totally physical. I hadn't appreciated the sheer power that boxers deliver. Most soft people like me toddle off to the gym once a week and spend half of it in the sauna. Boxers hit with menace.

When I arrived at the gym and said I had brought 'my gym kit', the way Matty responded I think he imagined I was straight out of *Chariots of Fire*, maybe about to top off my outfit with a college scarf. The fact that the director later thought it appropriate to use 'The Sugar Plum Fairy' as the soundtrack to this scaled-down version of *Rocky* was, I thought, a particularly low blow.

Exhausted from hitting the practice pads, I undertook my three-minute round with Matty. In a titanic struggle I hit him as hard as I conceivably knew how, summoning up strength I didn't know I had. But by degrees my imagined triumph turned into one of those nightmares I had often had as a boy, where I was in a fight and couldn't land a hit or seemed to be running through treacle. Bang, bang, bang, trying very hard, I made absolutely no impression whatsoever on Matty (he later said he thought he couldn't hit me too hard, that a single gust of wind would have knocked me over), and then I think he kissed me, very worryingly. I gave him no encouragement.

This rumble in the jungle with Matty – though it was more of a scuffle in a spinney – was a key moment in the process of getting to know the people of South Oxhey in Hertfordshire, where I was going to be spending the next nine months creating a community choir. It proved I was prepared to get stuck in. Once again I was going to be asking people to potentially make fools of themselves, to stand up in front of their friends and sing, which for a lot of people feels like a dangerous thing to do. So just as I had tackled my fear of heights by climbing up on the high ropes with the Northolt School kids, going into the ring with Matty was me saying, 'I am not theorising. I am prepared to get my hands dirty.' And my gym kit too.

Matty Leonard was a true son of South Oxhey. He seemed to know everyone, and was exactly the kind of person I wanted to draw into my plans for a community-wide choir. For this new series I had really wanted a different kind of challenge.

For the time being I felt I had gone as far as I could as a school choirmaster at the Northolt and Lancaster Schools. After the Royal Albert Hall performance I had worked very hard to preserve the legacy of all that work, returning many times to Lancaster School and the area to work with the local primary feeder schools on singing projects with the local music service. Crucially I had an able successor, Simon Lubkowski, in place well before I had gone, to keep the choir running. Simon is the extremely tall gentleman who appears at the edge of frame in many of the rehearsals. He's now head of music at the school.

As a result of the series and the work we did to ensure that the word was spread widely, many children chose, or at least their parents did, to come to Lancaster School over the following years, yes because they had seen the choir on TV but also because it was now known that it supported a large, strong and active choir. That was a sea change for a sports specialist college. Helen Collins left the school to teach at another school in the area at the end of the school year. I felt that it was time to broaden my horizons too.

When the *Boys Don't Sing* series ended, I knew I had gone through a period of growing up in my professional life, by taking on a more adult responsibility for my work. This was the way I wanted to work and how I wanted to be known. I remembered the blogger whose criticisms had helped influence the way I set about the second series and thought, 'There you go, there you go, Mr Florian Gassmann.'

I had done my best to answer those criticisms, to adapt and change and be better at my job. Imagine my delight when Mr Florian Gassmann wrote on the TES website: 'I thought this second series was very much better than the first, not least because Gareth Malone himself understood why his first project was flawed – lack of sustainability, insufficient contact with the kids and an over-ambitious goal that was as embarrassing for the viewer as it was for the kids.' In truth, nobody was embarrassed about the goal, but we must agree to disagree. I must have him over to dinner; I think it would make for a really entertaining evening. Sadly after the second series Florian Gassmann ceased discussing my projects.

I went away from Lancaster School with a sense of a job well done. I had had so much support from the school, I respected the staff and I felt that I was handing the choir over to people who were not only completely competent, but committed to continuing it. This time I was comfortable with the idea that I was leaving the choir. In any case, the Lancaster School choir were all boys. They didn't open up. The boys were not as emotionally astute as the Northolt girls Rhonda and Laura had been in China, coming up to me, doe-eyed, 'Please don't go, Mr Malone.' So even if we had a tear in the eye when we said goodbye, we blamed it on hay fever.

In the aftermath of *Boys Don't Sing* there was a massive spike in letters. It still surprised and delighted me that people were taking the trouble to write. But now it was turning into a deluge and many of them were up to six pages long. I was going through the fan mail for the best part of six months. I had boxfuls of letters asking me to go to different places and set up choirs. I did my best to reply but there were just too many. In addition to the letters responding to the series we had also emailed various community groups announcing that we were thinking of making another series based around a community choir. I was passionate about community singing: I had been running the LSO Community Choir in the Barbican for six years. I knew the impact communal singing could have in bringing the people in an area together.

This had been the original idea that Ana DeMoraes pitched to me back in summer 2005. Now it was mid-2008 and the idea didn't seem quite so lunatic. Besides, we had a fair wind in our sails; not one but two BAFTAs encouraged us to think bigger.

One morning I took the rickety London Overground train from Brondesbury to Camden Road where the Twenty Twenty office was based. It was a journey I relished because it was always exciting to go there. It had the feel of a newsroom. It was open-plan with creative types sitting on the edge of desks doing blue sky thinking, drinking frappuccinos and speaking animatedly into phones. Upstairs was a gallery with the executive offices and editing suites where the programmes were being cut together. The whole place was a bit of a shambles, with props from previous series strewn here and there, and a bookcase with a broken shelf creaking with the previous month's newspapers. There was no running water so tea was made in an urn apparently retrieved from a 1950s school fête with a slops bucket in the corner. The warehouse aesthetic of the place belied the brilliant creative work that was going on. It was a million miles from South Oxhey.

I was in the office to see somebody about a programme idea I'd had about sea shanties for BBC Four when Vicky Mitchell, who was the assistant producer on *Boys Don't Sing*, approached me by the water cooler. She had been ploughing through the responses to our email. She said, 'Oh, Gareth, just look at this – you've had a letter. I think it might be worth a quick read.'

As soon as I read the letter I thought, 'This is brilliant.' It was from the Reverend Pam Wise (who has since been made a Canon of St Albans Cathedral and awarded an MBE for her services to the community). Pam wrote that she was a vicar in South Oxhey in Hertfordshire and described the town. The detail she included that really hooked me in was the fact that South Oxhey was an enclosed community completely surrounded by woodland, almost cut off from the outside world, even though it was only ten miles north of London. I was intrigued.

Months later, at the local archives in South Oxhey, I discovered that the area had been created out of nothing to provide a new home for the Londoners who had been bombed out of their homes by the Blitz. In the 1950s, one newspaper article called it a 'promised land of Cockney utopia'. But the dream had been a troubled one. There had been vociferous complaints from the area's existing residents. I could understand why there was such an outburst of nimbyism. Oxhey means 'field of cattle', and the new town's neighbours were people who had deliberately moved out to the countryside, to places like Carpenders Park, seeking their own patch of pastoral idyll, wanting to look out on lovely green fields where cows were grazing. Suddenly they were told that a massive council estate with a load of Cockneys was going to be plonked down next door – and they objected. It was literally on the other side of the tracks, a recipe for disaster.

For the new South Oxheyites the move was equally disorientating. It must have been very strange for them to be uprooted from the East End and inserted into a ready-made town. The urban engineers had created an artificial environment. Where most towns grow organically with a mixture of people from different backgrounds, South Oxhey felt like a true monoculture: very white, working-class and Cockney. There was a pretty low percentage of incomers. Many families had been there for 60 years.

The first day of filming arrived and I took the train from Kilburn High Road to Carpenders Park. The station used to serve a golf course where it was said that HRH Prince Philip once played. Well, if he ever had, as I got off the train that morning in late September 2008 I wasn't expecting to see any royalty. It looked like a tired housing estate.

What became clear was that many people viewed me with suspicion. Our soundman Dave Harcombe was attacked with a shopping bag by a member of the public after I had innocently asked the gentleman if he was interested in singing. We decided to take this as a 'no'. Another man pulled his trousers down for the camera. We were warned away from a certain pub. As I wandered around South Oxhey I found that most of the working people were out of town during the day, so I was asking the unemployed, housewives and the retired if they'd like to join my choir. It was a slow start.

From the outset I found widely differing views about what South Oxhey represented to the people who lived there. Pam, the vicar, was involved with a local charity called Ascend, helping those people in the town who needed picking up after crises in their lives. For others, including Matty, it was a salt-of-the-earth place where everyone looked out for each other.

During my time in South Oxhey I learned that a community needs an idea that everyone can subscribe to, in the same way that I call myself 'British' because I know what that means to me. It might mean something completely different to somebody else who considers themselves to be British, but for me it is basically a simple idea: we are an island race, the Queen is our figurehead, I have a British passport, there is an idea that binds us together.

That, it seemed to me, was what South Oxhey lacked. When I talked to residents about what South Oxhey meant to them, a surprising number would say, 'No, no, I'm from South Watford.' They even didn't want to sign up to the idea of being from South Oxhey. And if I asked outsiders whether they knew South Oxhey, they'd laugh and say, 'Oh yes, I drive through it but I wouldn't leave my car there, I wouldn't go there late at night, I wouldn't send my daughter there.' The general impression seemed to be that it was, 'Full of yobs, drugs, drink and single mums'. That is a terrible thing to say about a place. The whole dynamic of this series, *Unsung Town*, was as much about changing South Oxhey's perception of itself as it was about building a choir.

Compared to going into a school with a fixed timetable and rules and where singing with Mr Malone was an agreed, and eventually acceptable, activity, arriving in South Oxhey, a town with a population of 12,000, with no real starting point was seriously daunting. I doubted we could make any impact on it whatsoever. The scale of it felt huge. Getting all those people to sing, my God, it was like pushing a rock up a hill at times.

My first week in South Oxhey was all about trying to get the numbers in to make sure I had enough people to start a meaningful choir. We produced enough flyers to leaflet the whole place. I went out and about the highways and byways of South Oxhey, into the shops and cafés on the Precinct, its central, somewhat deserted, shopping area, to raise awareness of the fact I was setting up a choir and to stir any interest I could. I don't mind that kind of hustling: I am always happy to go straight up and talk to people I haven't met before, and I have never run out of words. I went everywhere. I spent an afternoon receiving an involved lecture about crime statistics from the local desk sergeant at the police station – did it yield me a single singer? No. My morning gallantly mopping up phlegm and singing nursery rhymes (or should I say 'nursery rhyme', as the repertoire appeared to be limited to 'Twinkle, Twinkle, Little Star'?) at the mother and toddler group was equally unproductive, although I did meet Carly, who was to become a key part of the choir.

Haplessly I stood for several fruitless hours outside the Carpenders Park train station accosting the commuters streaming back from their day jobs in London and barely got a response, let alone a smile – it felt like an onslaught of the disinterested. Remaining positive, I gamely went on a wild karaoke night with Matty. This got me a lot of interest but most of it out of curiosity rather than actual commitment to turning up to choir practice.

118

Battle-hardened and ready for a cup of tea, I arrived at a genteel senior citizens' coffee morning at the Clitheroe Club where I met the delightful Kitty Lee and Fred, a retired engineering manager who had lost his wife Betty only four weeks earlier.

Fred had a fine voice, and as soon as the others prompted him, launched into a rendition of 'The Wonder of You'. Fred clearly knew why I was there and was sitting there itching to be asked. He could really sing. With Fred and his friends we ran through song after song that morning, Mario Lanza hits, songs from another era, which made me understand better what South Oxhey had been in previous generations. These were the children of the Blitz, of that East End now displaced and a generation that had always sung, particularly in a crisis. Their children and grandchildren may have lost the habit of singing as a community, but they were about to find it again.

I think I had hoped that in South Oxhey everyone would simply roll over and let themselves be tickled into singing. This time, I thought, it will be easy. Yes, this time, working with adults rather than children, people will respect me. But despite having had two successful previous series, as I walked around South Oxhey I immediately realised nobody knew who I was.

Pride goes before a fall, as they say. My first arrival at the BAFTAs was similar. I didn't feel like a TV person at all at that time – and I'm not sure I do now. When the first series was up for a BAFTA Award I decided to splash out on a nice suit and borrowed a smart Lancaster School tie – a red lion rampant on a black background – from the lost property bucket. We were in the middle of filming there and I thought the school would appreciate it if I was able to get this tie on camera during the awards ceremony (they did).

I went with the other members of the production team from a bar that was no more three minutes' walk from the London Palladium. But because this was the BAFTAs we had to go in a massive Audi with blacked-out windows – the most excessive vehicle I'd ever seen. It took 15 minutes to arrive because all the streets had been shut off by the police ... for the BAFTAs. It was very rock'n'roll; I felt as though I'd arrived. The build-up was immense. I felt like Michael Jackson arriving at Wembley Stadium in 1988.

After weaving our way around the one-way systems of Oxford Circus we turned into Great Marlborough Street surrounded by policemen, screaming adolescents and eager autograph hunters. I took a deep breath. What would their reaction be to the bespectacled individual about to emerge?

There was an enormous cheer as the car pulled up and the paps started firing off their cameras, snap, snap, snap, snap. I stepped out of the car. The crowd fell *totally* silent. Nobody knew who I was, and within half a second they were looking eagerly at the next car down the road. Somewhat downcast I walked up the red carpet trying to fight my way through the crowd and past journalists who ignored me entirely.

South Oxhey proved neither as reluctant nor as suspicious of me as I'd first thought. As I got to know the place and its residents, many spoke of the outside with a hint of resentment. They knew that people from neighbouring towns had a very negative view of their home town. This felt unjust. It was evident there was a spirit here to be tapped into; a spirit created out of an oppressive atmosphere. This was not overt, but the town felt invisible and to the South Oxheyites the outsiders seemed opulent, manifold and separated by the dense woodland surrounding the town. This was a solid reason to start singing and I felt that if I stirred a sense of insurrection in them, then through singing we would be disturbing the social hierarchy. It was exciting.

The place was full of open-hearted people. Kitty from the Clitheroe Club, for example, was a wonderful, wonderful woman – I parked my car outside her house, no problem. South Oxhey had had some bad years but there were now community programmes and the police had got a handle on the crime. The place was changing. It was certainly not perfect yet – Dee, a young black woman and a single working mum, had recently moved in and been subjected to some brainless, but unpleasant, abuse from a gang of local youths, the first racism she had ever encountered – but it was at least open to the possibility of change. 'I didn't want to join the choir at first,' she says. 'I didn't know anyone and hadn't had a very good experience of living in South Oxhey. The first rehearsal was the first time I had ever left my house to go to a venue in the town.'

The new South Oxhey Choir got off to a flying start. Nearly 200 people turned up to the first rehearsal on an October evening in Oxhey Wood Primary School. The hustling and the flyers had spread the word. Pam Wise was there. Matty had turned up. So had Kitty and Fred. I felt great about it. It was going swimmingly, but after the first couple of rehearsals I realised that Matty was not showing up any more. I went over to his club and sat down for a natter over a pint sitting next to the dartboard. What Matty told me took me aback.

He said, 'I came to your rehearsal and I have never seen any of those people. It didn't feel like my South Oxhey.' He could see I was a bit crestfallen – I had just got this choir together, it was feeling fantastic and yet Matty's take was, 'Yeah, but I don't recognise any of them.' Although a part of me felt, 'Well, that choir *is* South Oxhey, there are 200 people in it and they all live in South Oxhey, so you just haven't seen them, Matty,' I knew that in essence he was absolutely right: we were only getting half the picture. It meant going back to the recruitment phase, a prospect that filled me with the dread of having to pound the streets once again, but his comment helped me refocus on the real aims of the choir.

It was that sense of Matty saying, 'No, Gareth, it's not my South Oxhey. You are not getting to my mates.' Without that kind of endorsement, without his involvement, it felt like the whole thing was going to fail. Looking back I wish I had seen that earlier, but I think the reason I hadn't was that I had just spent the best part of a year concentrating all my efforts on the boys at Lancaster School. I had done the 'let's get blokes to sing' thing. In South Oxhey I had turned my attention elsewhere and forgotten to engage properly with Matty and his mates.

I determined to address that problem as soon as possible, but it would have to wait for a while because I was busy preparing the choir for a public performance in front of their friends, family and neighbours in the Precinct. We were going to sing Jackie Wilson's '(Your Love Keeps Lifting Me) Higher and Higher' and I hoped I could persuade Dee, who I knew sang regularly with a gospel group, to take the solo. Dee didn't fit into South

Oxhey and she felt it. She was one of very few black women in the area. Her sense of isolation was intense and she found it hard to overcome her natural shyness to speak to people at rehearsals. I felt for her.

During one rehearsal I tried valiantly to give her an opening, by asking if anybody would like to volunteer to try out the solo for this gospel song. 'Anyone out there with a good gospel voice?' A few brave souls got up and had a go, but Dee was being very backward in coming forward. She said later, 'I could feel Gareth's eyes on me. I was trying not to give him eye contact. I was more nervous of singing in front of 200 people, none of whom I knew.' In the end I had to call a break in the rehearsal so I could have a chat with her and talk her into having a go. She was very reluctant to stick her head above the parapet, with very good reason.

As her hand, finally, went up I got that feeling in my stomach that it was going to be good, followed by another feeling of concern that she'd mess up her moment. She began apologetically at first, but I could sense the potential and it was clear to everyone in the room that she was the right choice for the solo. It was a statement from me about who I felt should represent South Oxhey and she did her solo alongside Russ, who was white and from the area.

There was nowhere in the whole of South Oxhey that could fit a choir of close to two hundred people and an audience, so, despite it being November, we decided to go *al fresco*. The performance in the Precinct was on one of the coldest days I have ever experienced in the UK. It was freezing, far from an ideal environment for the vocal cords. We warmed up in the school and made our way to the shopping street. We didn't know what to expect. Would they be hostile?

As we rounded the corner past the Ox pub we could see a good audience: five hundred South Oxheyites wrapped up to keep warm. It wasn't an ideal gig, but nevertheless it was a successful one – I was winning them over.

I always like to talk to the audience before doing a performance. I love that connection early on, because you can see them, you can hear whether they laugh at your jokes or understand your points. You can instantly gauge their mood. When I said, 'We are singing for your town, this is your community choir,' I could sense the audience thinking, 'Right, we accept that,' and then the choir sang, Dee performed her solo, and I sensed that music was working its magic on them. It was important that they had performed on their own patch. They needed the rubber stamp – 'Yes, you are the South Oxhey Community Choir.'

Being part of the choir had already had an impact on Dee: 'I didn't know who was going to turn up for that first performance, or what was going to be said to me. I am so glad I did it. I stood up, and people saw me for me, not for the colour of my skin.

Fred was visibly moved: 'If my Betty had been here, she'd have been proud of us.' Even cynical Matty, who turned up to watch, was impressed. 'I'm proud of them,' he said. 'They're only going to get better and stronger. Who knows where they will go.' There was hope for South Oxhey.

Really Care for Music

After we'd all thawed out following the performance in the Precinct, it became clear that here was a choir who could sing. They needed work, of course, but it wasn't going to be the same struggle as I had faced in *Boys Don't Sing*. I had a choir. It was time to challenge them.

Just a few weeks later the South Oxhey Choir were to be special guests at a sell-out Christmas concert in the Watford Colosseum. But what to sing? I'd been collecting a list of songs for South Oxhey for several weeks, jotting them down on my phone's notepad whenever I heard something suitable. One song that had wheedled its way on was Leonard Cohen's 'Hallelujah'. I was pleased with this choice because I'd fallen for the Jeff Buckley version (although I'm ashamed to admit that I first heard it in the film *Shrek*).

Within a few weeks of starting rehearsals I was having a hurried breakfast in Sunny Boy's Café on the high street when Vicky Mitchell, our producer, strode towards me clutching a copy of the *Sun*. 'X-FACTOR SINGLE TO BE "HALLELUJAH" BY LEONARD COHEN', ran the headline. Grim-faced, I tucked into my full English and cursed my luck.

This time the solo spot was to be taken by a rather nervous Mikey, a retiring youth with a shock of dyed blonde hair. I had first met Mikey on my first or second day in South Oxhey when I was canvassing in the street handing out flyers. He and a friend were immediately interested. 'Give us a song, then,' I asked cheekily, and serendipitously they let rip with 'Hallelujah', *a capella* and in harmony. That was the first singing I had heard in South Oxhey.

It was a sign: *X Factor* or not, this was our song. 'Hallelujah' became one of the highlights of the Colosseum performance: the choir received a standing ovation, the first I had ever had. A large part of the success of that concert was the element of surprise. We were appearing alongside a well-established local choral society. After listening to them for several minutes we got up and comparatively South Oxhey let out a lion's roar. Next to the genteel choral folks we had serious spirit.

I decided it was time to up the ante for the choir. They had learnt 'Hallelujah' in just a couple of rehearsals. I knew they could sing, and sing in harmony, so now I wanted to give them something really challenging.

Classical music, I felt, was the right way to go. It had worked with Fauré's *'Cantique de Jean Racine'* for the Northolt choir and *'Ombra Mai Fu'* at Lancaster School. With the South Oxhey choir I saw an opportunity to do something demanding yet at the same time simple, if that is not too much of a contradiction. It is a standard musician's technique to perform something within your ability and do it to the highest standard you can achieve. It is only the most exceptional performers who can consistently work at the outer limits of their technique. For amateurs I think it is important that they feel comfortable going on stage and performing music that is within their reach.

I had been mulling over what this choral challenge should be, thinking as ever of pieces that both really moved me and which the choir was capable of singing. When I sang in the Bournemouth Symphony Chorus we had tackled a number of choral adaptations of well-known classical pieces, including 'Nimrod' from the *Enigma Variations* by Elgar and 'Agnus Dei' by Samuel Barber, a choral setting of the adagio movement of his string quartet. It's a searing piece that I've loved since I was a teenager, and not just because it was used in the film *Platoon*.

At the first rehearsal after the Christmas break I put on a CD of the piece and played it to the choir. As they listened I am sure they were thinking, 'We'll never be able to sing it, that's impossible,' but they were brave enough to take up the challenge. Their reaction afterwards was very good: 'It sounds amazing, I want to sing it.'

It reminded me of another piece of wisdom from my LSO mentor Richard McNichol, whose advice that if you trust kids they won't let you down had become a mantra of mine for the first two series. His other wise observation was, 'Whatever you do, it has to be an attractive challenge.' I thought that was a really good way of putting it. All my work has been about trying to make the challenge of singing choral music an attractive and appealing thing to do. You can't do that with a dull piece of music. It has to be something that people *need* to sing.

I place a lot of faith in a sense of challenge. It is easy to coast, to take the less difficult option. You usually know which option is which. I have a sixth sense, or a 'sick sense' as I call it: if I feel sick and I don't want to do something, it is probably the right thing to go ahead with it. It is only afterwards that you think, 'I am really glad I did that, and I feel better for it.' But right beforehand you just don't want to do it. Performing in China, appearing at the Royal Albert Hall, going onto a military base, conducting in public, all of those things filled me with a bit of terror, and that is a good thing, a good fear. Otherwise it is not a challenge at all. Ralph Allwood, the choral conductor and teacher, said to me, 'Call it excitement rather than nerves.'

This does, of course, put me under a huge amount of pressure. I remember Howard Goodall remarking after watching my first series that he wouldn't want to be that vulnerable on television. I can understand why he said it: after all, I'd just blubbed in front of the nation. A great many people who are excellent at television presenting are showing one particular side of themselves, their presenting self, their expert self. It's why *Who Do You Think You Are?* works so well, because we get under the skin of people like Jeremy Paxman who in their regular presenting demonstrate only strength and certainty.

My job is different. I am not a presenter. I'm actually going through the experience with the choir, commenting as I go – it's a very different skill. So I put pretty much my whole self, warts and all, on screen. I try never to pretend I am something that I am not, and I guess that is something that someone like Matty Leonard responds to. I am not putting on airs and graces, I am just coming to give them an offer. And I believe that if you do it in that spirit, then you can't really fail, because people appreciate that it is an exchange: we sing and you teach us how.

Here I was again potentially setting myself up for a fall. How would I steer these novices to sing a piece of such sustained intensity? To help me tackle the 'Agnus Dei' challenge I went to seek advice from David Hill. I had been aware of David ever since he had been involved with the Bournemouth Symphony Chorus when I was just starting to sing with them in the 1990s. When I was at the Royal Academy of Music, he also ran a workshop with young conductors and I was singing in the choir for the session. In those couple of hours I had learnt so much just from being conducted by David, about blend, getting the ensemble right to the nth degree, the importance of a really good ear and meticulous preparation.

My reason for going to see David was that he conducts one of the greatest 'big' choirs that we have in the UK, the Bach Choir, with over 200 singers. Now that the South Oxhey Choir was getting larger by the day, how should I handle them? He offered sage advice: if at the end of the evening he had not made eye contact with every single member of the choir, then he felt he had not done a good job.

I have always tried, whenever possible, to conduct from memory. There is an eminent conductor called Mark Wigglesworth who in performance always conducts without a score, and I admire the connection he makes with the players and the feeling that nothing can get past him. As a conductor, if there isn't a score there, then you don't have a safety blanket. It is much better, as David said, to be looking at every single member of the choir. In the moment of performance you can sense when things are going wrong and make an adjustment, and if you are looking right at the choir you know what they are thinking. Also it's so important to enjoy the performance and I find that much harder with my head buried in the notes.

Initially the South Oxhey choir found 'Agnus Dei' extremely hard work with almost no reward. Since they were not at all experienced there was nothing to draw on. It was an open access choir and there were very few already accomplished singers. It wasn't as if we had dozens of incredibly competent singers secreted away within the ranks. I remember one particularly dismal rendition in an early rehearsal where we got through about four bars. It sounded like an orchestra of cats. My big dream seemed a long way from realisation: 'This piece has an effect that grabs people by the guts. That's what has called out to me. This choir needs a soul, a heart,' I said at the time. Well it wouldn't work like that singing as they did in those early rehearsals.

On top of the musical demands I was making of them, they also had to sing in Latin, which ramped up the difficulty factor significantly. In truth it's easier to sing in Latin than in English because the vowels are purer, but their perception was that this made it more of a challenge. Carly, who I'd first encountered singing 'Twinkle, Twinkle, Little Star' at the crèche, was throwing her hands up in the air. 'People were saying, "We just can't do it", laughing, "It's ridiculous".' It seemed preposterous. And just to make it a little more frightening, the choir would be singing this piece in St Albans Cathedral. When I announced the venue there was an audible gasp from the singers.

We slogged. I sang and recorded every part (soprano included) and they all toddled off to get it into their heads. I wrote the note lengths onto every part. I went to their houses. I badgered, encouraged and tentatively pushed them towards the goal. With two weeks to go we were all near despair. They were still with me, just – that trust was hanging by a thread. It felt as if we were on the precipice of disaster. But the Blitz spirit of the older generation was an inspiration to all. The octogenarian Kitty Lee knuckled down to this huge piece. 'I'll get there, Gareth. I'm determined to get there.' She had never sung in a choir and I hope that when I'm her age I have half her pluck. Kitty passed away in 2011, and I know that being able to sing in St Albans Cathedral was an experience she revelled in.

With characteristic determination, the choir fought to get it right. They were all in it together, helping each other out, practising in small groups. Mark, one of the tenors, said, 'That was the point where it felt to us like, "Wow, this is it, we are a choir".'

The choir, which had been formed out of a community, now began to operate within itself as a small community. Russ Clancy ran one of the karaoke nights in the town and had a fantastic set of tonsils: he and his wife both gave the choir absolutely everything. Terry Petit, who became the chairman of the choir after I left, was another of those members who I thought of as the lifeblood of the whole thing.

Christine Wyard worked for the local charity Ascend and helped so many troubled South Oxheyites. She had given her life to the place for years and years and brought all of her sympathy and understanding along to choir rehearsals. If someone was having a problem, you could guarantee Christine would be the person who would go and sit next to them and help them out. It was starting to feel like the Utopian vision I had set out at the beginning.

In adult choirs I often find that if somebody in the choir is not a strong singer, some of these adults can start behaving like children, pulling me to one side, and whispering, 'There's that woman in the back row, she's absolutely awful and she's putting me off. What are you going to do about it? Are you going to kick her out?' I have to gently explain that because it's a community choir and open access goes to the heart of the whole exercise, we can't do that. Christine was always excellent at dealing with those sorts of issues and finding a way to resolve the differences, in the same way that Rhonda Pownall had helped me within the Phoenix Choir. It was vital that the South Oxhey choir included the full range of backgrounds, attitudes and above all abilities. Without that it wouldn't have been a community choir. All these high ideals only made my job as a musician more difficult.

As the adult choir started to gel, I also started putting a children's choir together. This choir drew on all six primary schools within the South Oxhey area and Colnbrook, a special needs school where I worked with the individual children alongside Val Hall, one of the teachers, who was also in the main community choir. I spent a lot of time in Val's company observing her in action. What a giver she was; a really good, truly decent woman.

At the rehearsal where I was looking for a soloist to sing at the Precinct gig – hoping that Dee would rise to the bait – I was staring at a sea of faces with not one hand going up. 'Anyone want to do the solo?' Not a soul. There was an uneasy pause where it looked like I was going to draw a blank, and then Val, bless her, said she would try. And the only reason she sprang up was that she could see I was dying up there. She had no intention of being the soloist whatsoever, but thought she needed to go and help me out, which I felt very grateful for – and then the footage of her audition made it to screen, much to her chagrin.

Val taught a lovely girl called Sibel who became my soloist at the first performance of the children's choir. Sibel reduced the whole room to tears with a touching rendition of Eric Clapton's 'Tears in Heaven'. I don't know whether the other children knew that Sibel went to the special school. Even if they did, it didn't matter when she opened her mouth to sing. I remember meeting her for the first time, talking with her as she had lunch in the school canteen and being struck by her disarming openness. Singing was something that Sibel clearly excelled at. She outsang the best of the mainstream children and I was absolutely delighted for her. She skipped to the first rehearsal and sat on the front row, beaming at me. I'd found a fan: 'He seems really friendly. Nice hairstyle. Funny. Talented. Very entertaining.' If only the rest of them had her attitude.

I had worked with young children before and run a children's choir at the LSO, but that had a strong element of self-selection – a streak there of middle-class parents who had wanted to push their children into the choir. Here in South Oxhey it was a free after-school club and a chance for some of them to get on telly, which meant there were a fair few chancers in its ranks. That was fair enough: they thought they'd turn up, give it a go, see if it was any fun. In fact, I was rather fond

134

of the chancers – they brought a bit of colour and excitement – and so I worked to keep them involved. Mind you, they made me work hard as they were impermeable to instruction. They had the fidgety quality of children with too much tartrazine in their diet.

One particularly smart boy, Louis, had announced he was there because of 'the fit girls'. I respected his candour if not his application. I knew he had not come along for the singing at all, only for the glory, so I made him and his mates Sidney and Louis the compères for the choir, giving him an opportunity to shine in front of all the girls, fit or otherwise.

To make the singing fun, I worked closely with the lovely Libby Marshall from the Hertfordshire Music Service. Libby was able to get them singing simple playground songs, an idea supported by a government initiative called 'Sing Up' that had been started by Howard Goodall – him again! – around that time. The whole point was to make singing a normal activity for kids to do, just as it used to be before Xboxes and Walkmans (remember them?) took over. At the end of the rehearsals, we would do a singing game that everyone, including me, could join in: 'Shake Your Mama', 'Here Comes Sally' and any other number of fun songs with actions. This was a welcome refreshment from the rigours of the Samuel Barber.

However you can't coast along just playing games. In the same way that the adult community choir were singing at St Albans Cathedral, I wanted the children to take part in a proper authoritative concert, which would give them a local seal of approval. I arranged for them to sing alongside the choir of the nearby Merchant Taylors' School.

135

Merchant Taylors is about one mile from South Oxhey and yet couldn't be further in terms of atmosphere. It is an independent school with a reputation for academic excellence for boys aged 11 to 18, housed on grounds that seemed to me to be almost as large as South Oxhey itself. This would be the aspirational challenge I was seeking. The day I visited Merchant Taylors' School it was bathed in glorious sunlight. The place reeks of opportunity and is fearsomely resourced: the Great Hall where the concert would take place had enough room to take a massed choir and orchestra, and there was a music department that made me salivate. I wanted the South Oxhey kids to have a chance to see this.

Richard Hobson, the head of music at Merchant Taylors, agreed that they could join in a performance of the mighty *Carmina Burana* by Carl Orff, again with words in Latin (when I told the children this, one of them, Megan, said I was 'nuts'. 'We're English, not Latin').

Come the night, there was a wonderful moment during the concert. I was standing at the end of one line of South Oxhey kids, part discipline enforcer, part conductor, but mostly just to sit and enjoy their moment. I found it incredibly moving to look down the line and see every child singing their hearts out. And I knew *why* they took it so seriously.

In preparation for this challenge I had taken them along to a county choral competition – a scene that didn't make the final cut on the TV. At this event the adjudicator wore a bow tie. Nothing wrong with bow ties, of course. But thereafter he became known to us all as Mr Bow Tie Man. Mr BTM had been absolutely on the money, giving very objective feedback in order to help the children improve, making suggestions about the range of the pieces and whether we should have done a particular song in a different key. But he also made three major points regarding the children's level of engagement, whether they were watching the conductor enough and whether they all knew their words.

I thought his comments were utterly fair, but as I looked at the teachers and some of the children I could see that they felt let down. I'd taken them to this competition and I think they thought they'd win it, not that I'd given them that impression. It was interesting that they felt so aggrieved by constructive critique. There is a danger that children, particularly in a place like South Oxhey which has a sense of isolation, are rather patronised by well-meaning people who think, 'Don't the poor things have it hard?' and therefore never tell the children straight truths. Anything difficult is immediately sugar-coated.

Mr Bow Tie Man didn't do that; he pulled no punches. His comments upset many of the kids, so we had a big pow-wow at the next rehearsal, sat them down in a circle, and asked them, 'What did you think of Mr Bow Tie Man?' A couple of them were angry: 'He was really mean. He criticised us.' I gently said, 'Well, do you think he was right?' Then one by one some of them started piping up, 'Well, maybe we could have done better.' After about 15 minutes of talking it through I persuaded them that all of his comments were things that it was in their power to improve on: learning words – anyone can do that; not fidgeting – most children can limit their extraneous movement; and singing with commitment – that would take work.

What this episode gave them was a determination to prove Mr Bow Tie Man wrong, by improving all the elements he had pointed out. It gave me some leverage. I could say, 'You can't stand like that because that's what Mr Bow Tie Man said.' 'Aaah, OK,' and then they would all stand up a little straighter.

By the time Richard Hobson from Merchant Taylors came to listen to them in his role as 'the conductor' the kids were absolutely switched on and ready to do battle. He generously said, 'You're better than us,' which he got some stick for back at his school when it went out on TV. At that point his choir had not even begun rehearsals, which is what he meant – not that our choir were *actually* better! But I felt that because we had such a solid *reason* to sing, the South Oxhey choir brought into Merchant Taylors an extra dose of liveliness and pride. They behaved better than I'd ever seen before and I was proud. The reputation of South Oxhey was done a good turn that night by those children.

As I looked down that line of young singers I knew that they were not just singing for me or for their parents in the audience, they were singing to prove their right to be there, and to thumb their noses at Mr Bow Tie Man, who would of course be absolutely delighted because his comments had had precisely the effect he had hoped.

The children in the choir had fire in their bellies, but I needed to get the same level of it in the adult choir. To incentivise them we had the spectre of Moor Park. If you go from the train station through the main precinct in South Oxhey you hit its main road, with the police station, the Catholic church and the school where the choir rehearsed. And if you follow that main road up the hill, it goes through the woodland that surrounds the town. When you emerge on the other side and go just past RAF

Northwood, there, less than a mile from South Oxhey, you find yourself in Moor Park, which feels like Millionaires' Row. I sent sorties into the enemy territory of Moor Park to hand-deliver leaflets advertising the choir's concerts and events. I don't know to this day if any of the residents came to see them. Certainly nobody ever came up to me and said, 'I'm from Moor Park.' It was a completely different environment. But it gave us a focus for improving.

I am a great believer in a common enemy for bringing people together. I have seen it time and time again: when you are building a team, you need purchase, you need something to fight against. The perception within South Oxhey was, rightly or wrongly, that Moor Park looked down on the neighbouring town, a throwback to the original nimbyism when South Oxhey was built in the late 1940s. Matty Leonard commented that Moor Park residents were 'not better than us, just richer', and one Labour Club regular said, 'They call this Beirut.' Whatever the truth, and I apologise to the good people of Moor Park for casting them in this role, they became the common enemy that helped bond South Oxhey's community choir together. It's a cheap trick – but an effective one.

We gathered in the stony crypt of St Albans Cathedral, ready to sing the Samuel Barber 'Agnus Dei'. I summoned up the demons of Moor Park to help cleanse South Oxhey of its damaging reputation. Could they pull off a truly classy performance? As Lorraine, one of the choir, asked, 'Are we going to smash it?' The audience comprised people from Hertfordshire who'd come to see the excellent Hertfordshire Chorus perform the Verdi *Requiem* under the baton of David Temple. They were a tough act to follow. South Oxhey sat in silence through 90 minutes of Verdi before they could have their moment.

Nervously they shuffled onto the impromptu stage in front of the carved stone screen erected by William of Wallingford in 1484. A screen traditionally hides the choir from the congregation to make the voices seem more celestial. But not that night. We stared Hertfordshire in the eye and produced moments of splendour. I was proud that South Oxhey Choir were standing where singers have stood for almost 1,000 years to be heard by their town, by their county and by the world. The cathedral echoed with the sound of the voices of ordinary men and women and, to me, there was something heavenly about that.

A Better Place to Play

There are some places you just don't go to. For many people South Oxhey was one of them. There are places in the places you don't go to where you just don't set foot in unless you are particularly brave. The Grapevine pub on a Friday night was just such a place.

You could feel the pounding of the electronic drumbeat from a hundred metres away. As you approached there was detritus strewn around the environs: bottles and cigarette packets. There were girls dressed in apparently little more than their underwear. It was a typical night in a lively pub for young people in the heart of South Oxhey. Even for Matty Leonard, champion boxer, this struck a note of fear. Would he and I dare to take singing to such a place?

I was struggling to engage with the young adults of South Oxhey. 'The people that you actually really want to sing are the people that would never dream of singing and would look like complete idiots if they were ever caught singing,' was Matty's typically astute summary of my dilemma as we chatted about the problem over a pint.

Having realised that I had failed to draw Matty and co. fully into the idea of a community choir, I set about working to encourage him and his mates to participate in some way. Matty agreed to approach the 'young guns of South Oxhey' and help me put together a sub-set of the choir, to be called Matty's Men. We would do a tour of the pubs and clubs in the town. This would really sort the men from the boys.

Matty and I set out on a cross between a PR drive and a press gang, circling round South Oxhey in Matty's car to round up some likely suspects. In the end we found a dozen or so willing volunteers and then spent many happy hours trying to co-ordinate an evening that they could all make, which seemed virtually impossible.

When Matty's Men were ready to go out on the town, the one night I did not want to do was a particular Friday, because the following day I was due to be in Wells Cathedral, singing in Bach's *St John Passion*. I had been adamant that that Friday had to be a sacrosanct day as I needed to keep my own voice in pristine nick for the Saturday concert in Wells. I simply could not do anything on that date, I told everyone. Then, of course, I was worn down drip by drip: 'That Friday is the only date we can possibly all do – please can you do it, Gareth?' I reluctantly acquiesced, desperate to avoid singing a single note as I knew that I would be singing some very demanding top As and B flats in Wells.

It was going to be Bach vs Bacchanalia: the night with Matty and his Merry Men was, my God, an anarchic, anarchic evening.

We met up beforehand to have a quick curry. The drinks bill alone came to just short of £100. The die for the rest of the night was well and truly cast. Our first venue in South Oxhey was the Labour Club, where we'd been told the Rolling Stones and The Who had appeared in their early years, so we felt that we were following in prestigious footsteps. A sort of male voice choir in bastard form. We arrived and found that there was literally one man and his dog in attendance – Matty's men would need Dutch courage for this audience.

We sang a few songs – from 'Don't Look Back in Anger' to 'Can't Help Falling in Love with You' – had a lot of fun, and the Men came out really elated and slightly more merry. At each venue, the first stop was the bar and another intake of courage. The pockets were emptying quickly and Matty was 'getting the beers in' with terrifying largesse. Things were going well. We'd manned up to the challenge, dressed like the Blues Brothers in black hats, white shirts and wide red ties.

Cue dramatic music: our final stop was the Grapevine. By now things were seriously out of hand. It reminded me of a previous occasion early on in my time in South Oxhey, another bonkers night out with Matty when I was trying to ingratiate myself with the South Oxhey regulars. Matty and I had sung a karaoke version of 'Don't Go Breaking My Heart' at the Dick Whittington pub (known to all as 'The Dick'), which must surely rank as one of the weirdest love duets of all time.

Bathed in a warm alcoholic stupor I found myself saying, 'I may seem a little bit posh, but I think they are less suspicious of me ...', which I am sure I would never had said sober. In truth I'm less 'posh' than people think. I was state-educated, born to

144

parents from relatively humble backgrounds – no family silver at any rate. Yet because I like choirs, singing and classical music people make assumptions about me in much the same way as people made assumptions about South Oxhey. Nonetheless I was intimidated by the thought of walking into any South Oxhey pub to sing – let alone the Grapevine. It could have been that same night that one girl flashed her boobs for the camera and a man tried to give me a kiss, but the South Oxhey evenings have blurred into one hedonistic continuum.

We approached the Grapevine with bravado, but just before we were about to go in, Patrick from Matty's Men lost his nerve and was about to chicken out. He was saying, 'I just don't think we should go in there.' Even for this lifelong South Oxheyite the raucous atmosphere inside seemed a stage too far. The others were bullish, though. 'We should go in, come on.' It felt like we were going to get massacred. I thought, 'In for a penny, in for a pound. Let's give it a go, what's the worst that can happen?', totally forgetting the *St John Passion* by now.

Even Reece, one of Matty's kick-boxing buddies, himself pretty useful in a spot of bother, looked ashen-faced. 'When we got to the Grapevine that was when it all went outrageous.' As we stepped inside, the DJ cut the music to much jeering and catcalling. Here Matty came into his own: he was in his element, dancing on the pool table and whirling around like a dervish. Either that or he was so pissed that he was past caring.

I ended up trying to play the piano squeezed between a bevy of drunken beauties, while balancing a hat precariously on my head. This affected my piano skills somewhat – it was hard to concentrate. It was a far cry from my piano duets with Helen

Tulloch when I was eight-and-a-half. Their sheer physical presence meant that I had to play at a strange angle, and because they were encroaching on my space I had to assert myself pianistically to prevent them from joining in. Matty looked back fondly on my discomfort: 'The look on Gareth's face, the smile on his face, all these girls behind him, dancing and ruffling up his hair.' That look was one of determined concentration.

Afterwards Reece said it had been one of the best nights of his life, and I detected a real tenderness in the camaraderie between the guys. The outward display of macho behaviour seemed to be all about bravado. I felt I had made a significant step forward in making a connection with the young men of South Oxhey. We had survived and so, thankfully, had my vocal cords: I made it down to Wells in one slightly fragile piece.

This male bonding was something of an eye-opener for me. Matty is a man's man in the same way that Alex Foreman and Paul Craven at Lancaster School were. I just don't have a lot of blokey mates. All that rough and tumble, it's never been me. There is a lot of female company in the world of choirs.

I increasingly grew to understand and like Matty. His was a very rich character. He is an exceptionally interesting guy, very clever, full of to-the-point observations and smart analysis of what I was trying to achieve with the choir. And, of course, he was right at the heart of South Oxhey. Now that he was onside once again, I felt that my original idea of bringing the whole community together might just be achievable. If I could keep them all sober ...

My most extraordinary blokeish moment was when I had been touring round South Oxhey's various locales trying to recruit likely members for the choir. After spending time at the police station, the toddler group and among the commuters piling out of Carpenders Park station, I had pitched up at the local football club. I ventured into their changing rooms while the chaps were having their showers and one of the team kindly performed 'the helicopter' for the camera. I hadn't heard the expression 'doing the helicopter' before, but I imagine the description is self-explanatory. If not, let's just say it was a hands-free rotation of a particular and exclusively male part of his anatomy. There is a kind of man who has the expression 'doing the helicopter' in his vocabulary, and until I went to South Oxhey I was not one of them. I have no desire to do the helicopter in public or in private, and certainly not on national television.

When we were just about to put the series out on air, some bright spark at the BBC looked through all the footage and chose a couple of clips to put on YouTube to whet people's appetite. There were two sequences. One was of me standing outside Carpenders Park vainly trying to rouse interest in the idea of a community choir. The other was the 'doing the helicopter' scene. I was staying with some friends when I had a message saying, 'You must have a look on YouTube.' I watched the trailer and showed it to my friends. We were in fits of laughter because it was not only uproariously funny but totally unexpected for *The Choir*, which made it even more brilliant. I then emailed the link to one of the executives from the BBC. Within 20 minutes it was pulled from the YouTube site, because it gave a lopsided view of the series, as it were, although the sequence stayed in the actual programme.

The saga continued. When the series was later shown in America it had to be edited down from one hour to 40 minutes because of the ad breaks. The US channel re-edited it and they took the 'helicopter' scene out as part of the edit. Last year a schoolteacher wrote to me from a small conservative town in America to say she that having seen the series she had bought the DVD version from England and had it shipped over to America to show to her class. She had been utterly horrified by that scene because, of course, it hadn't been in the American version. Suddenly there she was, showing the gents in the football club changing rooms to a class of 15-year-old girls. Choral singing has never been the same since.

The South Oxhey choir was evolving a cast of intriguing male characters. I am always fascinated by character. I did a degree in drama, so I have always been interested in acting and theatre. This extends to how people are made up, what people think about themselves and how they demonstrate that through their actions. Dealing with Matty's Men was, at times, like dealing with a cast of Shakespearean comic characters: anarchy prevailed but they had heart and I wanted to see them fulfilled.

In all my TV shows I've been sent into new and unfamiliar settings to create something from nothing. This requires me to pick up on the mood of the situation and run with it. I liken it to an extended improvisation where I'm playing myself. The camera is running – you never forget that – and it's time for me to go and badger some unsuspecting local into doing my bidding.

For my own part, when I sense a tricky situation or awkward silence, I feel compelled to dive in and break that atmosphere.

Standing in a diagonal line was my idea but it took ages to get everyone in position – we had a lot of trouble getting the choir into height order. The basketball hoop adds to the feeling that we were fish out of water. Vicky Savage and I studied together at the Royal Academy of Music and she played for us from the first rehearsal until we arrived in China.

Here we are fully kitted out in our silky pyjamas for a brief appearance on a Chinese youth TV station. You can see from how close everyone is standing to each other how much we'd pulled together. This was after we'd performed in the competition and you can see that I'd started to unwind.

Formal shots with a hundred boys from Lancaster School took some doing; we were there for about an hour getting everybody to look at the camera and stop doing bunny ears. This was a proud moment – a photo that says 'we've done it!' Very few of the boys or the teachers had been to the Royal Albert Hall before and a couple look overexcited. The range of haircuts was truly awe-inspiring.

Above and left: Tojan Thomas Browne (far left), Michael Moray (left) and the choirmaster holding the second of two BAFTAs awarded to the series. The first BAFTA took me completely by surprise but the second time I thought it was impossible that we'd win. Somehow we did it. You can see that I'm wearing the same school tie as Tojan for good luck.

South Oxhey precinct, late April 2009. The high street was rarely this full. On the left you can see the recently bankrupted Woolworths and various charity shops. But it's not the shops that make a place – it's the people, and by this point the choir had bonded into an energetic unit. This had been the scene of our early triumph, but here we are readying ourselves for the festival performance.

Here I am in St Albans Cathedral a couple of months before the end of filming. I'm contending with the choir in rehearsal for the 'Agnus Dei' and, despite trying to look comfortable, I'm as unsettled by the surroundings as the choir.

The Beatbox Choir outside the Royal Albert Hall. I often referred to them as 'the playground MCs', a name they were less keen on. I'd say this is one of the most incongruous photos I've ever been in. Imran (on my right, next to the boy with letters on his t-shirt) is more soberly dressed than some of the others, who look set for a rap concert. Without question the most difficult group I've worked with, yet also the most rewarding.

At the Radio 2 studios on Great Portland Street, December 2011. At Chris Evans' suggestion, I'm dressed in some ill-fitting combats (this prompted much hilarity from the wives). Paul Mealor clearly didn't get the memo and it wasn't until later on that he found himself dressing as a Navy Commander, thanks to a helpful member of the armed services hotfooting it into the studio live on air with 'the full rig'.

Right: Exalted company. Gary Barlow OBE and Lord Lloyd Webber. Oh, and me. Here we are launching the Jubilee single on the Chris Evans show.

This was actually taken a year before when I took a group of kids to perform live on Chris' show. It was the first time I'd met him and neither of us had an inkling of what was to come.

Far left: Behind Gary and me you can see the huge stage specially built on the Victoria Memorial for the concert outside Buckingham Palace. We were giddy with excitement.

Left: (from left to right) Kerry, Sam and Jenna, all from Chivenor, on stage at the Jubilee. What an extraordinary eighteen months it had been. It's hard to describe how proud we all felt to be involved.

Mission accomplished. We'd finished our performance and were relaxing on the stairs before returning to the stage of the Royal Albert Hall to sing the final hymns. The women thought this was the end. How wrong they were!

Back at Abbey Road, this time with a choir massed from ten of the Military Wives Choirs in existence at the time. One of the finest group of singers I've ever conducted and a very special day. This group represented all the work that Chivenor and Plymouth had put into supporting the development of Military Wives Choirs around the country. I'm surprised Gary didn't wear a bow tie...

All together now... Finally the *Sing While You Work* choirs go head to head for choral glory. I'm the one in the middle. Left to right top: NHS, Royal Mail. Bottom: Manchester Airport, Severn Trent Water.

That is something I've learnt from my dad; he's an ebullient character, the life and soul of the party. He has a skill and the confidence to say, 'OK, everyone cheer up, we're going to do some singing.' It was this element of my character that came in handy in South Oxhey. If it was a rainy day and no one was feeling very cheery, it was my job to cut through that and alter the dynamic.

My antennae are not always as finely attuned as I would like to think. At the first BAFTA awards night, when the crowd and the paparazzi had been completely uninterested in who *The Choir* team were, I had struggled through the gauntlet of the red carpet, brushing shoulders with the likes of *Coronation Street*, *EastEnders* and Jonathan Ross. I stood on Paul Merton's foot, and made it to the doors of the Palladium, feeling slightly humbled but exhilarated nonetheless. And who should I see but Alan Sugar, then Sir Alan, standing at the doors looking for his wife, who had also got caught up in the affray. I was an Amstrad CPC464 owner in my youth and he had been a bit of a hero of mine.

I knew what my dad would do – he'd go up and speak to him. 'Now is my moment,' I thought, 'I might not get another chance.' I had a pretext: *The Choir* had been nominated in the same category alongside *The Apprentice*, *Dragons' Den* and Gordon Ramsay's *The F-Word*. I was the minnow in such company.

I puffed out my chest, walked up to Sir Alan, and said, 'Excuse me, Suralan, you don't know me, but we are in the same category together, and I just wanted to say, "Best of British."' He looked quite shocked and really rather gruff, growling: 'Oh, I thought we was up against *Dragons' Den.'* I stuttered, 'Yes, yes, that's, that's right, you are, but, we are also ...', spluttering and stumbling over my words. 'We're also up for it, a little programme called *The Choir.'* And he went, 'Oh,' and stomped off, barely making eye contact. I thought this was brilliant – I knew I'd be dining out on this for years. Why should he have had a clue who I was?

Much to our mutual surprise *The Choir* won that night. We trounced *The Apprentice*, picking up the award for best feature (BAFTAs are *incredibly* heavy by the way). There was a cut-away shot of Sir Alan in his chair looking slightly puzzled, though it was hard to read what his expression actually was. He may well have been thinking, 'I can't get out of my chair for another hour now.'

Nothing in life really prepares you for these moments. It's hard to know *what* to say. I looked for Ramsay and Sugar all evening but I think they went home early. I stayed to the bitter end. There was a rumour that I was dancing with Ant and Dec at the after party, but that was pure fabrication.

I honestly thought that was it. I thought I could read the writing on the wall – a BAFTA, a pat on the back – now be on your way. I was wrong. A couple of years later we were up for another BAFTA for *Boys Don't Sing*. I reasoned with myself, 'OK, we've got absolutely no chance whatsoever this time. Lightning doesn't strike twice.' That year the awards were being presented at the Royal Festival Hall. I wore my wedding kilt and the Lancaster School tie, which had been a lucky charm for the first BAFTA. As I stepped out of the car, up pulled this black Rolls Royce, the one that you see at the beginning of every episode of

The Apprentice, and I could almost hear the theme music playing. By now I think Sir Alan was a Lord or just about to be a
Lord, and certainly significantly more important than when I had
last met him. To my astonishment he stepped out of the Bentley
and made a beeline towards me. He clapped me warmly on the
shoulder, patted me enthusiastically and wished me the best of
British luck. That was all rather pleasant, and then we beat him
again. Cut to more puzzlement on the Sugar table. It seems that
Lord Sugar's radar was a little off that day. I swear he thought
he'd beat us on the second pass. Better luck next time, Lord
Sugar.

I always thought Alan Sugar would fit in well in South Oxhey:
an East End boy, probably not big on singing. He'd have got on
famously with my assembled cast of male characters of whom
Matty was the most prominent, though there were others who
were equally interesting.

Mikey, who sang the solo on 'Hallelujah' at the Watford
Colosseum, had lost his way a bit. He had been intending to go
to college to study music, but for one reason or another – family,
funding – had not. I got the impression he didn't have the get-up-
and-go at that point to really fight for it; when he first sang with
the choir he was quite passive. The way somebody sings says so
much about their personality. Finally, after being dragged through
an hour's singing lesson, he opened up and let rip with this big
voice that had been lurking in there all along. Mikey was like so
many of the other men, hiding his bright light under a bushel.

Fred, who had sung 'The Wonder of You' at the drop of a hat
when I popped into the senior citizens group at the Clitheroe
Club, and who had lost his wife a few weeks before I arrived in

South Oxhey, found that the choir filled an enormous and painful void in his life. The same was true of Dean, who was separated from the mother of his children, and had a number of difficulties in his life but equally a lot of talent and much to give to the choir. I remember being struck by the thoughtful look on Dean's face as the choir listened to a recording we had made in the Abbey Road Studios.

The Abbey Road session came about because, following what felt like the triumph of singing the Samuel Barber piece in St Albans Cathedral, I was looking for a way of sustaining the momentum the choir had now built up. The concert had gone well; everyone was on a high and they felt like a proper choir, so what could we do next? Several of them suggested doing a recording because they felt frustrated that they hadn't heard themselves. In a gung-ho mood we decided, 'Why not aim for the top? Let's go to Abbey Road.' The Beatles album *Abbey Road* was a favourite of mine, and given the size of the choir we needed a large studio. Abbey Road was perfect.

The only problem was choosing which song to sing. We went round and round the houses, right up to the point that I got a text from Dollan Cannell, the series producer, one Sunday afternoon. He said, 'Don't choirs that sing at Abbey Road sing the Beatles?' Of course! We had been trying to resist, because we thought it was too obvious, but Dollan was spot on. So I plumped for 'In My Life', which seemed appropriate because it's about 'place' and what it means. I encouraged the choir to sing the song as if it were about South Oxhey, although I'm fairly confident that the Beatles never made it there even if the Stones did.

On the day, I walked to Abbey Road from my house. We lived about 30 minutes away. Stepping in for the first time was like walking on hallowed ground. Elgar recorded there when it first opened and here we were, 78 years later. What an honour. It was magical.

As you'd expect the choir added their graffiti to the walls of the Abbey Road studios like every tourist who ever visits (the studio tolerantly whitewashes the walls on a regular basis). We had the requisite photo taken of us all walking across the iconic zebra crossing, while passing taxi drivers waited impatiently for us to cross. And then we were inside Abbey Road's main Studio One, the huge orchestral space you need for a large choir.

I pulled in a few favours and asked a handful of my favourite musicians to play: Belinda MacFarlane on violin, Liz Burley on piano and Jez Wiles on drums. They were all players I'd met through the LSO, so it was fun for me to make that contact again, but there was a more serious reason for getting great players in. When George Martin recorded the song with the Beatles in 1965, he found that he could not play the piano solo at full speed so he slowed the tape down to half speed and recorded it down the octave. This had the effect that when played at full speed the sound came out at the correct pitch. Liz Burley got it in one take. Sorry, Sir George.

The choir were a different matter. I worked them to the bone. They were so excited they were all on the ceiling. For all of us it was a real treat to be spending time in that space, but it is always a very different discipline for a choir to go into a studio. Like the Northolt schoolkids, everyone expects to go in there and find that the producer and the engineers can sprinkle some magic over the recording, whereas actually what happens in a recording studio is that you just do it over and over and over again until you get it right. It is very hard work. For an inexperienced group like the South Oxhey choir the concentration levels required are hitherto unexplored and unimagined: they were all exhausted.

After about an hour we had a fainter; somebody went down, straight down, doink, hit his face on the floor, bloody nose, the works. It was that intense. He had been so buzzed that when the red light went on he felt that he couldn't possibly put his hand up and say, 'Sorry, I am about to collapse.' (I have learnt my lesson now: I let choirs in the studio have plenty of breaks.)

After a punishing afternoon we ran the playback and they heard their voices for the first time through the massive speakers of Abbey Road. There's no better way to hear a recording, and it was clear that this had touched them to their very core. It was a unique achievement and they had held their own. The true measure of success? Afterwards Lorraine had 'South Oxhey Community Choir 2009 Abbey Road' tattooed on her arm.

Don't It Feel Good?

There's something about old home videos: the speed, the colour, the lack of sound and the way nobody quite knows how to deal with the camera. Watching a film of the South Oxhey Festival held in the 1950s was a glimpse into a simpler time. Neat haircuts, pretty dresses, boys in shorts with dirty knees and postmen with crisp ironed uniforms; South Oxhey looked like an idyll. Bunting was everywhere and the people looked filled with hope.

Inspired by this now long-forgotten festival, the remainder of my time in South Oxhey was spent organising the Sox Fest festival in early May 2009, which the community choir would headline. The idea had come from going through the local archives and finding newspaper articles about the festival, which had run annually in South Oxhey through the 1950s and 60s, but eventually fizzled out. With a dedicated team of helpers we had spent months planning and preparing for the day, but, of course, in the long and honourable tradition of organising outdoor events in Britain the one thing we could not plan for was the weather.

I woke up in my flat in Kilburn on that May Bank Holiday Monday, 4 May (Star Wars Day – 'May the fourth be with you') and looked out of the window to see that my worst fears had materialised. It was raining. I called up Vicky Mitchell, the producer on the series, who – by her own admission – is normally fairly highly strung. Vicky was feeling the pressure like me: 'OH MY GOD, what are we going to do?' she implored. This was meant to be the high point of months of work, effort and time, the finale of a major BBC Two series, and an event that had gone way beyond the boundaries of the community choir: half of Hertfordshire was going to be there! Who would eat all the food? Who would go on the bouncy castle in the rain?

By the time I reached the South Oxhey playing fields where the festival was to take place that afternoon, the weather had intensified: a fine mist had turned into droplets of rain splodging down. It was early May and by rights it should have been swel-tering. In my mind's eye I had imagined the festival like a film from the Woodstock era, full of lens flare, dreamy sequences of groovy (naked) festivalgoers skipping through the fields in glori-ous Technicolor, but no. It was just grim British greyness, tarpaulin and cagoules. There was nothing to do but soldier on. God bless the Brits because they turned up – all 6,000 of them.

A local recording studio had sponsored a second stage at the festival, and boy, you could hear it from across the other side of the field. I popped in to have a look, but was forced to retreat in seconds to protect my hearing. It was a competition to see who could be the loudest, that typical teenage band thing of ramping it up to 11 and beyond. We had some major problems with the sound on the main stage: it was still a relatively unusual phenomenon to have choirs playing at festivals so there was very little expertise in amplifying choirs. Trying to mike them like backing singers or pop singers doesn't really work – it sounds too close. But moving the mics away to get a bit of distance, our soundman began to pick up the howling wind. Swearing and sweating profusely, he kept putting more and more furry socks over the microphones in a vain attempt to muffle the wind noise: it was blowing a gale – 'an absolute wind tunnel', Maggie called it – and was also freezing cold. I think I remember putting on the thermals that day.

Setting up the festival had involved an enormous amount of logistics. I had never done anything like it. There was plenty of support, but it was definitely my biggest moment of artistic direction to date, though much of the planning was far removed from anything artistic. A few months before I had sat down with a gruff gentleman at the local Three Rivers Council offices in Rickmansworth who was in charge of licensing the event. He talked me through all of the liabilities and responsibilities involved. It was a lengthy list; we talked for the best part of an hour. He told me what my personal liability was, and what access was needed for ambulances and fire engines in the event of a *force majeure*, an Act of God or just Matty and his mates getting a bit carried away. These were public amenity issues that I had never dealt with. He was eloquent on the placing of the temporary morgue, a somewhat chilling detail.

After that meeting I have to say I walked out feeling pretty alarmed. Apparently for an event of that size, 6,000 people at one location on one day, there is a significant statistical chance that somebody will die, and you just have to hope it is not at your event. I am very happy to say that nobody died and no animals were harmed in the making of the South Oxhey Festival.

The choir had all pitched in to help turn the festival into something they could be proud of. Carly suggested getting a fire engine in for the kids; one sub-committee went off to create a logo. We had to select the bands for the other stages, work through the niceties of stage design, agree the PA set-up, make decisions on all the facilities that were needed – where *would* we put that morgue? We had to make this a day beyond the community choir, a day that would have been successful as a festival in its own right even if the South Oxhey choir had not been part of it. This was a tall order on its own, disregarding the challenge of preparing the choir.

Thankfully, preparing for the festival was not entirely about morgue location. We had a lot of fun too. For 'Walking on Sunshine' we brought in a young local choreographer, Jazmin, to create some dance moves for the choir. Jazmin was hilarious, very much on the Matty Leonard spectrum. She was a proper South Oxheyite, of good South Oxhey stock, and so understood and could handle the likes of Matty perfectly well in spite of the fact that she was only 15 years old. She was remarkably self-assured and organised. She even taught me the dance.

I was surprised at the end of one rehearsal when a few of the choir, Maggie and Magda and some of their friends, came up to me and wanted to know why I was making them learn this silly dance when they were there to sing. Maggie remembers: 'We wanted to give a really polished performance. We had barely got our heads round the song, and the dancing was going to compli-cate things even further. I thought Gareth was pushing it too far. It was a heated discussion.' We nearly came to fisticuffs over that dance because the pressure of May the fourth was pressing down on everyone concerned. They were very direct and robust in their view. I didn't mind. It showed me how much they cared, how much the high standards I had set mattered to them. They wanted everything to be good – all their friends, family and neighbours would be coming after all. I asked them to trust me, promising that I would cut the dance if it looked bad. But the dance absolutely worked: this was not a formal choral setting, it was an outdoor festival. It felt right to have a bit of fun in there.

Throughout the run-up to the festival I had been buoyed up by the commitment of all the choir members. Ever since setting them the challenge of the 'Agnus Dei', I had seen them at work in their houses, putting in long hours of practice outside the main rehearsal times. I would go round to various sitting rooms lugging my trusty Korg keyboard, which weighed a ton (the very first synthesiser I ever had, a present from my uncle, was a Korg, and I am a very loyal person).

Visiting the choir members and rehearsing with them at home is an opportunity that choirmasters rarely have. They glibly say at the end of a rehearsal, 'OK, if you could polish up the next six pages at home, I'll see you next week,' and off they go. They don't see that some choir members are really fright-ened by the prospect because they don't know how to go about it. They don't realise that some of them are taking the trouble to get together in small groups to go through the music together, or using their daily drive to work to sing along to a CD of the pieces. That was a real eye-opener – or perhaps an ear-opener – for me and very heart-warming.

I had continued trying to broaden the scope of my work by reaching out to other groups within South Oxhey. One of the town's biggest problems, it seemed to me, was that it did not have its own secondary school; every child in South Oxhey from the age of 12 to 16 or 18 was put on a bus each morning and shipped out to the nearest secondary school, which is in Bushey. It wasn't in the same league as segregational bussing in the Deep South, but I wondered what that did to you psychologically, the idea that your town somehow was not *worthy* of having a school. At 3pm all the kids would flood back, alighting at the same time. They inevitably collided and it could get pretty lively around tea time. I wanted these kids involved, too, so I went to the local secondary school and asked to work specifically with all the ones who came from South Oxhey, to make sure that they were involved. They were totally up for the challenge and very vocal about what their town meant to them – no 'Matty-style' persuasion needed there.

Working with Colnbrook School, the special needs school, was a particularly rewarding experience. We found some real gems for the choir there, including the delightful Sibel, and one autistic boy who had the most incredible singing voice. My only problem was that I could never guarantee that he would want to sing on the day I might need him to perform. I would teach him a song and he wouldn't sing it, but listened hard while looking out of the window. The next day his mum would come into the school and say, 'Well, what's this song he was singing last night?' He was processing it in his own way and it was all coming out several hours later. I worked extensively with him and had quite a few wonderful moments of success and also a few wonderful moments of disaster, but in the end it was just not possible to get him involved in the choir proper because of the unpredictability.

I think he was the only singer in South Oxhey not lined up backstage at the festival. As we hit the stage Dee remembers looking out across the playing fields from her vantage point, and seeing them 'filled with people with umbrellas, people with blankets, bless 'em, little children. The crowd was still behind us – it was like it was a hot, sunny day.'

And then a miracle happened. As if in a film script, exactly at the moment that we went on, the sun finally came out. I stood on the stage looking up, thinking, 'Somebody up there is smiling on this enterprise.' There was a lovely vibe because the whole crowd had felt the same emotion at the same time, that feeling where you take your hood off for the first time after it has been raining hard and think, 'Great, it's brightening up,' which happened to be the very moment when the choir started to sing.

We did a set of eight or nine songs, including, appropriately enough, 'Walking on Sunshine', and the children's choir sang too. We had an absolutely partisan audience, all totally on our side, friends and family of the choir willing us on. It was unforgettable.

There are always any number of unsung heroes involved in each series of *The Choir*. The South Oxhey choir, the people I met through working with them, the people who had so willingly helped – Richard Hobson from Merchant Taylors, Richard

Hill at Colnbrook School – all contributed to a feeling of great togetherness. Meanwhile, long before we got to the festival I knew that, as usual, there was going to be a point where I would have to leave.

During one of the last rehearsals and out of the blue, Maggie stepped up and gently commandeered my conductor's podium to ask me to stay. Although she says she was 'petrified: I don't do public speaking – it was really emotional', she was eloquent and sincere. I had, she said, given them 'the gift of self-confidence'. I had not had an inkling she was going to do that. Maggie did it of her own volition, which was really pleasing, because it felt like the whole enterprise now belonged to them and she was seizing her chance to say it. She says, 'Without Gareth's enthusiasm and sparkle we thought the choir would just fizzle out.' They had a petition with 150 signatures on it. OK. Yes. I did cry. Just a little bit.

Since South Oxhey was only half an hour from my flat, the prospect of remaining involved with the choir did feel possible. I was keen not to make promises I couldn't keep in the heat of the moment and I knew that I would not want to stay with them for the rest of my life, but I felt that I wanted to help them with the transition from TV choir to functioning community choir – a difficult process.

I decided to stay as long as I could – making the announcement just after we came off the festival stage – and, in the event, I carried on working with the choir for over 18 months, which was more than twice as long as I had actually been there for the programme. To guarantee there was continuity, I worked with Simon Wookey, a talented conductor I'd met through an LSO connection who happened to live nearby. Simon worked as my associate and took over as musical director after I finally had to move on because of the pressure of other commitments.

But before I left there was time for one further shindig. The choir performed at Central Hall in Westminster and later at the Voices Now festival in the Roundhouse in Camden. I strongly felt that they had reached the point where they could move on and have their own musical life. I had mixed feelings about letting them go, rather like a parent watching their child taking its first tentative steps. I know how difficult it can be for choirs: every choir has ups and downs as it goes through changes of personnel. But the South Oxhey Community Choir is still going strong, and I take a lot of pride in knowing that. As I said at the time, 'We need music in our communities because we need music in our lives.'

One thing I am sure of is that the takings of Sunny Boy's Café in the Precinct must have dipped after I left. I ate a huge number of breakfasts at Sunny Boy's, bacon and eggs, the works, virtually every morning I was in South Oxhey, fuelling myself up for whatever challenges the day had in store. The café was the central meeting place where we would plot and plan, re-group and re-think. We were always in there, and the owners and staff were really good to us. Alas they couldn't come and sing in the choir, because the place never shut – they were always working. A couple of times we did head out up the road to Norwood to Pizza Express, and had a huge guilt trip as if we were about to be exposed as traitors. But then there are only so many fry-ups one man can eat.

At the beginning of the series, involving 6,000 people from South Oxhey in a celebration of song had seemed like a pipe dream. There had been a step-up in the ambition of the series. Of course the idea of creating a community choir was what Ana DeMoraes at Twenty Twenty had had in mind when she first contacted me in the summer of 2005, but I had dissuaded her from it then because, not knowing what was possible, I had thought the scope was too large, too uncontrollable.

Within the setting of the two schools the aims and ambitions were relatively simple. I remember people saying to me about *Boys Don't Sing*, 'That must have been terrifying,' but actually it wasn't as terrifying as going into a community. With the boys, I knew a few of them would say 'Eff off' and some of them would be very interested, but it was essentially just a normal group of average teenage boys, whereas the sheer variety of people in South Oxhey meant the unknowns multiplied exponentially.

Unsung Town was about taking the whole community on a choral journey. To experience and share in the pleasure of that festival crowd was not only a satisfying reward but proof positive that we had overcome the difficulties and forced many residents to re-evaluate what their town meant to them.

In the eight months I spent working with South Oxhey my own life went through some major changes, too. In the October, a month or so after we had started filming, my grandmother had died. I had always been very, very close to her. I went back to work a week later, carried on filming, and explained to the choir what had happened. The people of South Oxhey were lovely about it, very supportive, very understanding. At Christmas I had

165

a short break of two weeks, like a school holiday, in the middle of which I got a norovirus infection, which is not pleasant, as its alternative name, 'winter vomiting bug', makes all too clear. It was probably a symptom of working too hard.

Between the second and third series of *The Choir*, I had fitted in making two documentaries for BBC Four, both highly enjoyable for me in terms of the subject matter: one called *How a Choir Works* and the other *Shanties and Sea Songs with Gareth Malone*. I came straight out of that and back onto the treadmill without a break. Recovering in time to start back in South Oxhey after the New Year, I then went straight through to the festival in May with another short break at Easter. Somewhere in the midst of everything Becky and I did manage to find the time to get married, and that was a very good thing indeed.

One great advantage of television is that it brings a wider public awareness of an enterprise like this. So many more people have now heard of South Oxhey and I hope they have all learnt that it is a good place. Maybe we helped change a few preconceptions and prejudices. But if I just think about the project on the ground, holding that festival, where the entire town came together for one enjoyable occasion – something that had not happened, certainly not on that scale, for well over 40 years – that made a massive impact. It was the kind of event that changes how people think about the place they live in. If you live somewhere that has a successful festival, because you are trusted enough by the local council to put one on, that makes you feel very, very different.

When I left South Oxhey there was a tangible sense of civic pride. At that level the community project that we had set out to establish around the choir had really worked. Somehow we'd done it. We'd created a choir capable of uniting a town: perhaps only for one day, but the legacy remains.

Swear to Art

'Dithering is for schoolboys; men decide.' I was in a dark corridor somewhere deep within the Glyndebourne opera house, during a cold March snap. It was a crucial moment in bringing together a teenage chorus for *Knight Crew*, a new opera with a storyline where Arthurian legend met the language and violence of the street.

My task in *Gareth Goes to Glyndebourne* had been to go out and find kids for the chorus who could identify with the story. Glyndebourne did not want children who sang nicely with no real edge or presence – they told me they wanted the real thing, or as near as I could find: kids with street energy. It would mean dealing with teenagers who had no experience of professional performance or the demands it would make on them. So I scoured the East Sussex countryside, turning up unlikely rocks and watching teenagers scampering away from me like beetles.

Cesca Eaton, the series producer, and I had taken Glyndebourne at their word and gone straight to the young

offenders centre in central Brighton. Here we would find youngsters who had direct experience of what the opera entailed in all
its gruesome, bloody, tragic reality. This was not the
Glyndebourne of tuxedos and champers on the lawn.

And so it was that I was now in the middle of a do-or-
die attempt to persuade my nemesis, Korrel Kennedy, one of
my most challenging chorus members, to decide once and
for all whether or not he could make the necessary
commitment.

I had met Korrel at the young offenders centre. The staff
there tried to help youngsters get back on the straight and
narrow; they had some successes and they had some challenges. Korrel was one of the challenges. He had been in trouble
with the law – somebody later told me he had 'terrorised half of
Brighton'. There was a compelling argument for not including
him at Glyndebourne, but I felt that since Korrel had been
through the penal system and had worked with youth offending
teams he deserved a chance. If this opera was going to be about
street crime, Korrel would have a lot to say and it would be a
story he could really contribute to. If he couldn't be involved just
because of his background, the whole project did not make any
sense. I badly wanted him to be part of it.

I had previously done some work in a school for kids who
had been excluded with emotional/behavioural disorders. On
the day of the performance many of the kids either had not
turned up or got themselves kicked out by behaving abomina-
bly, even though the whole project had been going smoothly up
till then. A very experienced teacher said to me, 'These young
people don't know how to succeed. They are afraid of success

so they sabotage it for themselves.' All too late, I realised that was the pattern with Korrel.

Korrel is extremely intelligent, able and very gifted in many respects, but utterly uncontrollable. He had little self-discipline: he would turn up for rehearsals in the wrong frame of mind or after being up all night the night before, and that was completely impossible, because in order to get this teenage chorus ready in time for the first night of the opera we were driving them very hard. Korrel would sit in the corner looking bemused, not knowing if it was OK to enjoy this experience and without understanding how to handle the attention. It was very frustrating. The artistic team *loved* him – he could act, sing and had an electrifying presence on stage. He brought the authority of the street to the whole production.

But pretty soon things began to unravel. Two or three weeks before the first night Korrel told me he had to miss a rehearsal because he wanted to go to a tattoo fair. A tattoo fair? I didn't know they existed. It seemed to me a ridiculous reason to skip a rehearsal. John Fulljames, the opera director, seemed slightly intimidated by Korrel and allowed him the time off.

A couple of rehearsals later things came to the boil. On the train down from London I had been on the phone to Korrel's youth offending team for an hour. I had just discovered that Korrel had been offered a reward for being in the opera: the youth offending team so wanted him to enjoy the opportunity of working at Glyndebourne that they had promised him an incentive, arranging to get a passport sorted out or something like that – a financial incentive.

As soon as they told me this I knew it was a critical mistake. It had artificially prolonged Korrel's involvement beyond what was natural for him. If someone like Korrel did not have the maturity to see that he would gain something from an experience that had no monetary value but masses of personal value, he shouldn't be there. I told the team, 'Korrel can fly with this, but he has to be at the rehearsals and he must be in the right frame of mind.'

That same night he turned up, late, giggling, messing about, and the whole mood of the rehearsal changed. I had been putting the thumbscrews on the choir to make sure they were very disciplined and turned up to every rehearsal, fully prepared. As soon as Korrel sauntered in they became uneasy, angry and irritated about him being there, since they knew he'd missed so many rehearsals. Why wasn't I calling him to account? At one point Korrel asked a question that would have been obvious had he been at the previous rehearsal. That really grated. I told him, 'You missed that. You're too late. You do not have the right to interrupt my rehearsal.' There was a confrontation brewing in his tone.

Korrel walked out. I went running after him. It was one of those moments where instinct takes over. This was now just about Korrel and me and doing the right thing by the rest of the cast. That is how we ended up in a gloomy corridor thrashing things out. We talked for a long time. I gave Korrel ample opportunity to make a commitment, but in the end I made it absolutely about choice. This was within his power. I encourage young people to take responsibility for themselves and make their own decisions. 'It's *them* in this opera, not me. If you don't want to do it, don't do it. It's the arts, and no one can force you to sing a song.' He had the choice to be in or out. And in the end he chose to be out. As far as Korrel and *Knight Crew* was concerned, that was that.

The outcome of this confrontation was that I could then go back in to the rehearsal and announce, 'Korrel has chosen to leave.' It was implicit that I had forced the issue, but I wanted him to make the choice. The other kids probably thought I had asked him to leave, although I hadn't. Suddenly all the discipline was back and everyone was, frankly, relieved.

The road had been a rocky one, especially – and I realise this has become a central theme in this book – for the boys of the chorus. Before Korrel left I'd already had one tricky moment where a few of the boys left in a short period of time. I had been very excited about another singer, Lewis. He was a gentle giant of a young man with a huge voice who I had found through the same young offenders group as Korrel. He too had all sorts of difficulties with attendance, self-organisation and motivation. He went off to see his family and, sadly, we never saw him again.

These two contrasted sharply with the delightful Sol who was unerringly positive. The instant you met Sol you liked him. He has an open face and a lovely way about him. He had been in foster care and spoke movingly about his foster parents to whom he felt he owed so much. Sol was totally committed ... right up until the point where he left. He was a highly talented beatboxer but he decided to concentrate on his A levels. It struck me that Sol had music in his life in the shape of beatboxing, to which he was devoted, and he'd grown up enough to realise that he was in danger of spreading himself too thinly. In the long

174

run it was probably the right move, although I was disappointed he didn't just knuckle down to it and work harder.

Luckily there were others from the group of teenagers I was so keen to involve who were able make a lasting commitment. Desi had a cheeky-chappy, happy-go-lucky attitude that made him a favourite with the rest of the cast. He was always joking around but never pushed it too far. He usually turned up with some joke on his mobile phone or singing the latest pop song while running round the impromptu football pitch that had been created on Glyndebourne's hallowed turf. He was fun. Desi came from the Whitehawk Estate in east Brighton, which ten years earlier had been a more difficult place to live. Desi himself had been stabbed in an incident of street violence and was lucky to be alive. A nicer bloke you could not hope to meet, and he was a really good performer and singer. The movement director for the show said Desi could easily have been a dancer because he had natural physicality and a sort of earthy edginess that I, for example, definitely lack. Desi was always positive in rehearsals, was clearly loved and cared for at home, but happened to live on a tough estate.

Stefan was also an inspiration. I have worked with many young people, but I never met anyone like Stefan. He stood bolt upright whenever I saw him and had a dependable quality about him. He was a sergeant in his local army cadet corps and hoped to go into the military. I remember watching the series back and noticing that he had a Union Jack duvet cover. Sweet.

Stefan's tenacity amazed me, because he was vocally hopeless when I first met him. But he had incredible drive and great discipline. He proved to me that it is possible to make massive leaps and bounds in singing however low your starting point. During our first individual session Stefan could not get anywhere near the notes I wanted to play. By the end of the project he could sing in harmony, and had achieved that by sheer persever-ance, bashing it into his brain, firmly establishing the patterns of notes. At the beginning he really wasn't good enough; by the end he was. I was so glad because he had a phenomenal pres-ence and energy on stage. By earning the right to be there he typified the spirit of the choir.

Vaz was another interesting young man. Elfin, with thick dark hair and a cheeky grin, he had arrived in the UK from Bosnia and seized all the opportunities on offer in his new coun-try. He had picked up English quickly, and to a very good level, in only four years or so. Vaz was intelligent, talented and enthu-siastic, but also as a younger teenager quite impressionable. He was always looking up to the alpha males. This is why it was so potentially dangerous for the overall group dynamic when somebody like Korrel came into the group and started under-mining me, because a boy like Vaz who was on the fence might tip the wrong way. Luckily, Korrel, for all his wiles, was not the alpha male in the choir group – not least because he wasn't there enough to exert control – so Vaz looked to the others like Desi and Stefan, who were looking to me, and that gave me a kind of authority. As a result, the mood of commitment in that group was like nothing I have experienced before. It was extraordinary.

••••

The first conversations about doing a project with Glyndebourne had started as the South Oxhey project was still filming. Cesca Eaton, an executive producer at Twenty Twenty, lived near Glyndebourne, loved the place and was thinking of doing a programme about it. Cesca bumped into me in the TV company's office one day and said, 'I think your next series should be at Glyndebourne.' I'd been to Glyndebourne a few times and worked there on occasions in the education department. I knew that the place was synonymous with quality opera.

Off we toddled on the London to Lewes train to meet the opera house staff. I knew that many had seen *The Choir* but I was sure there would be some reservations about making a TV programme. I was right: we found nervousness at Glyndebourne about the prospect of a documentary because of *The House*, a notorious fly-on-the-wall, behind-the-scenes BBC series about the Royal Opera House from the mid-1990s, which had been quite controversial at the time. It uncovered the power struggles and diva-like behaviour behind the scenes, much to the shock of the public and the unease of the arts establishment. There are long memories in opera and so the relationship between television and the arts remained unsettled. Glyndebourne were, quite sensibly, concerned about anything negative coming out of our involvement.

Nevertheless they were prepared to talk, if cautiously, about the possibilities of a Gareth Malone-type series. 'Funnily enough,' they mentioned, 'we have a project coming up called *Knight Crew*. Would you be interested in being the chorusmaster on it?' Every few years Glyndebourne have commissioned a community opera – previously *Misper* and *Zoë* had hit the main stage there – but *Knight Crew* was to be their most ambitious project. They had been looking for a chorus leader for this new opera; evidently my name was already on their list as someone to approach since I had worked in the education department there a few years earlier alongside Katie Tearle, the head of education. Seeing *The Choir*, they had been reminded of my existence.

The idea immediately appealed to me because it was a completely different style of project to the South Oxhey series. *Knight Crew* was a brand-new piece and would be artistically led by Glyndebourne. The opera was already being written by the composer Julian Philips, head of composition at the Guildhall School of Music in London, and the libretto had been developed from her own book by the award-winning young people's novelist Nicky Singer.

On *The Choir* series I could bend the project towards what I thought would work. I had the freedom to say, 'They can't sing that, so let's drop it down a key.' The *Knight Crew* opera was largely unbendable, the schedule dictated by the opera company, the music set, the story fixed. I would have to work within those constraints.

It was a strange sideways move for me after the success of *The Choir*. The project was back in the area of music education and a return to the world of high-level music and real musical excellence I had been part of at the Royal Academy of Music. It was also about theatre, and I had done a drama degree, so I would have the opportunity to be in a working theatre, taking rehearsals and coaching talented young people who had been chosen because of their ability. This, I thought, should be a doddle.

The South Oxhey experience had been about teaching people who had never sung before to master four-part, even eight-part harmony from scratch – an extremely rewarding challenge – whereas the young choir at Glyndebourne were able to sing in harmony in the first session. The problem I faced was teaching them a piece of music that was technically very difficult, turning a disparate group into a believable chorus, and at the same time trying to make it a genuine outreach project.

That had been one of Glyndebourne's key criteria: they wanted the choir to include the unlikely kids, the regular kids from places that didn't have opera houses. They wanted a chorus of teenagers who hadn't all been trained, who hadn't learnt the bassoon to Grade VIII, but who did have potential. John Fulljames had said at an early meeting that *Knight Crew* was the story of the chorus. No pressure then.

So I really tried. Assisted by a brilliant theatre director called Karen Gillingham, we went out to schools in the less salubrious areas of East Sussex. As well as the young offenders group where I met Korrel and Lewis, we visited young carers groups, and youth clubs with forlorn karaoke machines in the corner where the writing was on the wall as soon as I walked into the room. On those occasions I knew we were in for a miserable evening, and that none of the kids there would be interested, but we persevered. Other clubs were fantastic: the difference seemed to come down to how the youth worker had sold the idea to the kids before we arrived. That's how we found Desi – a music worker called Kevin Grist at his local youth club recommended the project to him. Thanks, Kevin.

Glyndebourne itself had never penetrated the Whitehawk Estate, where Desi lived, to the degree that Karen and I could. The 'telly' factor helped, of course. It provided an extra sheen that Glyndebourne could never hope to achieve without us, and it drew in those kids who liked singing and dancing, but might otherwise not have put themselves forward. What Glyndebourne was providing and putting on for them was an incredible opportunity for those who signed up and saw it all the way through. By the end of that process I think we achieved a pretty good balance between my new recruits and the kids from the existing Youth Opera group who were drawn from a wide range of schools Glyndebourne already worked with.

To create that mix, and because this was going to be a professional production by a prestigious opera house, we ran auditions, but first we got all the kids who had expressed an interest in taking part to give a performance of the 'Toreador Song' from *Carmen* for their families. That was Karen's idea and it struck a chord with me because I remembered the difficult re-auditioning process I had been through before the Phoenix Choir headed off for China.

We wanted to make sure that after the audition process, even if they had not been selected, the kids could go home and say, 'Well, I tried out for it. I wasn't chosen but it was still quite fun. I didn't get through to the main event, but we did do that show at Glyndebourne and my mum and dad came along to watch me.' There is never a really pleasant way to package up saying, 'Sorry, you didn't make it,' but you can at least try to make people feel better about it.

The whole process had been a joy – Karen and I had brought people into Glyndebourne who had never been there before and we had several young performers to be excited about – and so far Glyndebourne seemed delighted.

At the final auditions, however, there was a marked change in atmosphere. The evening before this final selection took place John Fulljames, the director, and Nicholas Collon, the conductor, had been to hear the latest version of the opera with the composer Julian Philips. They had looked in detail at the nearly complete score and been quite shocked by its complexity. It was full of difficult time signatures and key changes. John and Nick arrived at the audition that morning looking stressed. They wouldn't talk about the previous evening on camera because I think it had got quite heated. They were worried that we could not possibly teach this music to a chorus of amateur teens in the short space of time available. Nick Collon remembers: 'The piece was very fast-paced, a huge amount of music, and we didn't yet know the standard of the singers. There was sense of apprehension, suddenly realising and hearing musically what we would have to achieve, and not knowing the forces we would have to achieve that with.' They asked Julian to go away and reconstruct the piece to make it more achievable and easier to work with (which Julian duly did), but their fear remained: would Gareth have found enough capable youngsters?

Nick and John were joined on the audition panel by the head of education Katie Tearle. Between them they had the last say on who was going to make the final selection. Even Katie, who had commissioned main-stage youth operas before, was concerned about the musical level.

Suddenly all the fluffy talk ended. 'Yeah, let's bring in all these kids; Gareth, go and find us this magnificent chorus of rough diamonds' was right out of the window. Unless we chose kids who could come in exactly at the right time, on the bar line, we were stuffed. There was a danger that this new opera could fall apart on stage. For John and Nick (as well as me) this was their big Glyndebourne moment, a major opportunity in both their careers. Karen and I had been unaware of this shift in their thinking, so suddenly all these kids that she and I had thought would get through were absolutely off the list. The level of expectation had shot right up.

When I look back, thank goodness Nick and John made those tough calls. It was the right way to go for the piece. At that time, having not seen the score, I couldn't have known that the piece would require such a high skill level. But it was disappointing to think that so many fantastic young people weren't going to make it into the chorus because their voices weren't up to it.

On that audition day we found about 80 per cent of the chorus – which would be 50 strong – but we were still lacking musical experience. We had plenty of diamonds in the rough but we also needed those who had the backup of musical training. After a further trawl at local music courses I found a few who played musical instruments and rushed them through some auditions to check their aptitude. We were edging closer to our full complement.

This fundamental shift towards musical excellence and experience only goes to show that for Desi, Stefan, Vaz – and Korrel – to have made it through this rigorous selection process was a significant achievement. Knowing that they had got there on merit made all the weeks driving round East Sussex going in and out of youth centres worthwhile. There was a special satisfaction from knowing that we had got kids in who had never thought about opera before.

One of the moments from the *Knight Crew* project that still moves me to tears was when the chorus were performing a particular line from the opera, 'We swear, we swear to Art' (Art was the name of the main character – a King Arthur figure). Desi, who had been stabbed on the Whitehawk Estate and narrowly avoided death, pumped his fist into the air, breaking into the most magical smile. It was a fantastic moment, a beautiful piece of music, and you could see him loving it all. Here he was, on stage at Glyndebourne – who ever would have thought it? He was mesmerising. And that is why I do my job.

(A footnote: at the tattoo fair that Korrel skipped a rehearsal for, he was scouted by a modelling agency and subsequently did some work as a model. For him the fair *was* more important than the rehearsal. For about a year the future looked bright until sadly during 2011 Korrel was arrested and charged with a crime involving a knife. Ironically, Nicky Singer's storyline for *Knight Crew* focused heavily on the evils of knife crime. At the time of writing I read in the *Brighton Argus* newspaper that Korrel was sentenced and imprisoned in 2011. Very sad. I wish him well for the future: I hope he manages to turn things round and that he learns not to look a gift horse in the mouth.)

Someone
Has to
Believe

After seeing how tough the auditions for the chorus had been, it hit home that *Knight Crew* was a very serious undertaking. We were not messing around. There were hard-nosed and high artistic aims for the production. John Fulljames and Nick Collon, as director and conductor, were under scrutiny, being observed by the Glyndebourne music staff. Nicky Singer, the writer, had a track record of successful theatrical adaptations, including *Feather Boy* for the National Theatre, while Es Devlin, the designer, had worked with Kylie Minogue. It felt like the big time.

The way the artistic team, including me, responded to the pressure and dealt with that environment, and the tone they set, might feasibly affect our future careers. Of course my job was different from theirs – I was to look after the chorus, train them up and make sure they had a good experience, whilst they were responsible for the artistic aims of the production. At times there was naturally a tension between the needs of the production and the needs of the young people. I was in the middle.

Ultimately I wasn't in charge. Nick and John were. That meant that they could run things as they saw fit. At times this resulted in situations where we were nearly at loggerheads. I remember getting the spreadsheet of the advance schedule. I slowly counted my rehearsals. On paper I had three rehearsals to teach the music, basically a week on my own without the distractions of director or conductor to drum this music into their heads. It sounded like a tall order but I thought there'd be some wiggle room ...

The real difficulties began early in 2010. On 6 January *The Guardian* ran a prophetic story: 'UK faces coldest winter in 30 years'. The nation was already running out of grit for the roads and dire weather was on its way. In my first week of rehearsals there were about four inches of snow in London; I didn't even make it out of the flat and so I lost all three of the music rehearsals that were scheduled. Since the chorus had been drawn from right across the East Sussex region, there was no way we could get them to Glyndebourne (even had I been able to get there myself). I was stuck, knowing that we'd be hugely behind. I began to feel incredibly frustrated.

In the world of opera there is an expectation that by the time you turn up to rehearsals with the director everyone should know the notes, at least to some degree. Because of the snow disruption, the chorus went into the stage rehearsals seriously under-prepared. I felt aghast that I hadn't got them up to scratch, but the whole artistic team was also feeling under pressure.

It was infuriating and yet nobody's fault specifically. It felt as though I had two per cent of the time I actually needed. Gone were the luxurious choir rehearsals of previous series. This was turning into a mad dash for the finish line. How should I respond? What should be my approach? I couldn't keep the entire artistic team waiting while I calmly taught the music, so we developed a more dynamic way of working. I would rush through a few bars, trying to teach the music to the chorus during any little gaps in proceedings, and then the director would set the movement. I learnt to leap in and correct things where necessary – it felt difficult at first, as though I was being impolite and interrupting. But this was the only way to proceed, and by degrees we began to master sections of the opera.

I remember singing the music into the kids' ears as we stood in the wings, 'No, it goes like *this*.' One minute I'd be in the auditorium, then I'd race round to the stage and climb up the scaffolding to check a harmony line. My score became surgically attached to my hands and I could find any page of the opera within seconds. I was learning to play my part within the artistic team, nurturing the choir while Nick and John struggled with other pressures. For the youth chorus it meant they had to give up every Saturday and a couple of nights a week for rehearsals, which came as a shock to the system. At the first morning rehearsal, one of the teenagers said, 'I want to cry, it's so early.'

Nick Collon knew that there was an enormous amount to do: 'From very early on, because of time, we were already staging things while the chorus were learning their notes. It was a bit of a tussle. In opera there is always that tension. It's not going to be easy, ever.'

These initial tensions did not disappear overnight. In addition to the *Knight Crew* youth chorus there was an additional smaller chorus in the opera, who were meant to be the mothers of the Knight Crew. Glyndebourne were very keen on asking the actual mothers of the teenagers if they could sing and were willing to take part, so that it really was a mum's chorus. I thought this was a great idea and would be very moving, especially since their music reflected on the consequences of street violence. Could I get Desi's mum to join? Would she be able to sing the music, knowing that her own son had been involved in a stabbing? In some ways this was the precursor to the Military Wives Choir – the material that Nicky and Julian had written was emotionally very powerful.

For the sake of the series, the director Harry Beney filmed every phone call I made to each parent of the Knight Crew. It took hours: there's a lot of wasted tape somewhere at Twenty Twenty. Some were definitely not interested – one said she would rather pull her nails out and walk over hot coals – but I managed to persuade a few of them to join in, including Karen, Desi's mum. I was excited about conducting a group of adults. Here was my chance to show everyone at Glyndebourne what I could do. I'd have enough rehearsals, there'd be time to teach the music and properly build their confidence.

The auditions went well: I found there were a number of strong singers in among those who had potential but no track record of singing. The women were very nervous, however, more nervous than I'd anticipated, in fact, and more than their children. They would clearly need careful handling after all.

But unfortunately the reality of time pressure began to bear down on us all and the schedule took a turn for the worse: the mothers' chorus were given, if it were possible, even less practice time than the *Knight Crew* kids before being thrown to the lions. I had handled the first rehearsal with the mums on my own in my usual manner, going through the material very lightly once or twice, planning to revise it in greater depth at the following rehearsal. Based on my own gut instincts about these women and previous experience of working with amateurs it felt necessary not to bombard them with detail and to keep spirits buoyant.

That week Nick Collon quite rightly said that he was worried about the mothers, because of the tiny amount of time we had available, so he asked to come and run the next rehearsal. As the conductor of the opera, Nick was my boss in this situation, so I was not in a position to say 'no'.

Nick is the artistic director and conductor of the Aurora Orchestra, a young and increasingly in-demand ensemble who are at the vanguard of the London music scene. He is a hugely accomplished and very personable guy, who is on the path to being a great conductor, but at that point in his career he did not have much experience of working with young people or of community work – neither did John Fulljames, the director – so he was on a learning curve, just as I was. Nick was in a very difficult position dealing with so many amateurs: 50 or so young people, plus the mothers' chorus and a youth orchestra. Even a couple of the professional singers were struggling with the music in terms of rhythm and timing. From Nick's point of view he just needed to know that the opera wasn't going to come off the rails as it did so often in rehearsal.

Worried about an absolute car crash on the night, Nick took the opposite approach to mine. He went forensically through every bar of music for three hours with these women, who had no musical experience. He went over and over a few scenes to the point that their brains could not take any more in. The women looked beaten by the intensity of the rehearsal. After their third rehearsal it was time to put them onto stage: it all fell apart. I was out of the room at the time preparing another group of singers. A decidedly worried-looking Mr Collon came to see me afterwards to tell me that it had been 'absolute carnage'. 'Did I say that?' Nick now asks, 'The music for the mothers' chorus looked innocuous on the page but it was difficult. They did just get there but only at the last minute. In the end they did as well as they could have. I won't take anything away from them as individuals.' We knuckled down and made a plan to get ourselves out of this tricky situation.

At the following rehearsal the mums were back to me, less confident than before, saying, 'We have just been told off.' They had, if truth be told, been shockingly bad. But the more Nick tried to admonish them, the more they collapsed, because the stern schoolmaster trick does not always work with people who have no experience of performance. They have nothing to fall back on. Panic was in the air and Nick and the ladies were concerned that it wouldn't be all right on the night. Glyndebourne had carefully enticed these mothers, some of whom had been quite reluctant, into the project. I had tried to help them over-come their nerves by telling them it would all be all right. It was now up to me to prove I could get these women up to speed because the orchestra had arrived and Nick had bigger and more pressing matters to deal with.

Over the previous series and during my time with the LSO I'd found out the hard way that learning the notes is only ten per cent of the story. How people *feel* about them is absolutely crucial. In many ways I had more directly relevant experience than Nick, but I don't know if at that stage he fully trusted me to get the ladies ready on my own and I'm not sure I trusted my own instincts enough to tackle him on his approach. I didn't speak up at the time.

In retrospect I should have had more confidence in my own experience. I was probably a little bit dazzled by working so closely with Glyndebourne. In this operatic setting I felt everyone else there were the experts and I was the new boy. Of course I had already done a huge amount of community work and should have stood up more strongly, saying 'I am good at this. This is what I know about.'

In my view Nick made an error with the ladies of the chorus by being too demanding, too soon. But since we had so little time, it would have been difficult to take my slower approach – it certainly hadn't been possible with the *Knight Crew* chorus. All that mattered now was building the ladies' confidence in time for the upcoming performance.

So the ladies and I found a quiet room away from the others and went back to basics. I employed the time-honoured technique of repetition; over and over they sang their parts until they became automatic. They needed a little TLC too – they were at a low ebb and about to sing under pressured circumstances. They wanted Nick to be pleased with their singing. We crammed in extra rehearsals and the ladies went up a few gears.

On the first night I can vividly remember watching the mothers' scene from the back of the auditorium. From the top of the gods the small group of singers looked very small indeed. My heart was in my mouth. Somehow they managed it. Theatrically it was a beautiful moment. All the mothers wore white shirts, and as they sang a plea to stop the gang culture that had decimated the lives of the characters, photos of their own children were projected onto their shirts. The pictures moved slightly as the women sang. It was a powerful image with some beautiful music by Julian. They sang so movingly. Finally we had moved beyond note bashing – this was theatre.

To Nick's credit in the middle of the preparations he took time out from all this stress to give me a conducting lesson because I had to conduct the chorus offstage at one point. (Nick describes offstage conducting as 'a thankless task. I hate it with a passion. If it goes well you have just done your job. If it goes wrong you have really screwed up.') Nick gently took my conducting to pieces; it was like being back at music college except with an instrument I couldn't play. His verdict? 'Not bad at all', though I think he was being generous. I could barely move my arms afterwards. I went home and spent hours in front of a mirror and watching conductors on YouTube trying to improve on my slightly lacking technique. The problem for me was that this was operatic orchestral conducting, very different from the choral conducting I was used to. I had to learn.

I spoke to several people about this in preparation, including a visit to the Guildhall School of Music to see the eminent conductor Paul Daniel for a lesson. Paul said that he thought offstage conducting was the most terrifying job in opera because you can't see or hear properly and yet everyone is relying on you. It's like skiing in the dark. I took some comfort from that. Still, I'm not sure I'd have wanted to do what Nick did. He came into his own once the orchestra began, flying around the score like a mad professor.

It wasn't all slog: for several weeks the youth chorus had been coming into its own. There was a growing sense of enjoyment and they were starting to feel like they owned the place. It was time for them to meet the man who actually did. Gus Christie is the owner of the old house at Glyndebourne and the executive chairman of the opera company. He also happens to be from an operatic dynasty as he is the grandson of the founder of the opera house. Gus, short for Augustus, is like a youthful, springier version of Prince Charles with a gentle wit and plenty of charm. He's married to the glamorous opera singer Danielle de Niese and the man has been brought up with music all his life. Gus's grandfather built an opera house in his garden when the house's 'organ room' proved too small for the performances that he and his wife, the soprano Audrey Mildmay, would put on for friends. This was in the 1920s and 30s, and although the original theatre has been replaced with an astonishingly beautiful theatre, the organ room remains.

For kids more used to the youth centres of Hastings and Brighton, walking into a wood-panelled room full of antiques and oil paintings was a rare treat. They all packed in, wide-eyed, and gathered round the piano to sing to 'the boss'. Gus was fantastic with them, speaking very honestly about the place he clearly cares so deeply about. I think he enjoyed having these young people in the house livening the place up. It was a very satisfying moment when they sang to him and filled that room with their voices, a really strong sound. Gus said it really 'blew the roof off'. Rather charmingly he told them that the room was

194

where his grandmother had been seduced by his grandfather. They loved that.

The youth chorus were by now starting to become a gang in their own right, working together and getting into the storyline. For Nicky Singer, the writer, the experience was proving to be an emotional one. I often found her at the back of rehearsals crying over aspects of the production – at times I felt because she was moved, at others because she was lamenting what had been lost from the novel in the adaptation to the stage. John Fulljames, the director, had been instrumental in boiling down the story to its essential elements, because a novel can be complex whereas simplicity works best onstage. I think Nicky, like most writers, found it difficult watching her beloved story be hacked to bits.

The music too had to be simplified: Julian Philips had reworked the score as John and Nick had requested, cutting difficult harmonies and putting in new bar lines to help people read his music. He had written the original score in quite complicated ways because he is blessed with an ability to read music very easily. You could turn a piece of music upside down and Julian could probably still read it, whereas none of these young people had that level of skill. Some could read music enough to know that it was difficult, which was almost worse. The kids like Desi, though, who didn't read music at all, learnt it by rote.

Julian cleverly composed all the music for the Knight Crew around one theme based on a little angular cluster of notes. Once they had mastered this theme, learning the rest of the music became easier. The theme took over my life. I started hearing those notes everywhere; if someone tapped a cup or a glass or the doorbell rang, the theme would start off in my head. We were doing so much rehearsing to be ready in time for the first night, it had become embedded in my brain.

One line of the opera was for a female solo voice with the lyric 'Someone has to hope, someone has to believe'. It was just a short solo for a girl with a strong enough voice to be heard in the auditorium. The girls were at times in danger of being over-shadowed by the boys: I had specific problems with Korrel taking up time. Besides, the piece had something of a macho gangland swagger anyway, something the boys took to more readily than some of the daintier girls. In the story it was the female charac-ters who spoke most sense (naturally), and so at the end hearing a strong female voice singing about the future felt like a natural choice in the composition.

I auditioned several of the singers following a rehearsal one Saturday and put forward three to sing to John and Nick. There was much deliberation but they decided on Elsie and Jess to share the soloing duties. Elsie had an extraordinary voice – strong and clear to the back of the room – while Jess had a pure, sweet sound. Both of them knuckled down to the task and did not buckle under the pressure. The girls were generally less feckless than the boys, more obedient, harder-working, etc, etc. Same old story.

Kiya, Gaile, Becky, Millie and so many of the others were terrific and will have moved on to great things, while some of the boys are most probably still learning to take responsibility for themselves. It was the same when I was growing up. What does go on in boys' heads?

One teenage boy did, however, seem to have himself under total control ... until it all went wrong at the last minute. On the day of the dress rehearsal, Stefan of all people – who had started out practically tone deaf and had made *incredible* improvements – failed to show. This was a boy who had been to every single rehearsal. He was very focused, never missed anything. On this occasion he simply got his times wrong: it happens to everyone once in their life, especially teenage boys!

We were really worried, calling him and getting no answer, phoning his family, his college. We couldn't find him anywhere. He was happily trundling in with his phone turned off and arrived at the opera house just as the final curtain was going down. He sobbed his heart out because he felt so bad about letting us down. Of course it was fine; no one was really angry with him. Frankly I was relieved that he was all right. His reaction and abject apologies proved how much the opera and the experience meant to him.

Whatever it was that was absorbing Stefan I had my own worries: a few days before the final performance I was able to tell everyone that Becky was pregnant. I'd known since the beginning of rehearsals, but I'd not been able to say anything until the first three months were safely over. I will never forget John Fulljames announcing that we needed extra rehearsals on Friday, which would mean me being away from home while Becky was going to all the hospital appointments and just not being around to check she was OK. I had to negotiate my way round yet another scheduling dilemma, without being able to tell people what was going on.

During the previous summer season, before I started working on the project, I had taken Becky along to see a production of *Carmen* at Glyndebourne, and our visit was filmed for the series. I wasn't sure whether I wanted Becky to appear on screen – and neither was she – but I suppose there was a tiny bit of an agenda behind our night out. At the time I was getting endless questions about whether I was gay or not; every single bit of press was along the lines of 'Everyone thinks Gareth's gay'. This was particularly tiresome – it reminded me of the sort of bullying I had been subjected to at school for being in a choir. Here was an opportunity for Becky to come along, and in a fairly low-key way we could demonstrate, 'Look, this is my wife and we are very happy together. Now you stop wondering.'

I genuinely think that people – or at least a certain sort of person – saw my being prepared to open up in my job as a womanly or homosexual trait, because they are positively terrified by anyone who feels free to be expressive and wave their hands around or do silly voices in rehearsal. This has very little to do with sexuality – it's my job. Also it's just one side of me, a super-ramped-up version of myself I unleash during rehearsals. I am not like that all the time.

I feel it's important for young people, especially boys, to learn how to be *more* expressive. My role is to give them the confidence to be themselves and not worry about what people are going to think – or at least to persuade them that others might think what they are doing is OK. With *Knight Crew* the music and storyline was so tough that it ceased to be a problem. Julian's score required a strength and masculine quality in the singing that these young men found acceptable. I admired them hugely for the unselfconscious way they began to throw themselves into it.

So the performances of *Knight Crew* took place with me glowing at the prospect of fatherhood and feeling very protective of the chorus who had been through so much. The first night was a world premiere – Glyndebourne stuck this on every bit of paper relating to *Knight Crew* – and seeing those words gave me butterflies.

This was the moment where I had to let my fledgeling chorus go out on their own to sing and I had to trust Nick to be there for them on the night. Apart from a short piece of conducting, all I could do was sit, watch and pray. I conducted their first entry because they couldn't see the conducting podium from their upstage position. I dressed completely in black so that nobody could see me, and I remember counting down the bar numbers like a launch from Cape Canaveral before their first line: 'Five ... four ... three ... two ... one ...'. A hand gesture, and they were off. I exited speedily to watch them complete the act on their own. I stood there like a proud father watching his toddler learning to walk, beaming from ear to ear.

The chorus dug deep and produced something quite magical. Then, like all shows with a short run, it was over too quickly. Afterwards there was plenty of evaluation of the project at Glyndebourne, and I think that was wholly positive, but the sad thing is that the opera may well now just sit on a shelf, possibly forever. This is the fate of a great swathe of pieces that are commissioned by specific arts institutions. *Knight Crew* is centred around the chorus of teenagers, and not every opera house has the time or the resources to pull a chorus like that together. It has to be a chorus of young people. You could not simply slide the Royal Opera House's professional adult chorus into the piece. I attended a few meetings at the time where Glyndebourne talked to people who had come over from other opera houses in Europe, places like Utrecht and Frankfurt, to see the piece. I think they all liked it, but because it was a commission very specific to Glyndebourne and to the outreach project, to everything that the Knight Crew had been, I got the feeling no one was going to put it on (and I have yet to hear of anyone putting it on), which is a shame. They should.

I thought the opera worked incredibly well. What needs to happen is for *Knight Crew* to be put on somewhere else, because the second time around everyone could make small tweaks and improvements. Julian Philips might come back in and adjust the orchestration or the director would cut certain scenes that had not worked so well in practice. Opera is such a slow art form, it needs more exposure for something to really bed in and become a regularly performed piece. That process could then create a work to stand in the opera repertoire for the rest of time.

Katie Tearle, the head of education at Glyndebourne, had done the most incredible job in bringing her department out of a small cupboard, into the main building and onto that main stage. It was her vision that made those artistic ideals absolutely as high as possible, and got people like Nick Collon and John Fulljames to do the best quality production with top-flight designers and movement directors, and the rest of the main company, the wigmakers and propmakers. Yet there is still a slight prejudice about a piece that starts out as an education commission, which can stop it breaking into the mainstream.

The great exception to this is Benjamin Britten's music, whose *Saint Nicholas* and *Noyes Fludde* have found an ongoing life.

There are a lot of those pieces floating around, looking for schools or youth projects to take them on. The fact that *Knight Crew* is technically complex may not be in its favour. It was fiendishly difficult. We had top-quality répétiteurs playing piano at the rehearsals, and I remember one guy blurting out, 'Oh bugger!' in exasperation as he made yet another mistake. It is not something an amateur pianist could handle. *Knight Crew* demanded a level of professionalism that was unique to that small set of circumstances. The feeling at the end of it for me, therefore, was one of joy as it had been an amazing thing to be involved in, but tinged with a slight sadness because it was probably one moment in time. Jess Jackson, who was one of the two soloists, put a message up on Twitter on the anniversary of the show reminding everyone that it was two years since we had done *Knight Crew*, so it had obviously been an incredibly emotional and formative experience for her and the others.

On *Gareth Malone Goes to Glyndebourne* we had set extraordinarily high professional standards for the youth chorus. They had shown an equally extraordinary determination and commitment in trying to match those standards. All of that affected the following series, *The Choir: Military Wives*, because I came in with much, much higher aims for the wives from the beginning. From day one I thought, 'These women really can sing. We can go much further.'

Probably Break Down and Cry

In early 2011 Becky and I began to search online for somewhere to stay in North Devon. Not knowing the area we drew a circle around Chivenor, where I would be working for the next eight months, and picked somewhere that looked quaint. The place we chose was Mortehoe, a tiny, beautiful village out along one of the remoter stretches of the North Devon coast.

It was raining when I arrived towards the end of February: I had travelled down from London on my own to set up house. Becky and our then four-month-old daughter Esther would be coming down a few days later. As I drove into Mortehoe the visibility was so poor that I couldn't tell that there is normally a stunning view of Lundy Island. The locals say that if you can't see Lundy Island then it's raining, and if you can see it, then it's about to rain.

The little cottage we were staying in proved elusive on my first attempt to find it, so I ventured into a pub called the Chichester ('the Chich'), one of three in the village. I was warmly welcomed by a couple of beer-soaked regulars who I could see were wondering what I was doing there in the middle of winter. After a couple of pints of ale and a fisherman's pie I felt ready to brave the elements once more and eventually located the cottage.

Once I got the log burner up to temperature the living room was soon roasting hot. Heaven! I opened a bottle of red and sat in the silence contemplating the task ahead. Earlier I had walked over to the village shop: a sign on the door read 'Shut until March'. Reality dawned: I was going to be living in Devon for nine months. It was going to be a long year.

When Tim Carter, the CEO of Twenty Twenty, first told me that we had approval from the Ministry of Defence to film at a military base and that the base was actually quite a long way away – from a Londoner's point of view of course – the idea of living there took hold. At the time of the conversation, Becky was heavily pregnant, so faced with the prospect of my under-taking a six-hour commute to North Devon we both thought, 'Well, why don't we move to Devon?' Becky would be on mater-nity leave from her job as a teacher so it was eminently possible. We had this dream of wearing Hunter wellies and charging through the countryside chasing a Labrador – not that we have a Labrador.

In addition, the major commitment of decamping to Devon as a family, rather than me going by myself, felt absolutely inte-gral to the spirit of the new project, *The Choir: Military Wives*. During the series I would be working alongside the wives and girlfriends of serving soldiers, sailors, marines and airmen, who are routinely transferred to a randomly chosen new base every time their husbands receive a new posting. The Mortehoe experience would give us a small taste of that aspect of military life.

Neither Becky nor I realised quite how tough it would be, especially for Becky, a new and first-time mother, uprooted from the surroundings she knew and relocated to Devon, where I would be out all day filming and encouraging these other women to sing. There are worse places to be dropped. North Devon is a lovely part of the world – especially if you are outdoorsy – but it is definitely remote. It really was an upheaval. Speaking to the wives and telling them that I was living up the road, I showed that I understood a bit about their predicament. I was able to say, 'I know something of what you are going through.' Of course what I couldn't comprehend was how they dealt with their husbands being away at war, but several times the women of the choir told me they thought of Becky as an 'honorary military wife' because of her situation.

One of the strengths of previous series of *The Choir* was both the sense of total immersion and the obvious length of the filming period. The viewers could share in the change over a long period of time. I consciously wanted the project to be difficult for me because I knew it would be for the women. I didn't want people to have the impression that I just arrived by helicopter every day from London (for the record I have never been in a helicopter). I also loved the idea that I would see life unfolding; how the women's lives would change, that babies would be born, haircuts changed at least three times, the girls losing ten pounds. Real life happening in real time.

There was another reason for going. I had a sense that things were getting generally a little easier and cosier in my life, maybe too easy and too cosy. When I had phoned up Glyndebourne to talk about what became the *Knight Crew* project (some five years after previously working with them), I had immediately heard, 'Oh, hi, Gareth, how are you?' rather than a puzzled silence and a 'Sorry, who is this again?' That element of my life was getting easier. There were rather more taxis available all of a sudden, and people offering to get me a coffee, much more of that kind of behaviour than I had ever had before. Something about all of that made me slightly uneasy, because I did not think it was conducive to the way we made *The Choir*. I didn't want to get lazy. I wanted something that would be challenging, that would push me.

I went into Chivenor with a totally different degree of confidence in my own ability. I felt I had proved myself; I had proved that singing works, that I could create performances, that I knew how to do my job. My whole attitude from the outset was, 'Right, I'm here to help and do what I can,' knowing that I could make some kind of a difference. But I was uneasy about how singing would be received in *this* context.

This felt like a far more grown-up situation than my previous series. I already knew that singing improved confidence, and by now everyone else did because they had seen me do it, but what we didn't know was whether it could work in circumstances where people were bereft. That was a question with substance and a question I wanted to ask, although I was slightly frightened of the idea, because I would have to deal with military types and grown-up emotion.

The first day of filming was also my first day on a military base. Simply entering the place is intimidating: the guard with the gun at the gate, the CCTV, the barbed wire, the military vehicles thundering by, being met by a coldly professional security service with all the ruthless efficiency of the Politburo. I was not at home.

Once through these forbidding outer limits I was ushered through to meet Lieutenant Colonel Leigh Tingey, an impressive man with a steely gaze, an iron handshake and an efficient yet charming manner. He took me through the basics of what 24 Commando Engineer Regiment and Commando Logistic Regiment were going to be doing in Afghanistan's notorious Helmand province. If I'd been intimated by going into the sports department of Lanky Boys in Leicester, this was a whole new level. These guys could kill you with a toothpick – should the need arise.

Back then I knew next to nothing about the military, although there were a few connections in the family. I'm very proud that my grandfather volunteered to join the RAF during the Second World War and flew in Lancaster bombers as a wireless operator and second gunner. He takes great pride in being British, a pride he has instilled in me. My father was in the Territorial Army in Glasgow before he moved south. The TA trained him up and got him interested in running and fitness, something he passed on to me, although my dad ran marathons and I just go to the gym. When I was a child, as a family we always watched Trooping the Colour, went to exhibitions of miniature military aeroplanes (I was *obsessed* with Airfix models) and regularly visited the Imperial War Museum.

Like many boys I grew up with an interest in the military and was drawn to the sense of discipline – vital in any choir and its choirmaster, of course. I'd enjoyed being a scout, all that lining up, marching and saluting. However, as I became more and more interested in the arts at school, that enforced, codified separation between musical and sporty activities took over. I was not in the Combined Cadet Force, which was run by a rather gruff, bulldog-like master known as BJ. There was a feeling that the CCF was for the rufty tufty types and not for the likes of me; at my school, singing did not fit with the masculine surroundings. Conversely, I thought that CCF was for louts. Through my work at Chivenor I came across many people in the military with very fine brains, refined tastes and first-rate educations. Who knows, in another life, or with another set of opportunities, I think I would rather have relished the challenge of being an officer. It's just the actual danger I'm not too keen on ...

Leigh Tingey played down the danger. On the previous tour of 'Afghan' his two units had been lucky in not losing any lives. I felt reassured since I wasn't relishing the prospect of dealing with this aspect of military life. My boyish conception of the military was partly informed and inspired by my grandfather's great stories of derring-do in the Second World War (which in any case were toned down, I think, for my young ears). At the Chivenor military base I was going to be faced with families being split up when the serving men went off to Afghanistan. That is a very different and harsher reality.

Twenty Twenty had been developing ideas for the next series of *The Choir* and was looking at whether a military wives choir would work. As with the South Oxhey series, a letter rose to the surface above all the other mail. This particular one had been sent in by Nicola Clarke, whose husband was at Catterick Garrison in Yorkshire; she thought that setting up a choir would help the community of wives while the men were away on active service. This letter gave us the proof that we needed – that we had been looking in the right places. The interest and demand for a military wives choir was out there. Twenty Twenty was working with the MOD, scouting around for a suitable location, but for a number of reasons it turned out that it was not possible to go to Catterick. Then I got the call from Tim Carter saying, 'There's a place in Devon that looks quite interesting. Would you be prepared to go and work down there?'

Royal Marines Base Chivenor, not far from the town of Braunton in North Devon, seemed promising. Above all, Chivenor was a tri-service site, with members of all three armed forces based there. Originally a civil airfield, which had been taken over by the RAF as a coastal command base during the Second World War, it had been primarily a Royal Marines base for 15 years and was home to the Royal Marines Commando Logistic Regiment and Royal Engineers 24 Commando Engineer Regiment. A detachment of 22 Squadron – part of the RAF's search and rescue force – flew out of Chivenor.

With the logistical element of where I was going to be working set up and in place, I could turn my thoughts to the emotional side of the project. A few years earlier there had been a mass shooting at a college in the States. The students got together shortly afterwards to hold a midnight vigil during which they sang the college song. I remembered the TV news talking about the singing. My radar is always switched for anything to do with singing, so this item caught my attention.

What I found interesting was that these students were going through an awful moment, after some of their friends had recently been horribly and irrationally murdered, and yet what they wanted to do was sing. Thinking about the Military Wives, I had this hunch that even when your husband is in a war zone, even if, God forbid, the worst should happen, there is still a role for singing. Why do we sing at funerals? Because it is expressive and it makes us feel better by helping to let the grief out. I knew that from an intellectual point of view, but I didn't know it from first-hand experience.

The situation fascinated me, and when I met the women for the first time I was struck by their ordinariness – they were regular women who had found a strength because they simply had to. But they seemed quite zipped up about how difficult their predicament was. The 'Afghan generation' was ten years old in 2011. Ten years of bad news stories, casualties and fatalities had hardened these women. They suffered in silence while the outside world had little idea they existed. The project started off as an idea: I believed that singing would be beneficial to Chivenor. I also hoped that it would enrich my own experience of the role of singing and music. But what a point to arrive there – 600 of these women's husbands and boyfriends were just about to be deployed to Afghanistan for a six-month-long tour. I had a chance to meet some of them shortly before they left, at a fête they held on the base. That made the experience immediately feel more real for me, as I saw the couples together just before they were separated.

At that point the men were absolutely ready to go. Their training was complete and they had a little leave to spend time with their families. Many of the women told me that these last days were like being in purgatory. More than one was heard to say, 'I wish they'd hurry up and go.' The tension must have been unbearable.

I spoke to the men about what they would be doing. Most of the Chivenor guys were not at the forward operating bases, the FOBs as they call them. Those FOBs are the most dangerous places in Afghanistan, out of the so-called 'safe zone', right in the line of fire. This is not to say that Leigh Tingey's men were by any means out of danger. There were many times that they would be heading out to deliver equipment, to build or repair a bridge, or to collect a jeep that had broken down and needed bringing back to base. At any moment there was the possibility of an ambush or of being caught by an IED, one of the improvised explosive devices that had become the deadliest of weapons. Although not directly on the front line, there was still the possibility that during the course of filming one of the husbands or boyfriends might not make it back or be seriously injured. I didn't know what to say to them. I shook a lot of hands and simply wished them luck.

There was nothing we could do about that possibility – and I didn't feel that it should prevent me from starting a choir. As a TV production we had to be aware of it, but as a choirmaster I was becoming increasingly certain that the women might want to sing. In fact, at that family day I began to feel that my work of bringing singing to the wives was urgently needed.

The early rehearsals were brilliantly chaotic but there was a definite sense that these women could sing and wanted some relief from the stresses of their daily lives. There were children everywhere. I became a surrogate father figure around the camp and several of the babies would watch in wonderment as I waved my arms around.

By the third or fourth rehearsal I noticed that the women weren't leaving quite as quickly, that they were hanging round to chat with each other. At the Hive, a little military café near the church, Jenny, one of the singers, would make extra cakes on choir days and the choir would all head there to drink instant coffee and eat brownies. They were starting to bond.

Initially the overriding emotion I encountered when I arrived in Chivenor was one of stoicism. At the first rehearsal I had imagined I would find a group of women who were all quite gutsy, but in fact I detected a reticence. All their true emotions were hidden away. This is hardly surprising given the depth of emotion relating to their position, but it also revealed an embarrassment about their feelings that I thought was unfounded. They didn't speak openly about having their husbands out in Afghanistan because it was too painful, but when it came to singing surely they could let themselves go a little?

The traditional role of military wives in this country has been to keep the home fires burning, as the song goes. Children, jobs, chores kept these women from falling apart. They did not like to cry in front of each other. Stoicism was their coping mechanism. Their uncomplaining fortitude was necessary because they needed to make it through each day and get on with their lives. I wanted to demonstrate to them that it is acceptable when you are among friends to let emotions out. I hope that one result of all the choir's success is to encourage people to do that, because in my opinion it is not that helpful to hide everything away and not talk about difficulties. It may be typically British, but I am not sure it is psychologically very healthy.

I remember the first fully teary moment was announcing that their recording would be played on BFBS (British Forces Broadcasting Services), which airs in Afghanistan. The thought of their husbands hearing them sing over the airwaves was like breaking a hole in a dam. And once they started, they just didn't seem to stop.

Over the months the crying began to change, from painful, personal sobbing to a sort of less awful welling-up. Women continued to cry regularly but they didn't tend to run out of the room in embarrassment; they just carried on singing. Sometimes I'd catch their eye as they were singing and crying at the same time and then they'd start to laugh at themselves. It was a peculiar mix of emotions that was eased by being in the choir.

Musically they were immediately strong, probably because there were no men singing to put them off. Since they were so good so quickly, I organised a performance for the wives choir (we called it the Military Wives Choir even though it was technically wives and girlfriends, because that name got too long-winded and suggested a WAG-style veneer, which didn't seem entirely appropriate). During one of the early rehearsals I announced that we were off to the base to perform to the rear party, those marines and soldiers who had remained at the Chivenor base. You could have cut the air. The wives didn't enjoy being surprised – unsurprisingly they liked their lives to be nice and ordered. Unfortunately for them this would be the first of many shocks I would spring on them.

I had chosen a song I knew they'd all know: despite its origins as a rock song, I had arranged Guns N' Roses' 'Sweet Child O' Mine' for the performance. I don't know whether the prospect of performing it was more intimidating for the choir or for me. As the hangar door rose to reveal the rear party in all its splendour I felt a heavy sense of responsibility. This was like the Year 11 assembly in the first series, only in full camouflage kit. I hadn't seen a room full of 200 soldiers before. Most of the rear party are replacements who will be sent out in the event that someone on the front line is injured, so they are all battle-ready, prepared to go out with very little notice; a fearsome group.

We were singing in a huge hangar full of tanks and air ducts. I had thought the sound the choir made might be lost within its size, but it had a gorgeous acoustic, rather like singing in a cathedral. The performance worked very well and the wives had a great reception – it didn't feel like a joke, but serious and worthwhile – and I could tell the audience believed in us. We had started earning our stripes. The enthusiasm we received there was the first inkling for me of what the reaction to the choir was going to be like; exactly what I had hoped for and more. I had wanted the choir to be good enough for everyone to get right behind them. I was not prepared to settle for a level of basic competence for which they would get the support simply because it was 'a nice thing to do', a slightly patronising 'Aren't the girls doing well?' attitude.

From that very first rehearsal, where 40 of the wives, including Kerry Tingey, the CO's wife, had turned up, with all their assorted babies and children in tow, I sniffed real potential. I thought that people listening to the choir might actually be taken aback and realise these women really could sing. I would have to set my sights very high indeed.

Keep Holding On

As a general rule I don't drink things that are blue. Toilet cleaner, aftershave and mouthwash are, to my taste at least, not suitable for consumption, so as Penny, one of the livelier military wives, forced me to knock back some ghastly iridescent concoction I should have turned on my heels and run. Going head to head with the wives for an evening's serious drinking in the Sergeants' Mess was my toughest challenge during the first few weeks at Chivenor. I had previously been out on an exercise drill for a gruelling cross-country yomp with the rear party soldiers, which had left me exhausted, but this night of boozing was truly something else. These women 'went large' with a vengeance.

There were various kinds of liqueur involved. One bright pink drink turned out to be some sort of Sambuca, and aniseed is definitely not my favourite flavour – in fact it makes me gag. The other was green and ostensibly apple-flavoured, although it tasted unlike any apple I have ever eaten. However, surrounded by a phalanx of military wives, I was left with no choice. There was no dodging the bullet and I had made the terrible mistake of having a pint or two when I arrived at the Mess, thinking I would drink those and then be allowed to skulk off. Just as I was eyeing the exit, the shots arrived. I think I had about eight of them, and then another pint because I was feeling all right. Silly man.

It was at this point that they brought the Flaming Sambucas round. Very luckily Steve, the director, intervened and said he was terribly sorry but he was not allowed to let me drink anything even remotely flaming because if I set light to my face and ended up in hospital he was going to be in deep trouble with the BBC (bless him for that white lie). However, he did not prevent me from doing The Nails, a military tradition involving a massive block of wood, like half a tree trunk standing to about hip height, a box of nails and a massive hammer. The idea is that you tap a nail in just far enough so it stands upright, then place one hand behind your back and whack your nail as hard as you can with the hammer. Everyone takes turns at this, and the last person to knock their nail in has to buy the next round or down a gazillion drinks or something equally awful; absolutely standard operating procedure in the Sergeants' Mess. We all did The Nails. There were sparks flying and nails shooting through the air. Kelly Leonard, a seemingly mild-mannered soprano who is ex-RAF, was transformed by The Nails into a violent maniac. I feared for my soft tissue.

The wives told me that I might have run with the big boys but now I was playing with the big girls. They are dangerous, they really are, and they are married to hard-drinking dangerous men. It was shocking for a choirmaster, frankly. This was not like being at Glyndebourne. There are no Flaming Sambucas at the opera house as far as I am aware. Eventually Steve said that it might be wise for us to leave. I could hear them carousing from 200 metres away.

The next morning I woke up and realised that the whole thing had been a dreadful, dreadful mistake. I was due to be at one of the local schools at 2pm. I ordered a cab, because there was no way I was in a fit state to be behind the wheel of my own car. I knew the local taxi driver quite well, so when he turned up I warned him that I was feeling rather unwell, and that he might have to stop en route. I made it to within a mile of the school before having to get out and walk. I then spent an hour working with 60 young children. That was a very difficult session.

That evening with the wives made me look back to my workout with the Marines with something approaching fondness. It had been a suggestion from some of the guys on the base and everyone thought it would be fun to watch me suffer. I was a little embarrassed that I might be quite out of shape and seriously worried that I would look a complete idiot by collapsing and being ignominiously carted off.

It was a very hard session, the long yomp and then over to the Marines' 'playground'. There was not much fun to be had in that particular area as it involved pounding up a very steep hill and then sprinting down the other side trying desperately to stay in formation and not fall flat on your backside, knocking everyone over. Finally, there was an enormous amount of trudging through lots and lots of mud. The hardened regulars cooled off afterwards by jumping into a very deep, freezing-cold swimming pool, but the military advised me against it. In fact they said they would not allow me to do it. It was good advice. I think that might have pushed me over the edge. Unless you are blisteringly fit, jumping into that ice-cold water on a chilly February morning could stop your heart. I snuck off for a hot shower.

I am glad to report that the physical trainer did say afterwards to our director that he thought I had done well. He may have been being nice but I am a determined sort of person: I pushed myself ridiculously hard, like a middle-aged man about to have a heart attack playing squash with a 20-year-old; embarrassing really. Still, I came out elated. It was enjoyable despite being shattering: although my heart was pounding, and I was boiling hot after ploughing through the mud, I felt alive. I quite liked that. It reminded me of my days of scouting, except with guns.

The military didn't *need* to recruit a choirmaster but taking part in the training session and being seen to have a go was a great way to break the ice with everybody. All the wives loved hearing about it. 'We heard you went and did a training session?' 'Yeah,' I said as nonchalantly as possible. 'How was it?' 'It was a nightmare.' They laughed. 'Oh, you are so unfit, Gareth. You are so weedy.' All their husbands are built like machines. I resolved to get back to the gym as soon as the project ended.

By now I was starting to build a good rapport with the wives, and they were seeing themselves as a choir rather than a disparate group of women who happened to live near each other. They called the family quarters 'the Patch'. Built some time after the 1960s, it looked like any council estate, except very, very tidy. All the houses were to the same design and were painted and decorated by the MOD. It was all a bit eerie.

In my early days the place was relatively quiet during school hours, but after a few weeks as I walked around the Patch I would always hear someone indoors practising a harmony line or a random bit of one of the songs. That was a lovely change.

I was also beginning to understand who were likely to be the stronger singers in the choir. I had met Samantha Stevenson during one of my first visits to a playgroup on the base. Sam was one of the few who would admit to being able to sing, though she wasn't rushing to demonstrate her potential in front of me. At the early rehearsals she came across as being incredibly lacking in confidence. She would be irritated by every mistake and beat herself up over tiny errors. Her memory of the first rehearsal is at odds with my positive take: 'The first rehearsal was a disaster. With music, you have to really let go in order to enjoy it. As wives, holding the fort while our husbands are away, it's very hard to let your guard down. You have to keep a brave face on all the time. Letting go is a really big deal.'

Sam was pretty uptight, and this perfectionism mixed with general anxiety about her husband meant that when I was doing an individual session with her she must have apologised fifty times in half an hour, including apologising about saying sorry ...

All the other wives had seen Sam get up and sing in the past, but there must have been something about me walking through her front door and asking her to sing for me, together with whatever authority I had, that made her terrified. She was afraid of being judged, I suppose, and what she was looking for was a sense of approval. My telling her she could sing well, that she was easily good enough and that we would work hard together marked the beginning of her personal turnaround.

Sam reflects, 'A turning point was the moment Gareth asked me in a rehearsal to sing the solo in *"Pange Lingua"*. He asked me to sing it with Hayley and with Emma first of all, and then asked me to sing it on my own. I knew his ploy because he was looking at me the whole time. That rehearsal, when I sang the solo in front of the whole choir, was when I knew I could do it. He picked the right moment.'

I really like Sam's singing. She was by far the strongest of the sopranos that Chivenor had, but she was quite untutored, so her breathing was a little shallow, and her voice was not absolutely rock solid. But she is an incredibly emotionally articulate person and a very good communicator. You always know how she feels. When Sam is angry or upset, everyone feels it. When she is happy, everyone feels that as well. That is what she brings to singing: an openness that I really respond to. I don't want to hear someone who is technically refined and dull; I want to hear someone who has got heart in their singing.

Nicky Scott also had a very good voice. Jon Cohen, who produced the Military Wives on their recordings, said that she had one of the most distinctive voices he has ever worked with. Her sense of pitch and the feeling that she puts into it is absolutely incredible. Her voice is lower than Sam's soprano: Nicky's is close to alto, maybe a mezzo-soprano, and she sings especially well in that lower, deeper part of her voice. She was at school in North Wales with the wonderful bass-baritone Bryn Terfel, and maybe some of Bryn's influence had rubbed off on her. Or maybe vice versa.

Nicky is ex-army herself, and had only just arrived at the base. She said in an interview for the programme that she had not even met the CO's wife yet, and there was Kerry Tingey sitting only a few chairs away from her in the rehearsal. They became great pals, and it showed how the choir could help to cut across all ranks as well as the different services represented at Chivenor to bring the women closer together. Kerry is the least rank-orientated member of the choir. She managed to be one of the girls but usually with the dignity appropriate to the wife of the commanding officer – except after a few Flaming Sambucas ...

Both Sam and Nicky were able to put their emotions into their singing and wear their heart on their sleeve. Furthermore, they had the confidence to do that while performing in public, which a lot of the other women lacked because they had spent so long clammed up and keeping a very stiff upper lip. And they were scared stiff of singing.

Following the successful performance to the rear party where I unleashed the Chivenor Military Wives Choir to the troops on the base, I now wanted them to perform before the general public. In fact, the original plan was for the rear party performance to be the end of the first programme, but quite quickly I realised that it wouldn't represent enough of a challenge. I shifted the bar up another notch.

Barnstaple is the main town in North Devon, and only a few miles from the base. The high street looks like most other British high streets except there are telltale signs of farming life round every corner – you know you are in the country. In the centre of Barnstaple there is a lovely Victorian marketplace called the Pannier Market and I was wondering if this might be a place for the choir to sing. I went to check it out because I was, as usual, concerned about the acoustic. It turned out to be perfect. On the day they cleared a space for us and put up some Union Jack flags. I expected a crowd of around 50 friends and family.

We decided to dress in blue jeans and white shirts to give the choir a contemporary feel and to fit in with the red, white and blue theme of the market. A simple stage was erected. With just three TV cameras we set up for the performance and waited.

In the event Barnstaple did us proud: the local residents turned up en masse. There were over 500 people crammed into a tiny space; it was extraordinary. Nicky took the main solo on Bob Dylan's 'Make You Feel My Love', singing it for George, her husband. 'I was so happy,' she says. 'When Gareth told me I had the solo, I thought I'd won the lottery. It lifted my spirits, and they stayed up there for the rest of the time he was with us.'

As I looked around the audience I could see several people in tears, including some grown men who were clearly ex-military. After the positive reaction on the military base, this was an indication that the general public were also going to be supportive. In front of my eyes the choir blossomed on that stage; they could sense the enthusiasm coming from the crowd.

During the opening bars of 'Make You Feel My Love' one baby started screaming and had to be taken outside. That was my daughter Esther, who had come along with Becky to watch proceedings. Becky missed the whole thing and then had to wait eight months to watch it on TV. I think that will be Esther's only TV moment for the time being, but the fact that I was now a dad affected my relationship with the wives and my attitude to the absences at the heart of military families. Becoming a parent changes your whole life, of course, and I felt that being a father gave me a greater authority in that situation. It made me more of a grown-up. I suddenly felt as if I had earned the right to be part of society, to talk to other parents, and understand family dynamics. I could never have managed this choir before the arrival of Esther.

Sam was sure that the women responded to me because they knew I had a daughter: 'Gareth was working with us when he could have been with his wife and new baby, so he had an understanding of what we were feeling. He knew what it was like to miss your family. It meant he could really relate to us emotionally. He could relate to the men too. They're out there in Afghanistan away from their families ... Gareth being a dad meant he could understand more easily how hard that could be.'

My conversations with the wives were often about babies. We ended up talking about all the usual subjects that parents talk about: where to get a good pushchair; the pros and cons of breast-feeding; the exhaustion of sleepless nights; midwives; hospitals; everything you start learning about when you become a parent. I felt drawn in, and they felt free to carry on their conversations about babies and children, which for many of them was a large part of their lives. I don't think they would have spoken like that in front of me if I had been still single or not yet a father. Certainly I had never been a part of those conversations in female company before. It seemed that parenthood allowed me to have a more privileged position within their community.

Before Esther was born I would have empathised with the wives and their feelings but it would have been in a more abstract way. You can't really understand it until you have your own child.

One of the choir members, Suzy Brady, whose father had been in the military, had both a husband and a son who were serving marines. Her 21-year-old son was in 42 Commando, based in Plymouth, which was having a very bad tour in Afghanistan: one of the marines had recently been killed. As a result, Suzy was on a different emotional level of awfulness from the word go. 'It was the first time my son had been away and the first time is always the hardest,' she says. 'It was heartbreaking.' For Suzy, singing in the choir was a very welcome distraction. But I want to be extremely clear that hers was just a different hue of what all the wives live with day in, day out; the separation and the uncertainty.

Obviously some of their men were more regularly in the firing line. When I first saw the group of women who made up the choir, I had no idea whether their husbands were based at Camp Bastion, the main military base in Afghanistan, on the front line in a forward operating base or had not yet been deployed and were alongside me on the yomp. Some of the guys were in the RAF search and rescue helicopter 22 Squadron. Their job is air-sea rescue, which is also incredibly dangerous: they could easily get caught up in a storm; anything could happen. And they were only based two minutes away. Being a military wife is a very pressured existence. There was an aura of anxiousness, and the snippets of news filtering back from Afghanistan made for a tenser atmosphere. During the months I was in Devon I was more aware of the news than I had ever been.

When we recorded three songs for broadcasting on the British Forces Broadcasting Service, Twenty Twenty arranged for a local cameraman in Afghanistan to film some reactions from the men out there. The footage never got used, partly because the way of filming *The Choir* is very specific – it's an observational documentary style, with the camera on the shoulder, moving around, capturing the sense of being inside the scene – whereas the cameraman in Afghanistan used a standard news-reporting approach: set up the tripod, mount the camera, get it in focus and press Record. It jarred with the overall feel of the series, but the truth was that we didn't actually need to see the reaction of the men. *The Choir* was not about the guys in Afghanistan, it was about their *absence*. By not seeing them, it underlined the fact they were not back in Devon. Their wives were missing them, so why should the TV audience suddenly get a privileged insight into these guys? The sequence was cut.

We heard anyway that the reaction to the broadcast was incredibly positive. There was constant communication via Facebook, Twitter and weekly phone calls. I was starting to get feedback that they were talking about the choir. 'What's been happening this week?' a husband would ask. 'I've been at choir rehearsals.' That was a big shift for those conversations. Nicky Scott's husband later said that was all she had been talking about.

In a short space of time we had collectively proved that singing could work wonders for these women. It felt like an endpoint. What would I do next? Since I received Nicola Clarke's original letter I had been thinking that choirs could work wherever there were military wives gathered in one place. Since there are dozens of bases around the country it seemed time to broaden the scope of the mission.

I made a plan to head off for another military town, Plymouth, and booked a date. A couple of days later we received news of a spate of recent casualties affecting the base. For a moment I choked. Should we be going to a town where the wives of those recently lost men were currently grieving? I sought advice from Chivenor and Suzy Brady, whose son was based at Plymouth, told me, 'They *need* this.' So with a degree of nervousness, the best of intentions and a desire to be sensitive we clambered into a minivan.

Plymouth is about two hours' drive from Chivenor across Dartmoor. I took a small number of the Chivenor women along for the ride to show what we had been doing, and when we got there, they surprised me by being quite nervous about performing to other military wives. To be fair there was a healthy turnout from Plymouth. I think one or two of the Chivenor girls had hit the bottle before we arrived for Dutch courage. The journey down was like a female version of the night out in the pubs of South Oxhey with Matty and his Men, except that we had to keep stopping for toilet breaks because several of them were pregnant.

Women had come from all over Plymouth. There was a much wider catchment area with some 2,000 military families drawn from the entire city. The Plymouth women had great confidence from day one, and that intimidated the Chivenor group, who were a little scared about how good the Plymouth choir already was after only about 30 minutes of singing. Had I taken the whole of the Chivenor choir and given a polished performance of something we had worked on maybe it would have been different, but much to my surprise the Chivenor women came away feeling deflated. This was the opposite to what I had intended. I felt that I had messed up badly.

Sam was not with us on that trip but felt its effect as word spread around Chivenor that there was a new kid on the block. She said, 'We were used to having Gareth all to ourselves! I think it made us pick up our game. We wanted to be the best. There was definitely some healthy rivalry between us.'

However, although there was an element of competition between the two choirs, which was purely human nature, a positive side effect was that each choir developed a very strong sense of its own identity. It seems to me that there is a human desire to form groups and bonds, and that we identify ourselves by what we are not. There is a need to say, 'I am British, there-fore I am not French,' or, 'I come from the south of England, therefore I am not a northerner.' The Chivenor choir drew even closer together by casting themselves in opposition to Plymouth, which I had not expected.

This was an issue that hadn't existed before the choirs had been set up, because when women went from one base to another one, it was simply a matter of thinking, 'Right, I am going to Plymouth, OK, now I am a Plymouth wife.' There was nothing for them to identify with strongly, in the way there now was with the choirs. There was perhaps a lack of team spirit because in order to have team spirit you need to have someone to set yourself in opposition to.

It was exactly like the people of South Oxhey defining them-selves in comparison to their neighbours from Carpenders Park or Moor Park. Channelled positively, that rivalry helped foster a stronger community spirit within each choir and pushed up the performance standards because each choir wanted to be better than the other, though it was never meant to be competitive. When I announced that I was also setting up a choir in Plymouth, Kerry Tingey looked darkly at me and pressed on me, 'You *can't* make this a competition.' I needed to unite the two groups.

I brought them together for the first time to perform a mashup of 'I'll Be There' with Bruno Mars's 'Just the Way You Are' at Armed Forces Day in Plymouth, which was the Plymouth choir's first public outing. The day had a fairly formal feel to it with much military pageantry. This was my first taste of what was to come and it made me edgy. I'm fine with a relaxed crowd but performing to the military was another matter altogether.

By the time we turned up the following November at the Royal Albert Hall, the choir was ready to present a united front. I deliberately mixed up the members of the two choirs. I spent a day sorting out who was going to be standing where and made Plymouth women stand next to Chivenor choir members. During my pep talk as we got ready to go on stage, I had a very clear message for all of them, 'We are one choir tonight.'

What Would Life Be?

The focal point of the year I spent in Devon would be at the Royal Albert Hall on 12 November 2011, appearing in front of the Queen and other members of the Royal Family, live on BBC One – a TV audience of around six or seven million. This was hugely ambitious, even by my standards. I was feeling more confident that the combined Military Wives Choir would be able to handle it, but until the actual day I wouldn't know for sure, because they couldn't rehearse together until the morning of the performance.

Given the scale of this event I had to get everybody in the right frame of mind, so as a warm-up I took the choir to perform at a formal dinner at Sandhurst in the very heart of the military establishment. This was not a gig, this was a ceremony. It would be a stern test of our mettle and a good indicator of how the choir would stand up to the pressure on the horizon.

All I knew of the Royal Military Academy Sandhurst was that Princes William and Harry had both been there. The place seemed to exist in some different dimension. I wasn't even sure exactly where it was until I looked on the map and found it was on the Berkshire/Surrey border, just north of Camberley on the M3. Entering Sandhurst is like stepping into the past. It's an intimidating place with even more security than the bases in Devon. Driving down several long roads I passed cadets out on exercise, red in the face and fully kitted out for battle despite the intense heat of the day. Nobody walks at Sandhurst, not unless they are very important soldiers; they do a funny half-march at all times, just in case the Major General is looking out of the window.

As I made my way down the corridors of New College, where all the cadets are based, I saw posters and information sheets with timetables listing classes in the theory of war, expeditionary operations, insurgency and counter-insurgency. It was like an old-style public school with a very serious curriculum.

I had a meeting booked with Lieutenant Colonel Lambert, in charge of New College. I rapped on the door as hard as I could, trying to appear manly from the outset. His standard issue officer's dog bounded towards me – all the officers above a certain rank seem to have them – followed by the man himself. I could tell this was an officer of significant rank from his dress and his manner. His uniform had large amounts of gold braid, medals and regalia. His boots had spurs. I gulped and shook the man's hand violently. We sat down for a chat like a headmaster speaking to his errant charge.

Lieutenant Colonel Lambert was incredibly supportive and open to us from the start. In truth, we'd been trying to get to talk to the Commandant or higher, someone who could really speak on behalf of the military establishment. I was told by one bureau-crat at the Ministry of Defence that this would require ministe-rial approval, but 'I will not be bringing this to the Minister's attention.' I think the man in question viewed it as a little bit of a distraction, which I suppose is correct: we were at war and I was talking about a small group of women who, at that point, had only performed in Barnstaple's market hall and on Plymouth Hoe.

But as I explained the idea to Lieutenant Colonel Lambert, I could sense his engagement with what I was saying. He wasn't performing for the cameras and he was not the type of man to speak when he didn't mean it. He instantly understood what I was trying to do and commended it warmly. This was what I was looking for, validation from somebody in a really cool uniform. If I couldn't get to the Chief of the Defence Staff at this point, then Lieutenant Colonel Lambert would do nicely. He understood that his own wife had been through many of the same absences, problems and emotions as the choir wives. This performance could spread ripples through the military if we got it right.

The night of the dinner arrived, marking the end of training and the beginning of the passing out ceremonies for the cadets. In the morning the rear party had given us a send-off with their own heartfelt rendition of 'My Girl', which made the Chivenor girls feel supported. We all understood how important this was going to be. After arriving at Sandhurst, we finished our rehearsal and got dressed up – the women in their posh frocks, 'the most beautiful choir in the UK,' as I told them (no exaggeration, they'd scrubbed up well), me in a properly tied bow tie (naturally).

I was standing outside the dining room with my nose pressed against the glass like a street urchin from *Oliver!*. I nudged the heavy oak door ajar to hear what was being said inside and was overpowered by a very distinctive aroma of men – there were very few women in the room. All the cadets were dressed in full woollen uniform in a very warm room. They were all getting tanked up and had probably been out on a run earlier. It smelt slightly better than a class of teenage boys, an odour I had become familiar with on a daily basis at Lancaster School, since there was a hint of expensive aftershave hiding the full horror. Into this bear pit I was going to bring 100 nervous women. It was a very strange position for all of us to be in.

I was going out in front of everyone in that room as the guy in charge and I was aware that this entire institution was about authority and leadership. Nicky Scott noticed I was nervous, that I had been 'pacing, hugging and chatting to everyone to make us feel better. I think it was fear of the establishment. If you get it wrong there, they don't give you second chances.' It was certainly frightening to be about to walk through that door. While I was hovering next to it, waiting for my cue, an officer who was very senior and extremely decorated announced us, 'And now, Gareth Malone and the Military Wives Choir.'

I walked in past all these chaps clapping politely, and at that moment I distinctly heard someone say, 'Yeah, whaddever,' in this really gruff, earthy and very un-officer class voice. To this day I don't know who it was, but in my memory I have the impression he was a big bloke, about eight foot tall and eight foot wide. The bottom dropped out of my world. I thought, 'Oh God, this is all going to bomb.'

Sam was about to do her first solo, singing a piece of plain-song written in the thirteenth century. It was as though she and I were in a competition to see who was the most nervous. Sam recalled my ashen face: 'At Sandhurst I don't know who was more terrified, me or Gareth! You could see the terror in his eyes! He had to stand and give a speech in front of 600 officers about to have dinner, who were probably thinking "Who the hell is this?" He is normally cool, calm and collected, but at Sandhurst there were moments where I saw him just sighing and sweating. Him trying to calm me down I think was actually him trying to calm himself down. We definitely both needed a drink after that.'

Another Sam, our soundman, Sam Mathewson, who had been with me ever since the first series, and had blubbed along with me on that night way back in China, later told me he had never seen me that nervous or lost for words before. I was really stuttering, 'Hello gentlemen, thank you so so so much for having us, I am sorry to take up your time,' getting more and more apologetic while trying to deliver a rousing speech, before we went off into a difficult set of music, some plainsong, a bit of Bach and a lullaby by choral poster boy Eric Whitacre, before finishing off with 'Boogie Woogie Bugle Boy'.

Despite my nervousness, especially about the Bach, the choir did a cracking job and the air of relaxation was palpable. We even managed to all miss out an entire bar of music and carry on unfazed so that no one other than the choir and me knew: the advice I had had from David Hill, the Bach Choir conductor, about looking everyone in the eyes had paid off as I had instinctively sensed their mistake and gone with the flow to carry them through.

Afterwards everybody in the dining room was looking to the Commandant and the senior officers on the top table to see how they would react before they showed their own reaction. There was one chap on the top table – goodness knows I owe him at least a pint if I ever find out who he is – who, regardless of anyone else, leapt to his feet as soon as we finished and then, of course, everyone followed suit.

I had been so thrown by Mr 'Yeah, whaddever' that I had forgotten how this choir of women spoke to everyone in the room by virtue of who they were and what they represented. As soon as I started to say, 'Behind me are a group of military wives, and you are going to have a military wife or girlfriend or husband one day,' that was very real to the audience. Most of the officer cadets must have been at that stage where they had long-term girlfriends, if they weren't already married, and were coming up to a crunch time when they would have to decide to make a commitment or not before they went off to serve in Afghanistan. These were very pertinent issues for them. In the course of the performance we shifted from, 'Who is this bloke coming in here with a choir of women?' to a genuine sense of appreciation.

At the end of the night we all went our separate ways, the choir back to Chivenor or Plymouth, me home to the flat in Kilburn. It was 10 August, Becky and I were fifteen days off completing on a new house and I was in the thick of *The Big Performance* for Children's BBC, another Twenty Twenty programme that took me all over the country. Alongside preparations for the Remembrance Day concert I'd been rubbing shoulders with Mel C from the Spice Girls – quite a contrast from Lieutenant Colonel Lambert. All of this seemed like small potatoes when I thought about the impending concert in the Royal Albert Hall. Success at Sandhurst was one thing, impressing the nation was another.

Appearing at the Festival of Remembrance seemed a piece of perfect timing because it happened just after the men had come back from their tour of duty in Afghanistan. The idea of taking part in the Festival had been mooted from the very beginning of the series. By the time we started filming *The Choir: Military Wives* in February 2011 initial conversations had already been held with the British Legion, Twenty Twenty and the BBC, and presumably at some point a note was dispatched to the Palace.

Every single person I met continued to badger me, 'Wouldn't it be great if the choir did a performance at the Festival of Remembrance?' Everyone knew that at the end of a series of *The Choir* there would be a major performance, so they were all trying to second-guess what it would be, especially the wives. I had to keep telling them, 'Just leave it with me until I can say for definite what is happening, all in good time,' but of course those women hate surprises because they can mean bad news.

I could not confirm anything until it was signed off, and there was a lot of paperwork to be sorted between the BBC, the organisers and the Royal British Legion. I went to the Legion's offices in Borough to talk with Tim Marshall, an experienced broadcaster, who runs the whole event and has done for years. Tim's opening bargaining gambit was to offer me the chance to bring forty women to perform. I said, 'I have got a hundred.' 'Ah, right.' Tim went back to the Royal British Legion and came back with an improved offer of sixty women, to which I responded, 'I have got a hundred.' How could I have turned people away? I held my nerve and with three weeks to go eventually they let us bring them all.

Before the Royal Albert Hall there was one extremely important performance for the choir – to celebrate the homecoming of the troops. I got some flak over my choice of song, Whitney Houston's 'I Wanna Dance with Somebody', from some of the choir. There was a lot of heated discussion over that. With the Military Wives every choice of song tested me as a musician, because I felt such a responsibility. This was a crucial moment where, after six months of being away, the guys were coming home and we wanted to show them everything that we had done during that time. What piece of music could possibly deliver all of that?

For reasons best known to the military, the men came back earlier than we, the film crew, were expecting. The upshot was that we had very few rehearsals to get ready for the performance – it seemed ridiculous that after six months we were in a mad scramble.

Given what the men had been through I didn't think they'd appreciate anything too funereal. I thought it much better to go frothy and do something fun and joyous, than too much down the route of 'You've been through the wars ...'. Whitney Houston felt right – and I loved Whitney's singing – but initially I had quite a negative reaction to the song. I did the arrangement on the train down to Devon and as we rehearsed the song I realised that I'd made it quite difficult; they were struggling with the harmonies. We had a few tricky rehearsals and one or two choir members got very irate with me because they cared about the

241

choir and wanted to do a great job, just as Magda and Maggie from the South Oxhey choir had been concerned about introducing the dance moves for 'Walking on Sunshine'. On the day, though, it was such a joyful happy occasion and I'm not sure what else we could have sung.

From the reaction of the returning men – especially with the addition of the children's choir I had been coaching at Southmead School, where 40 per cent of the kids came from military families – the Whitney Houston option seemed to have been the right one. The children appeared to be more excited about the glitter that we had prepared to throw on the final chord than about singing to their dads. My soloist Katherine Catchpole almost lost her nerve and arrived ten minutes late. 'I was having a moment,' she announced. It wasn't so much a 'choir' performance as a statement of how happy they were to see the men safely returned. Now we could concentrate on the Festival of Remembrance.

Sometime during the summer I sat down to think about repertoire for the Royal Albert Hall performance. Paul Mealor had written a wonderful song for the choir. When he sent me 'Wherever You Are', I read the words at the next rehearsal. As the women listened to the lyric, which Paul had constructed from letters and poems they had written to their husbands, there were tears almost immediately. He had perfectly captured the sense of strength and vulnerability.

It certainly got to Sam. 'Gareth sang "Wherever You Are" to us for the first time in a rehearsal. I don't think there was a dry eye in the house. Paul Mealor did an amazing job. Gareth singing our raw emotion made it all the more special. He had been on our journey with us, putting up with women crying, acting like a surrogate husband to all of us! So hearing him sing those words, *our* words, made it all the more personal, and heartfelt.'

The title came from the phrase, 'Wherever you are, you will always be in my heart', a quote from Mahatma Gandhi engraved on a bracelet worn by Stacey Clouting, a member of the choir, which had been bought for her by her husband Daniel. The other letters and poems provided the sentiment, the ideas and the music, the hopefulness of it and the strength of it. The song is in a major key, which feels very optimistic. If Paul had not read those letters and seen the strength, the humour, the wit and the life in them, I think he would have written something rather sombre. Intuitively Paul was able to get right under the skin of it. He has since said that he cried when he read the letters, because they were incredibly powerful. They weren't written to be published. They were written to husbands and boyfriends on the front line.

The day that I sang the song to the choir at Plymouth was a difficult one – there had been a funeral that day for a man who did not make it through the tour. Several of the singers knew him and his wife and a couple of the choir had been to the funeral. This was the first time the choir had heard the words of the song. I found it very hard to sing and it even got to tough-as-old-boots Alice Clarke, who was Sandhurst-trained and had left the army to be a mum. Alice comes from strong military stock – her father is a former Major General. Here she was crying like a baby. This was going to be very difficult to sing without breaking down.

I had asked Paul Mealor for a piece that was universal and which, on the very first listen, would tell you everything you needed to know about these women. He'd put it better: 'You want a good tune, don't you?' The Albert Hall performance needed to connect with a very large public and appeal directly to their emotions.

Of course I had to train the choir to sing it. Part of this meant thinking about the words of the song. There was one rehearsal, when I was really getting into the meaning of the text, where I had to call a halt. Nicky Scott says, 'It was a really emotional song but it took me about a month before it got to me. I was brave, brave, brave – then tears. It was like a chain reaction.'

Steve, the director and cameraman, was following a pack of tissues that was being passed down the line from one person to the other. It was a festival of sobbing. I knew from bitter experience that we had to have experienced those emotions within a rehearsal in order to be able to get through it on the day. That was my biggest concern: that on the night they would be overwhelmed and not be able to deliver the song successfully.

I was running out of time; the rehearsals were now very few before we had to get on the coach to London. During one of the final rehearsals, Stacey ambushed me in the middle of a rehearsal. 'Oh no. It's another Maggie moment,' I thought, resolving not to cry. The Chivenor choir had been preparing in secret. They launched into 'Thank You for the Music' by Abba. The women had asked Sam Abrahams, a friend of someone in the choir who was not a military wife but ran a choir in nearby Lympstone, to rehearse and conduct them. They did it in total secrecy. I had no idea what was going on. There was a hidden Facebook page where they could all discuss it and make plans, so I was completely caught on the hop. We were rehearsing hard and about to go on all night, when the choir stopped me and took over.

It was a lovely moment. They had changed the words a bit to make it personal, and had all bought 'Gareth' glasses to wear. The humour of the glasses diminished the sentimentality of the song, making it all the more moving. The Plymouth choir also organised their own similar moment and rewrote 'Wherever You Are' so they could sing, 'Wherever you go, you will go there with our thanks.' I was overwhelmed by them both.

In the week leading up to the Festival of Remembrance I fell ill. I had picked up a stomach bug on 9 November, my birthday, after going out for fish and chips at Squires in Braunton to celebrate – for the record it was nothing to do with the food! I'd been coming down with something for a few days, but I came home thinking, 'I really don't feel at all well,' and then I was bedridden until the Friday when I crawled into my car and fought my way back to London. Thankfully I woke up on Saturday morning feeling just about all right, and then had to get through this monstrous day. I arrived at the Royal Albert Hall for a rehearsal at nine o'clock, our first rehearsal with an orchestra.

If I felt exhausted I could not imagine how the choir felt. The day before had been the homecoming parade for the Plymouth men, which I couldn't attend because I was too nauseous. The women had gone to the homecoming event, then out for dinner that night and boarded a coach at 9pm, arriving in London at two in the morning, before they got up again at 6.30am and turned up at the rehearsal. It must have been a shock for them arriving to be surrounded by people in full formal military uniform, including bearskins. We were allowed two, maybe three run-throughs of the song before the stage manager said, 'That's it, we are out of time,' and there was nothing more I could do before the performance. We weren't ready – we hadn't settled the speed with the orchestra, who were taking it decidedly slowly.

Rather than reassure me, this rehearsal made me more worried as the introduction had come unstuck. At a previous meeting I had raised the need for audio monitors so that we could hear the orchestra, who were about 100 metres away from the choir standing in the middle of what they call 'the bull-ring'. In the event I think the monitors were forgotten about so neither the choir nor I could hear properly. I was given an in-ear monitor, which meant that I was in time with the orchestra. The choir, on the other hand, had to wait a few fractions of a second before the live sound reached their ears. That meant we were effectively in different time zones.

It was like conducting in soup: I was supposed to conduct and then the orchestra conductor would follow me and bring in the orchestra. It was very similar to the experience of conducting offstage at Glyndebourne, which had been such a nightmare, and I had vowed never to do that again. Here I was once more with Paul Daniel's words ringing in my ears: 'This is the most difficult type of conducting.'

I came off stage at the rehearsal in a cold stupor, unsure about how it would go. Technical considerations were running through my head and I was still feeling dodgy from my stomach bug. I hobbled over to Paul Mealor who had come along to the rehearsals. Paul was sitting at the back of the auditorium with some of his colleagues, listening to the piece for the first time.

He had tears in his eyes. He said to me, 'This is going to be amazing, the best thing of the night. It will bring the house down.' I thought, 'Really, are you sure?' I still didn't have that confidence because I was so focused on all the problems. Added to all of the musical pressures I had the most emotional group of women I have ever seen in my life. One hundred of them, standing in front of me, knowing that the Queen would be watching them perform. It was a recipe for a great deal of stress.

There were two shows that day, one in the afternoon – which functioned as a dress rehearsal – and one in the evening with the royals in attendance. The afternoon show had been fine, but in the evening the introduction fell completely apart: the orchestra set off too fast, while we went at the speed we had taken in the afternoon. It was on the verge of being a total disaster. My heart was in my mouth, but then, somehow, out of the chaos, somewhere around bar 8, it all came together. Everyone drew something extra out of the tank and won the audience over. For me that was one of the most nervous ten seconds of my life; absolutely horrible. This was a one-off opportunity, live on BBC One in front of the Royal Family. It was musical pressure of a very different order from anything I'd previously experienced.

I had chosen Sam Stevenson to tackle the solo for the song. It was massively demanding as she had to start the whole piece as the sole singer. Over the years I have become quite adept at spotting soloists. I know early on in any rehearsals, as I look down the line, 'You're a performer, you're a performer; you're *not* a performer.' And Sam is a performer through and through. The moment I realised she could really deliver was back when the Chivenor choir performed in the Pannier Market in

Barnstaple, even though Nicky took the solo. I was looking at the whole choir and yet Sam stood out. She was right there with me and loving it, displaying her love of singing to all these people with unutterable confidence. That is the kind of moment when I know whether someone is an instinctive performer or not. After that, it doesn't matter where you go, or whether it is five people or five thousand people they are singing in front of, it is the same process. I simply *knew* she could do it.

I'm not sure Sam had the same confidence in herself: 'Walking onto the stage I was filled with terror. I was the last person to walk out and all eyes were on me. Because I had to sing the first few notes, I felt so open and exposed – everyone was watching me. I also felt absolute disbelief. There I was on that stage with all those people, and the Queen, looking at me waiting for me to sing. I knew that Gareth was relying on me. I had to do it for him. He believed in me and I didn't want to disappoint him. I had to put my "game face" on.'

Sam swallowed right before she sang and I could sense her nerves and that horrible dry feeling at the back of her throat. Five thousand people held their breath in anticipation.

Under this most intense attention Sam delivered. In those circumstances, you have either got the right stuff or you haven't and Sam has it in abundance. The significance of it all, the emotion of it was extreme. I take off my hat to Sam. Her performance was something truly remarkable.

The audience erupted in applause. My life would never be the same.

Light up the Darkness

Two months before the Military Wives Choir appeared at the Festival of Remembrance, I was in Croyde, a surfer's paradise in North Devon. On most days I was grateful that the village has not yet been crammed full of Starbucks and Costa Coffees, but at that time I was urgently trying to find a wifi hotspot where I could download Paul Mealor's first version of 'Wherever You Are'.

Paul had texted me to say he had sent the file, which was not huge, only 60K or so, but without wifi access I could not get the piece onto my computer. I finally found the Thatch pub had internet and they let me do the download. I went back home, and played it through. The version was a simplified demo, using some piano with the three vocal lines played on a synthesised flute. I was reading the score, trying to sight-sing along with the demo and imagining what a final performance might sound like.

I listened all the way through and was really torn. I had seen the lyrics already so I knew the sentiment and was completely happy with that, but my first thought on hearing the music was to wonder whether Paul had gone too far, beyond the bounds of my own taste in terms of sentiment. I wondered whether the piece might be too slushy both for the Festival of Remembrance and for the women in the choir: would they believe it when they sang the song? I wasn't sure. I decided not to call Paul back yet. I needed to let this settle.

I knew Paul had created a really solid tune, one with that wonderful quality of a universal melody you think you have heard before, but can't put your finger on. I listened to the piece again, and a third time, and that was the time I thought, 'I've got this now. Maybe this really will work.'

I had first come across Paul's name earlier in the year. I get most of my news on my phone and, unusually, the BBC News website featured a story about classical composers. It was shortly before the Royal Wedding in April and details had been released of the music for the service. I scanned the list, eager to see what we could expect. There were a few standard choices: Prince Charles's favourite C.H.H. Parry was well represented. Yet among the pieces by Vaughan Williams, Elgar, Walton and John Rutter – a living and well-established composer – there was a new name and a new piece, 'Ubi caritas', a motet by Paul Mealor. All the website said about him was that he was 'a Welsh composer, who is currently Reader in Composition at the University of Aberdeen'. The link was that Paul's composing studio is on Anglesey, where Prince William was then based. 'Oh,' I thought, 'that's interesting, I wonder what that will be like.' I have to be honest, I imagined this piece would be an extremely modern music moment, sounding like squeaky gates, and thought nothing more of it.

On the day of the wedding we all sat down as a family to watch. I kept my daughter on my knee long enough to listen to the music, and for me there were two standout moments. One was Parry's 'I Was Glad', with an incredible aerial shot of the procession of the bride and the train of her dress. And then there was the piece by Paul Mealor, which I thought was absolutely exquisite, the perfect piece for the occasion.

A couple of weeks later I was at the Classical Brits, and following the celebrations went on to the after-party, which was in Roman Abramovich's Under the Bridge nightclub at Chelsea. I kid you not: it was the loudest place on God's earth. I do not know why anyone would put a speaker system big enough for Wembley Stadium in a room no bigger than a pub. In the gloom I was introduced to Paul Mealor on the dance floor, though I couldn't really hear a word. Somebody from a record company screamed in my ear, 'THIS IS PAUL MEALOR ...', 'HELLO ...,' Paul shouted something back at me and I just about made out that he was inviting me to come and visit him in Aberdeen. I nodded and smiled, but thought it was unlikely that our paths would cross again.

Sometime around June 2011 I began to think in earnest about the Royal Albert Hall concert and started to fret about what exactly we might perform. Which song could do the job of being appropriately sombre for the occasion and yet celebrate the achievement of these women?

I needed a piece of music that had all the grandeur of a state occasion. Immediately Paul sprang to mind. I fired up the laptop and found his website. The mad fool still had his direct phone number listed on his website, so I phoned him up and left a message. I think he called me back ten minutes later. I explained the story of the Wives choir and as soon as I told him about it he said, 'Great, I'll write something for you.'

His reply completely took me aback because my experience of working in the music business is that if you want to get something written, you have to go through a long commissioning process, find a pot of money and deal with agents. Paul cut straight through all that. 'I'll write it, it's fine – and I'll do it for free.' I can remember the look of joy on the face of Lucy Hilman, our executive producer, when I told her that I'd just secured a commission from the 'Royal' composer of the moment and for gratis. Paul had been immediately struck by the women's plight and wanted to get to work straight away. I've come to learn that he is a prolific composer and once inspiration strikes he doesn't mess about.

On a gloriously hot day during the summer I went to meet Paul at St Jude-on-the-Hill, the parish church in Hampstead Garden Suburb, where he was recording an album. For about ten minutes we sat and listened to the chamber choir Tenebrae ('This is the world's greatest choir,' Paul told me) singing 'Spotless Rose'. The serene surroundings and the rich timbre of the voices quite overtook me. I'd picked the right man for the job.

We found a corner during the coffee break to talk about what the feel of the piece should be, trying to project ourselves to the event in November. Paul half-shut his eyes and hummed some lilting phrase, saying, 'I am imagining something quite flowing.' His hands swept through the air as if conducting a half-realised strain. I could see there was a germ of the music growing already, maybe a snatch of melody, some harmonies, the pace perhaps, I don't know. But Paul had seized on the gist of the music.

As we walked out into the bright sunshine, with the cameras and radio mics off, Paul turned to me and said, very quietly, 'You want a tune, don't you?' 'Yes, please don't write something that is inaccessible. The audience is going to be mainstream BBC One. I'd like them to hear it once and immediately understand what the women are going through. It can't be any more compli-cated than that because we only have two and a half minutes to make it work.'

I think the experience Paul had had writing for the royal wedding, and understanding that national event, was a really good preparation for him as a composer for this song. He innately understood the audience; he wasn't writing to impress other composers – he was writing for the public.

When I heard the wives sing 'Wherever You Are' the only way I can describe it is to say the song sounded right coming out of *their* mouths. Suzy Brady put it really well, describing her reaction to hearing the song for the first time. 'I thought, "Wow! That's our song, written for us, with our lyrics." It was mind-blowing.'

The women connected with the song instantly in a way that was extraordinary. It is to Paul's considerable credit that he got the balance exactly right between emotion and something that was too British, restrained, stiff upper lip. The point of the whole exercise was that we were trying to get these women to open up and show the public who they were. It needed a piece of music of precisely the right emotional order to let everyone in.

As I listened to 'Wherever You Are' taking shape in rehearsal I started to feel it might work as a single, but I couldn't get anyone very interested even in some general discussions. I cold-called the record companies with my best pleading voice. 'A charity record, at Christmas time?' Tom Lewis from Decca Records told me that unfortunately the market became saturated with charity singles around Christmas. But he didn't close the door on the idea; he asked to hear a recording. Unfortunately I hadn't yet taught the notes to the choir, so a recording, however rough, was out of the question.

Besides I had other priorities, getting ready for the performance at the Royal Albert Hall. The song was in three-part harmony, with a large emotional and vocal range. It was taking a lot for the women to sing it and we were running out of rehearsals. With only a few days to go before the performance, as more people heard it, confidence grew, however. The film crew were starting to dream about singing 'Wherever You Are'. The ladies were in good shape so I invited Russell Thompson, the Royal British Legion's director of national events and fundraising, down to Chivenor to hear the song. He looked utterly swept away – and this was only with half the full choir. Back in London my executive producer saw footage of the rehearsals and called me to say how excited she was about the song. At last, the idea of releasing it as a single picked up some momentum.

My first thought was that if it did become a single, it had to be for charity, and specifically a military charity. I asked the wives which charity they would choose. They all said SSAFA, the Soldiers, Sailors, Airmen and Families Association, because most of them already had a direct connection with the organisation. In fact, my grandfather, thanks to his RAF service, had received some assistance from SSAFA at various points in his life, so it was a charity close to my heart as well. We also selected the Royal British Legion's Poppy Appeal, since that was so central to the Festival of Remembrance's very existence.

I called Tom Lewis a second time. Tom had been responsible for acts like the Fron Male Voice Choir (it turned out we would go head to head with the Fron Choir's reinvention of 'Grandad') and the Cistercian Monks of Stift Heiligenkreuz. I reinforced the idea and although I knew there was a growing sense that we very much wanted to record it, Tom still wasn't convinced. 'At Christmas time everyone wants to take on the *X Factor* winners, hoping for that Mr Blobby moment when for whatever reason a single catches fire.' Even the cast of *The Only Way Is Essex* were having a go. Nonetheless Tom spoke to his boss and told him about the idea. Tom's boss is Dickon Stainer, MD of Decca Records, and he came along to the afternoon performance at the Albert Hall when the choir received an amazing standing ovation. Dickon felt the power of that audience reaction, came to find me straight afterwards and said, 'We have to record this, even if we put it out as a download.'

Despite my excitement I couldn't yet tell the wives, because I was conscious of how much work there was to do in getting the go-ahead to make the single. I had to keep completely zipped up throughout the rest of the day, knowing that the only way I would then be able to tell them was by putting a posting on Facebook, because I was staying in London that night while they were heading straight back to Devon – at this point they all thought this was the end of the journey. As I said my goodbyes and mopped up the tears at the end of the evening I did at least have a sneaky hope that there was more to come.

Usually there is a lull after a moment like that, a few days at home watching TV and recharging the batteries. But this time there was little or no chance for rest. The Monday after the Royal Albert Hall show I began shooting the final programme in my CBBC series *The Big Performance 2*, which would culminate on BBC One that Friday in front of a TV audience of millions.

I also spent most of the spare moments that week trying to get everyone to agree that the Military Wives song could be recorded. I felt a bit like Bob Geldof and probably swore just as much, trying to get this person to phone that lawyer to get permission from so and so, talking to agents, publishers and the BBC. At that point it still felt very small-scale, so I was saying, 'Don't worry, it will only be for the women and their families, maybe a few of the viewers will buy one. I am sure it will all be fine, it won't blow up into a huge media hullaballoo ...'

The decisive moment came around Wednesday as Emma Willis, the commissioning editor at the BBC, threw her weight behind the idea. Now I'd got the big guns involved. The lawyers came up with their official answer: we could record it. Suddenly the flurry began – the song would have to be recorded that Saturday so all the women would have to get back onto the coaches to drive up the M3 again. The message went out on Facebook, the producer Jon Cohen began recording the piano part and Paul Mealor flew into town to conduct the orchestra on Friday. The machine was winding up.

On Friday I was on *Children in Need*, trying to bring together a choir of thousands of children being beamed in from all over the country to sing Avril Lavigne's 'Keep Holding On'. I went to bed at God knows what time, beyond tired, drained and emotional. I had done two of the biggest things in my life within six days of each other, and to cap it all I had lost my glasses. When I got home that was all I could talk about. Becky was saying, 'It's fine, the evening was a triumph.' 'Yes, yes, but I've lost my glasses, I can't see!'

I woke up at seven, getting ready to head over to the Air Lyndhurst studios in Hampstead, a fantastic space with a beautiful acoustic, one of the world's greatest studios for recording choirs. Although the idea was still to do a small digital download release only, with no fanfare, I had thought somebody should film this. But time and money were tight – the budget for the TV programme had all been accounted for and the record was a modest affair not requiring a fancy video shoot. There was one person I knew who might help me out: my best friend from childhood, Gratian Dimech, who just happens to be a music video director. I said, 'Look, here's the deal: we are recording this single, there's absolutely no money in it, everyone is doing it for charity, but it could be fun. Would you mind coming and filming it?' Gratian said, 'Sure, but I've got no equipment. I normally hire stuff in, so who's going to pay for that?' It was all so last-minute but as it turned out Twenty Twenty also came through and sent a small production team to film for the day.

As I left the house I grabbed my little digital SLR, the one I use for taking pictures on holiday, jumped in the cab to Air Lyndhurst and started the recording. Gratian turned up and said he'd use the SLR, so in the end we had footage recorded by Twenty Twenty on their equipment, on my camera and his mate

James's iPhone. This was edited into a video that accompanied the single, and Gratian and James combined this with photos of the husbands on active service. Despite its ramshackle beginnings, the combination of studio footage and personal photos was extremely moving and it was widely played on TV at Christmas time.

The women in the choir were both exhilarated and exhausted: they had travelled straight up from Devon that morning, a six-hour journey. The final piece of the jigsaw was Sam's solo, which we recorded last of all: she was broken by the end of the day. 'I was stood in this tiny recording booth with a microphone, but I still needed Gareth beside me. So we both had to squeeze into this booth the size of a toilet. He believed in me and I needed his support. I think he appreciated that I really wanted him with me when I was recording my solo.'

The next morning I was, unbelievably, flying to New York where *Gareth Malone Goes to Glyndebourne* was up for an International Emmy. I had decided to go, not because I thought we had any chance of winning it, but because it was an opportunity to go to New York, which I had only visited once before, and after all the excitement of the previous months, those seven hours on the plane seemed a good time to relax. I collapsed into my seat and slept. Meanwhile Jon Cohen, who was producing the single, was beavering away in the studio, trying to get everything edited, sorted and mastered, ready for delivery on the Monday.

On the Monday afternoon, I was in New York getting my hair cut for the Emmy ceremony, while BBC One was putting out the final episode of *The Choir: Military Wives* at 9pm UK time, including the Festival of Remembrance performance of 'Wherever You Are'. Twenty Twenty had edited everything in a week, a really quick turnaround; I had seen a version on the Wednesday and blubbed my way through the entire thing. Over in New York I got a handful of texts, one from my mum saying 'Fantastic', and a couple of others from friends telling me they had really enjoyed the series. That all sounded good. Click, I switched my phone off and went to the Emmys. The evening went extremely well (we won the award!) and I went to bed thinking, 'It doesn't get much better than this, does it?'

I surfaced next morning, jet-lagged and slightly the worse for wear and turned my phone back on, to find 40 missed calls and texts from practically everybody I knew saying that Chris Evans was desperate to get hold of me, 'Call him right now.' Of course I had missed the boat as his Radio 2 show had finished hours before – while I was sound asleep. However, one of his producers had left her number so I called her up to ask what was going on. She said that Chris had heard about the song from people texting in, they had patched the Albert Hall version in from iPlayer, played it live and had this most unbelievable reaction.

The audience for Chris Evans's show is around 8 or 9 million, so on top of the 6 million or thereabouts who had watched the original Festival and the audience for the final episode of *The Choir: Military Wives* the night before, there was suddenly a huge extra reach. Chris had played the song at the hot spot of his show at about a quarter past eight. He had managed to get Sam Stevenson on the phone; she was utterly bewildered as she was just about to do the school run and suddenly found herself talking to Chris Evans live on air. Chris is very much someone who shoots from the hip. His gut reaction was, 'They have to record this,' not knowing we just had. 'This should be the Christmas number one.'

His producer said, 'Why don't you speak to Chris tomorrow when you touch down?' I was due in to Heathrow at 6.30am after the night flight from New York, so we arranged for me to call him from the airport at about a quarter past eight. I woke up after another lovely deep sleep on the plane only to find that there was fog over London and the plane had been diverted to Cardiff. I was stuck on the plane, so I told the aircrew I needed to speak to Chris Evans. They were very accommodating and sent me up to the kitchen of the first class lounge. I sat there, barely able to hear because of the noise of the air-conditioning, and was put through to Chris. At that point I wasn't sure whether we could really announce the single. No one had put a strategy together. It was all incredibly reactive. Chris told me Decca had just sent them a copy of the CD, and when they played it that was the very first time I had heard the recording, listening down the phone on this plane thinking, 'Actually this sounds pretty good.'

Chris kept playing the song on his show, and very soon, both TV channels and the press started to run with the story. It began to take on a life of its own. I checked my phone later that day and found that one of the big bookies was offering odds of 50/1 on 'Wherever You Are' being the Christmas number one. It seemed that every time I logged in over the next few days the odds were shortening. Tom Lewis from Decca called and told me the record company were going to go for it, and we would have the full weight of the company behind us. For the first time

I thought it might be a possibility. From that point on it was mayhem.

After the series I had been planning to have a gentle month off, be based at home, take it easy, go back to the gym, get my head back together after what had been a very emotional and big year, and then in a calm way plan how to make sure the Military Wives Choirs carried on. Of course, I ended up conducting them more than I had ever done before. The single was launched live on the Chris Evans show. Chris, being the genius of PR, said we should dress up. I told him I had an old army uniform somebody had given me, so Chris decided to wear an RAF outfit. Paul Mealor turned up just in his civvies, and the wives said, 'Where's your rig? He's got no rig.' This was announced live on the air and a Commander from the Royal Navy brought over a uniform for Paul to wear.

That photo made the front pages of many of the nationals. In fact, a favourite moment for me in all the madness was discovering my photo on the front page of *The Times*, even though I was looking more than slightly dishevelled. I said at the time that I now know what it must feel like to be Justin Bieber, under the intensity of that gaze, everyone wanting to know what you are going to say, the press looking for a particular quote, in my case wanting me to savage Simon Cowell, while I was thinking, 'I don't want to savage Simon Cowell, I want to promote the single and make sure everyone realises *why* we are doing it. This is not about a phoney war with *The X Factor*, this is about raising money for a really important cause.'

All of this was happening over a matter of a few short weeks, so in retrospect much of it, the TV appearances, the interviews, has blurred together. The choir and I had decided to embrace the experience, knowing this would only last for a short space of time. It was an extraordinary moment: everyone was talking about the single, every time I got in a cab or went to a restaurant people knew who I was all of a sudden. Soldiers in particular would come up to me and say, 'We think it's fantastic what you're doing. We are behind you and we're going to buy the single.'

The first bit of news came in: we'd broken all presale records on Amazon. This was going to be a big single, but would it be big enough to assail the mighty *X Factor*?

We kept doing everything possible to promote the single. Suzy Brady says, 'For me, the best part of all the promotions we did was going to Number 10 Downing Street and performing in front of the Prime Minister and to the troops who had only just returned from Libya. It was our chance to show some of the most important people in the country that we are here and that we support our men and our families through thick and thin. And that we're human.'

Another stand-out highlight of those crazy weeks was attending the Millies, the Sun Military Awards, at the Imperial War Museum a couple of days before the announcement of the number one. The event meant a lot to the choir, since they all knew about the awards celebrating achievements by the military, and the organisers had asked the full choir to come along.

At one point someone from the *Sun* came up and said, 'The Duchess of Cambridge would like to meet you.' I went over and had my audience with her. She was very enthusiastic about the single and I told her that the wives really considered her to be one of them. 'Oh, I don't know,' she said, 'they are much more hard core.' I thought that was fair, they probably were more 'hard core', but the wives had a point: the Duke of Cambridge was on active service so she could understand the pressures and fears. Like any of the guys who fly helicopters, he was risking his life every time he went up. It is a dangerous job. She was eminently well placed to empathise.

By the critical mid-week sales figures on the Wednesday leading up to the announcement of the Christmas number one, it looked like we might beat Little Mix, the *X Factor* winners. For some reason their single had not quite captured that Middle England market for a Christmas single: the people buying the single for their grannies, mums and dads. 'Wherever You Are' had somehow managed to tap into the mood of the moment. The song and the words seemed to have a real resonance with and relevance to what people were feeling. Christmas Day fell on a Sunday, and it was announced that, just over one month after the Festival of Remembrance performance, the Military Wives had secured the much sought-after Christmas number one.

The choir's success had come out of nowhere. This was a choir made up of women whose daily life was far far removed from showbiz luvviness. When Nicky Scott heard the news, 'Because it was Christmas Day, there was so much else going on, but I remember thinking, "Should I be wearing leopard print leggings, drinking champagne and throwing my TV out of the window like a proper pop star?" Instead I went home and peeled the potatoes for Christmas dinner.'

The single had sold well over half a million copies in the final week, more than all the rest of the top 12 combined. It felt like a victory for the power of singing, its emotional impact and what it can achieve.

The word 'journey' is overused. I frequently switch on the TV to hear somebody who has just baked a cake, or climbed a very small hill, say, 'It has been such an emotional journey.' Now *this* had been a huge emotional journey. The question was, where to go next?

Home Again

I felt the effect of the overnight success story that was 'Wherever You Are' almost immediately. As well as squaddies stopping me in the street to say how proud they were that the song had been the Christmas number one and that their wives now wanted to be part of a choir too, the swell was growing on Twitter and Facebook: 'I'd like to join one of these choirs, where can I go?' I was also getting messages telling me, 'We've just started up a Military Wives Choir on our base.'

Just before *The Choir: Military Wives* went on air I contacted Nicky Clarke, who had written the letter that started the whole enterprise, to tell her about what we'd achieved. As I spoke to her I realised what a shame it was that she hadn't been involved with the filming: Nicky told me enthusiastically about the choir she had created at Catterick Garrison in North Yorkshire, who were getting more and more attention and creating their own stir. We both realised that this was becoming a movement and at the time it was absolutely out of control. It had gone from being a very small suggestion to something on a national scale in the space of weeks.

Nicky sensed that the moment was ripe to create a foundation for all these choirs to try and coordinate this increasingly chaotic situation. I agreed with her – this needed a plan. From our first conversations about the idea it was clear that Nicky had the level-headedness and sense to lead such an operation. In the end, Nicky managed something that I could not: she created her choir *without* the lure of TV cameras and without support – this would prove invaluable experience for the next stage in the development of the choirs.

In the weeks and days leading up to the announcement of the Christmas number one the media frenzy had been whipped into a tornado. This had made planning any kind of future impossible. Christmas itself was nearly a write-off – I was close to nervous exhaustion and the ladies had been rinsed through a series of increasingly high-profile TV appearances. Nicky and I had decided it was best to let the dust settle after all the frantic activity at the end of 2011 before we got together to discuss a plan for the future.

I didn't meet Nicky face to face until January 2012. On first meeting she came across as affable but stern. You could imagine Nicky as a headteacher that everyone loves and respects but secretly fears. It was clear that she was ready to take her idea to the national stage and wanted to work with me, Chivenor and Plymouth to ensure that *every* military wife, girlfriend or affiliate had the chance to sing.

In January 2012 Nicky and I brought all the parties involved together, along with wives from both the Chivenor and Plymouth choirs. Representatives from SSAFA and the Royal British Legion were there, along with Twenty Twenty, Decca Records and Jon Cohen, who produced the record. We sat in a boardroom feeling like we were in an episode of *The Apprentice*. It was an extraordinary moment as we all began to wake up to the realisation that collectively we had ensured that pretty much everyone in the UK knew about the Military Wives Choir.

Nervously Nicky took the floor, passing round a spreadsheet with a brilliant, but modest, proposal to create a Military Wives Choir Foundation that would encourage and enable more choirs to emerge. At that stage she and her colleague Caroline Jopp envisaged ten choirs in the first year. At the time of writing there are an incredible forty-seven.

Everyone at the meeting started nodding and agreeing that this was what was needed. The charities immediately stepped up to say, 'Yes, we see this as part of our remit, part of doing right by military communities and families. We will definitely support it.' Tom Lewis from Decca piped up, 'We'd like to make an album ... But we need to do it *now*.' He turned to Jon Cohen and asked him whether it was possible and, if it was, whether it could be done quickly. Jon replied, 'It's impossible, but let's do it anyway,' which became the unofficial motto of the project: This isn't going to work, but somehow we will make it happen.

Sitting around that table and listening to the discussion I started to form the idea that the album should involve as many choirs as possible, precisely because this was now growing far beyond the original choir, and the whole point had been for those women in Chivenor and Plymouth to be able to go and join another choir when and if their husbands and boyfriends were posted to other bases. Since part of my central mission running throughout all the series of *The Choir* had been to get as many people singing as possible, to do my bit for choirs and for singing, it chimed perfectly.

Over the Christmas period I had actually been questioning whether there was any point in doing an album, which seemed the next logical step after a single. Was there going to be any appetite for it, and if so what was the reason for an album? There had been a number of excellent reasons for recording the single: it had raised money for good and totally appropriate causes, it had allowed the Military Wives to have a definitive recording of 'Wherever You Are' and the chance to share their achievement with an even wider audience. I thought maybe this was the point at which to say, 'Job done.'

I wasn't convinced that releasing an album was necessary until I was at that meeting, when it seemed that the album could be an important first step in creating the Foundation. As soon as I got back home I sat in my office and started scribbling some song ideas on a Post-it note. Nearly every one of those songs made it on to the final album, but it also seemed essential for the project to ask Paul Mealor if he wanted to contribute another song.

In late January I was in Ipswich, doing a workshop for the Royal Opera House, and called Paul on the way to talk more about the idea, which I knew had already been mooted with him. I got his answerphone so left a message: 'Hi Paul, I hear you are up for writing this song, really looking forward to hearing from you, let's discuss it when you have a spare moment.' After the workshop, which lasted two or three hours,

I was driving back to London when Paul called me. He said, 'I've done it, I've written it ... It's all done.' 'Really, that's very quick.' He said, 'Yes, it just came straight out.' Paul later told me that he gets so caught up in the mood and the atmosphere of the words and the song that the pieces develop a life of their own. For example, for this new song, 'In My Dreams', he hadn't wanted it to have a chorus, but he just couldn't help himself.

When I got home, I downloaded the demo he had emailed me, played it through and thought, 'Brilliant. This is in the same emotional landscape as "Wherever You Are", absolutely the right piece.' Paul had got it spot on again. I played it to Becky, who began to well up just reading the words and hearing the tune, which I took to be an excellent sign that we were on the right track.

We had to move at high speed to prepare the album. For the next few days Jon Cohen was bombarding me with sheaves of sheet music and vocal arrangements. We were taking the songs I had listed on my Post-it note, songs that were very well-known in one particular context, and trying to adapt them into choral arrangements. At this stage Jon didn't know the choirs that well, so my role was to advise him who could sing what, who was capable of hitting which notes, where the lumps and bumps were. A constant stream of musical scores were turning up on my phone as PDFs and I was looking at them travelling between meetings on the tube. It was absolutely crazy. We were working at a frantic pace.

I think Jon was putting in 18-hour days in front of his computer, getting everything ready to allow him to go out on the road and record the choirs the following week. I had to miss the entire thing because I was on a trip to America, but Jon told me it was the most ridiculous ten days as he sped from location to location, setting up temporary studios for each of the Military Wives choirs. There was now a choir at the Royal Marines' Commando Training Centre in Lympstone, run by Sam Abrahams (who had conducted Chivenor's 'Thank You for the Music' tribute), and a choir in Portsmouth, which had only been in existence for about three weeks.

I called up Kim Martin, who wanted to set up the choir for Portsmouth, Fareham and Gosport, just to sound her out, find out what her musical experience was, and see what level the choir was at. I got a really good vibe off her – she was telling me, 'We are quite good, we've got some decent singers in there, we've had one rehearsal' – and I was wondering whether to drop the bombshell but left it to Tom from Decca to call her the next day and ask her whether she wanted her choir to be on the album singing 'Up Where We Belong'. She was absolutely bowled over, couldn't believe it. That was really lovely, just as it was to be able to go back to Nicky Clarke and say we wanted the Catterick choir to sing Coldplay's 'Fix You'.

The final decision was to bring all the choirs to sing together on Paul's new song 'In My Dreams', recording them separately and combining their voices using technology.

'In My Dreams' needed a soloist: various singers came into the frame but none of them quite felt right. Then, as I was on the freeway heading into New York on my trip to America, I got a phone call from Tom Lewis saying, 'What about Jonjo Kerr, the guy from *X Factor*?' I immediately thought that was a bizarre suggestion after the strange rivalry with *X Factor* in the run-up to the Christmas number one, although by this point Simon Cowell had admitted to buying not one but two copies of 'Wherever You Are' and I had had a tweet from Gary Barlow saying, 'G, massive congrats, what a great idea, Happy Xmas, Gary x' (I had to check twice that it was definitely from him!).

The reason Jonjo had been suggested was that he was a serving soldier with the Yorkshire Regiment. Once we had dug a bit deeper into this, we realised that he would be going out to Afghanistan in the middle of recording. It seemed like the perfect situation: a serving soldier duetting with the wives of other soldiers who were already out in Afghanistan. Jonjo needed little persuasion. He even took time out from his leaving party, jumped on a train, came down to London, was taught the song, sang it, shot the video – filmed by my old friend Gratian Dimech again – got back on the train and went back to the party. A week later he was on a plane to Afghanistan.

The album was released on 5 March. There was another mini-bubble of media interest, promoting the album, setting us up in competition with the new Bruce Springsteen album, *Wrecking Ball*. I felt there was a real danger that we might get carried away after the success at Christmas. Would people want to buy a whole album? New Military Wives Choirs were spring-ing up (not just in the UK, but already on bases in Germany) and we were really proud of the album. Everyone was patting them-selves on the back: isn't it marvellous? It seemed a long time since those early days in Chivenor with all those women worry-ing about the men while they were away.

I had noticed one email going round from one of the choirs wishing Jonjo good luck on his deployment, which said, 'God speed,' and that really choked me up. I realised I had grown accustomed, maybe even de-sensitised, to the real reason we had been doing all of this, the root purpose of the Military Wives Choirs, and that it had become a kind of patter as I did yet another round of interviews with the press. Something about that phrase in the email, somebody saying 'God speed,' really got to me. It felt so old-fashioned, so timeless, but genuinely heartfelt.

Two days after the album had been released I got a text from Nicky Clarke asking me if I had heard or seen the news. Six British soldiers had been killed in Helmand province by a massive IED blast, including five from the 3rd Battalion, The Yorkshire Regiment, Jonjo's regiment. I was in a taxi when I heard the news and I exclaimed out loud: it was heartstopping. I felt sick to my core. I was thinking about Jonjo's wife and how horrendous it was that we were in the middle of doing the promotion for the album while this news was coming in – what if she hears his voice on the radio, and what if something has happened to him? – and simultaneously thinking even if it isn't Jonjo, if he is safe, just how terrible it really was. It brought back the harsh reality of the military wives' lives.

There were a few hours of not knowing the details, whether Jonjo had been involved in the incident or not. About three o'clock that afternoon I got another text saying he was all right. He had only been out in Helmand for a week; he was in a dangerous place, absolutely on the front line. I was starting to question whether it had been the right thing to ask him to sing the solo, but later that day we took the decision that we would carry on publicising the album, but soberly and appropriately, not wanting to be too triumphal nor getting involved in some story about an imaginary rivalry with Bruce Springsteen, which seemed entirely irrelevant. We would focus on why we were doing it, which was to raise money for the Foundation.

At this very sensitive and difficult moment the spirit of the women shone through once again. Sarah Stenning, the CO's wife at Battlesbury Barracks, Warminster, where Jonjo's battalion was based, had been asked if, given the circumstances, she would like to cancel an interview she was due to give about the Military Wives Choir she was involved in setting up at the garrison there. Her response was immediate: 'No, I'd like to do it anyway, because the choir has been such a support.'

I was very moved by her comment because it underlined that when everything is at its most terrible, that is exactly when the value of a choir comes into its own, and that all the nonsense about the album and Bruce Springsteen and the single and *X Factor* was utterly, utterly irrelevant. What was important was the power of singing together to provide strength and support in the bleakest of circumstances, which is where the whole project had begun. Within the week we were number one in the album chart. There were more media opportunities arising; the ladies of Chivenor and Plymouth triumphed with their performance at the National Television Awards, receiving a standing ovation for their rendition of 'Make You Feel My Love'. They were turning into seasoned performers.

So what next? How could I follow the rollercoaster ride that I'd just stepped off? There was nothing for it. It was time to put *The Choir* on a back burner.

Keep on Turning

In the aftermath of everything that had happened in the run-up to Christmas, I think everyone involved with *The Choir* felt, not that it had run its natural course, but that *The Choir: Military Wives* had been such a strong series it would be very difficult, nigh on impossible, to top it. In terms of taking a group of people who had never done any choral singing and giving them a vision of what is possible through singing, I cannot think of a better example than what the Wives and I had achieved together.

I had taken a group of women who had never sung before and had a Christmas number one hit. We had got the first choral classical piece of music to be a number one ever, which was bringing choirs into the mainstream in the way I had hoped we might be able to through the TV exposure when I first started.

Alongside this I had seen people, weirdly, using the term 'the Gareth Malone effect', and more and more people turning up to choirs saying, 'Oh, I watched *The Choir* on BBC so I've decided to come and join.' I read an interview with Sam Burns, the choirmaster who runs the Gurt Lush Community Choir in Bristol. Sam said he had been an ex-pat in France running choirs there so he had missed the series of *The Choir*. He came back to the UK, put up a request asking for anyone interested in a community choir and was swamped with people wanting to come out and sing. He had not banked on this and wasn't prepared for the huge turnout; he said he was grateful as most of his work was now coming because of the effect of the programmes.

It proved that, especially with the chart success of 'Wherever You Are', everybody would now have different expectations. It would change the dynamic. In all the series of *The Choir* the majority of the people who were involved were not necessarily aware of the programmes. Now if I went into a community and said, 'You may not think singing is a good idea, but let me tell you it is! Hey, do you want to sing?' they'd all chorus, 'Oh yeah, like on the Military Wives – I'm in.' And then they would be hugely disappointed if they didn't automatically get a number one single. I was on a riverboat trip in the New Year and one of crew stopped me to say, 'Oh, all us blokes out on the river, we sing, we all love a bit of karaoke … How about making a series with us?' Everyone was coming out of the woodwork.

So, as is my natural desire, I wanted to do something slightly different. One option was to go down the path of being a thoughtful talking head on Radio 3 or BBC Four, following in the footsteps of the likes of Howard Goodall or Simon Russell Beale. I enjoy doing those kinds of programme, and I love talking about classical music anywhere, anytime, but it seemed to me that what I *really* like doing is bringing choirs to a bigger audience and a more popular audience. I felt I had found my niche, which is in a more general audience space. I wanted to do something that combined all of the above with the fact that I am really rather competitive, which I like bringing out of people. How could I tap into that?

I had also been doing some team-building work with companies – from a food company to an investment bank and a think-tank – encouraging their staff to sing as part of staff training days. This had all been off camera and proved an enjoyable way of doing extra work when I wasn't filming. I had had some good feedback from the companies about the effect it had, and what surprised me was how emotional it could be.

Twenty Twenty and the BBC had been developing some ideas for the new series, one of which was the concept of workplace choirs. They had thought that more choirs and a more competitive edge would be interesting, so ultimately all of these ingredients were merged into the idea for *Sing While You Work*. I would go to four British companies, set up choirs in their workplaces and then let them battle it out.

For a business to spend money, resources and people-time on larking around in a choir is a difficult proposition in economically lean times, when sending people on team-building events is becoming harder and harder to justify. The choir idea, based on the company premises, seemed better suited for straitened times, but it still required a significant level of investment from the company – they'd have to commit their staff to rehearsals during work hours.

In late February 2012 I went off to the Severn Trent Water company. On my first day I walked into their new HQ building in the middle of Coventry, a lovely modern office, and met the management and the inhouse teams who run the call centre, handle billing and deal with complaints – all of the admin people. I have to confess that the environment felt a tiny bit soulless, but then I don't usually find myself in traditional workplaces.

However, that afternoon I auditioned about 120 people: they were good. They could really sing. I was pleasantly reassured. The next day I went out on the road to spend time with the guys who actually dig the holes in the road and maintain what they call 'the network', all the pipes. Later on I visited a sewage works. Now, singing has taken me to some extraordinary places but I have to say the sewage works was one of the weirdest, and absolutely fascinating. I don't know what I expected to find, but in fact there was a great pride in the work there and a real interest in and enthusiasm for the subject. I wanted to make sure all these workers had a chance to join the choir.

On that day I unearthed an extraordinarily high tenor who had never sung before: he was ex-army, now a reservist in the Paras, who goes out and finds leaks in the system. He told me he didn't sing, and then hit a top B flat absolutely cold, without any worries whatsoever. That was very exciting.

We auditioned everyone in groups, maybe 25 people at a time, and they sang in front of each other. To make it fair I asked them all to sing the same simple song, one we had chosen to be appropriate for their area of work. The water company's audition song was 'Row, Row, Row Your Boat' (we later used 'A Spoonful of Sugar' for the staff at Lewisham Hospital, and 'Those Magnificent Men in their Flying Machines' at Manchester Airport). The audition material was only a tiny phrase from the song, so that even if you didn't know the number already, you could easily learn it if you had a decent ear. Then I played them a couple of notes to sing to me. This was back to Northolt High and Glyndebourne territory: testing my ability to quickly pick out potential from a large pool of possibles.

I was not necessarily looking for people with singing experience, rather people with musical brains and instincts who were going to be able to blend and come together as a decent choir. The first clue I had that it might be working was a couple of weeks in. We had a team of musical directors and arrangers helping out by conducting rehearsals with one choir when I was rehearsing with one of the others – this was a huge enterprise and required a large team of musicians.

One night I had a text from Lucy, a very experienced choir conductor, who was working with the water company. She said, 'This choir is AWESOME. I love them.' That was from somebody with real choral experience who had performed with choirs up and down the country and who was completely taken aback, as I had been, by the standard. But it wasn't just the standard that we were thrilled about, it was the way they'd come together and the energy they brought to their singing. The fact that they all worked for one company made them work as a choir.

And so to another workplace, Lewisham Hospital, where I found a very different group of people with a completely different range of singing experience. There were staff members from an African-Caribbean background who were experienced singers in gospel and church choirs alongside others who had studied music formally and been part of classical choirs. Almost immediately the sound they made was absolutely extraordinary, although they sang with less expression than the other choirs.

On my first visit to Lewisham it was very strange to enter the hospital doors and go 'backstage'. Just as in the water company, I was intrigued by the prospect of getting the behind-the-scenes staff involved alongside the people who are absolutely on the frontline dealing with the public, the nurses and the physiotherapists. We ended up with a choir including nurses and junior doctors from A&E, a vascular surgeon, the anaesthetist who worked alongside him, the theatre nurse who handed over the scalpel, the guys who pushed the medicine and food trolleys around ...

There were two further companies on the list: Manchester Airport and The Royal Mail in Bristol. The Royal Mail is a fascinating and huge operation, but the radical change and modernisation it's faced in recent years has led to a divided workforce. During the first rehearsal I noticed that the union representative was sitting and singing next to one of the senior managers. Would this ignite fireworks or bring them together? For a postie, here was a chance to represent the entire workforce, an empowering position for someone on a lower grade within a company hierarchy.

Manchester Airport Choir had a different problem. The division in their company was between those on landside and those on airside. Since you need serious security clearance to cross from one to the other there was very little opportunity for people from different sides of the business to meet. There are also several employers at an airport: the staff of the airport itself, air traffic control, the baggage handlers, airlines and ground staff are all employed by different companies. This made it difficult, if not sometimes impossible, to find a time when everyone was free for rehearsals.

By the end of the audition process we ended up with a good cross-section across the four companies from blue-collar to white-collar workers and management. In fact, in all the companies we found examples of people who had worked together for years but had never met face to face. Mick and Gill at Severn Trent had spoken countless times on the phone and were delighted to finally meet each other. CJ and Heather from the airport's security firm had never spoken about anything other than work and merely exchanged pleasantries. Now they were rehearsing together during their breaks, laughing and generally brightening up the security check area.

As soon as we got past the auditions and put the choirs together, I realised that we were in for a powerful contest. The standard was like nothing I'd had come across on previous series. Four-part harmony seemed no obstacle. I started talking about blend, about dynamic range, tone and vocal technique. This would be a joyous contest.

The choirs were strong but already very different. The Severn Trent Water choir was predominantly male – as the company itself was. At the Royal Mail it was also the men who dominated, whereas the hospital staff was around 70 per cent female, and at Manchester Airport we had the strongest of all the alto sections. And there were regional accents, the Bristol Royal Mail being the strongest and most obvious. As they sang their warm-up song (the theme tune to *Postman Pat*!) they sang with a broad Somerset/Bristolian accent that made me smile because it felt so idiosyncratic. I liked the regionality and tried to retain some of the individual sounds the choirs created. The Mancunians sang with a very open, flat sound that had plenty of energy but at times could be a little harsh. It seemed to reflect them as a group of people: they were fairly boisterous in those early rehearsals, especially Daz, an extrovert fireman.

Each choir also had its own sound: some were rich and technical, others gutsy and raw. Shaping them into choirs and bringing them up to scratch would be an interesting process both socially and musically. The next step was to select a challenging song that, as with the audition piece, related in some way to their field of work. For the Royal Mail it was 'Return to Sender', for Lewisham Hospital, REM's 'Everybody Hurts'.

At Severn Trent somebody suggested Take That's 'The Flood'. Everyone laughed out loud, thinking it was a great idea. Gravely a senior manager in the choir stepped in to say, 'Aah, I'm not so sure about that. We have had a flood, and it is not very funny,' which put the kibosh on that one. The next suggestion was made by one of the most junior people from the billing department, a girl who answers the phones but was quite authoritative in matters of music. She suggested 'Proud Mary' by Tina Turner ('Rollin', rollin', rollin' on the river'). That was taken on by everyone as a more appropriate choice. This is what singing can do in an otherwise hierarchical situation: bringing all those people together on a level – though thankfully not water-logged – playing-field to represent their company.

I had been determined to make sure that the challenge we set the choirs was really tough, so the music was technically far more demanding than anything we ever tackled on *The Choir* with close harmony and moments of *a cappella*. I love that aspect of programmes like *The Great British Bake Off* or *Masterchef* – those wonderful moments where the expert says,

'Your loaf has collapsed because the fibres of the bread haven't come together in the right way'; that level of genuine technical expertise. I felt that people had got used to the idea of choral singing being an interesting area; they knew that choirs were expressive and could see what could be achieved through them, but what they didn't know was *how* you do it.

Each choir had a different struggle. For the clinical and scientific hospital staff singing an emotional song was a stretch. For the Royal Mail to sing in four-part harmony was going to be hard work – they seemed to be the underdogs.

The thought of having all those choirs competing against each other, choirs that had emerged from an outreach project because they did not exist before, but drawing on the resources of the company, was exciting me. There were so many factors at play: the physicality of singing, the emotion and the intellectual business of actually learning how to sing as a choir.

What instantly became clear was that the idea of the contest brought out a competitive edge in everyone that made them work harder. Each choir knuckled down. At one point the Royal Mail Choir were rehearsing every night of the week.

The filming of each choir was happening concurrently so we were running from one company to another, a round trip of 500 miles each time. For a period of four months or so it seemed like I was never off a train or out of a car. I did the rounds of the workplaces, getting under the skin of the company ethic and helping the choirs to improve.

The way that each choir sang told me a lot about who they were as people. Equally, getting to know them as people helped me to understand how they should sing. The Manchester Airport crowd were very earthy in their humour, constantly bantering with me and each other. When we were batting about suggestions for their song they came up with a rocky number, 'Learn to Fly' by the Foo Fighters. I confessed that I'd never heard of it. 'That doesn't mean you shouldn't sing it, though,' I told them. Lisa, one of the sopranos, piped up, 'We can be your cool choir.' Much agreement from the floor. Something in their body language, facial expressions and open sound revealed their extrovert personalities, which came through in the singing from the start. Many of them were involved with jobs that meant dealing with the public – customer relations, security, first class lounge assistants – all roles which involve performance of a kind. Unexpectedly it made them very well suited to singing in a choir.

Each company worked towards a performance in their own workplace in front of the other staff. This would be a chance to get the whole company behind them. All over the country people began to gather: sewage workers, baggage handlers, nurses and posties crammed into venues not at all designed for choral singing. The airport choir had to contend with the noise of aeroplanes; the hospital didn't have a large space so we squeezed into the newly refurbished casualty department (before it was officially open). Only at Severn Trent Water was there a suitable acoustic in the cathedral-like space of their shiny head office. For the Royal Mail we headed to one of the larger sorting centres, like a ginormous aircraft hanger. I managed to get the noisy sorting machines turned off until we'd finished singing. A few of the other workers stood around in their hi-vis jackets with dazed expressions, not quite knowing what to make of this musical *coup d'état* that had silenced their workplace.

In each case there were surprises, there were nerves and, occasionally, blind terror. One member of the Royal Mail choir clung to her friend's hand with tears in her eyes throughout the ordeal. But generally, as is so often the case, they came off stage elated, exclaiming, 'I want to do it again!' I then had the chance to meet their families and co-workers. Quizzing them about the effect that the choir was having, I was interested to hear how it had become such a talking point. I had not considered how routine many people feel their jobs are: my own job is anything but routine. For all these singers, the choir was a break from the norm and taking part had encouraged them to evaluate what their company meant to them.

As a result of rehearsing and performing together, a bond was forming. The singers began to speak warmly about the other members of the choir and how lovely it was to meet people from other departments. People they had never met before from their own company could now be called friends. These groups of singles had been transformed into emblems of a cooperative way of working. This was most evident in the Royal Mail.

The weekend before filming started it was announced in the news that the Royal Mail was in danger of being sold off. When I arrived there was a combustible mix of heavy pessimism and bullish optimism in the air. Change had torn people apart. Families that used to work together had been troubled by redundancy. Some had taken it on the chin, but even these most positive workers felt huge trepidation about the future.

Sam has a portrait of the Queen in his kitchen (lifesize) – he and many other colleagues were genuinely upset that they might lose their 'Royal' title. Sam had served as a union rep through the worst of the industrial disputes. He told me that the workforce understood the need for change but that in the past they felt management had tried to push too much through without properly consulting the experts: the people that actually do the job. Happily this too was something that was changing. Tim, the senior manager in the choir, said that they were now road-testing ideas and consulting more widely before implementing change. I saw plenty of examples of this on my weekly tours around the company: new delivery systems, improved transport and modern trolleys to help posties carry all those Amazon packages we all love to receive.

The effect of this *esprit de corps* could be felt in the choir: they wanted to work together and as a group seemed determined not to let difference of rank interfere with the singing. We talked repeatedly about change and several members of the choir showed themselves to be passionate about the company. It reminded me of the passion shown by dock workers, steel workers and miners about their industries. Underlining this passion was a zeal that the company could once again be a world leader for mail delivery. For the most part it wasn't, as I'd suspected, a nostalgic view where a jolly postie rings the bell on his bike as he delivers a couple of extremely light letters early in the morning before popping home for lunch. Everyone seemed to understand the need to be competitive in the modern world and adapt to the changes that are happening in mail.

This new willingness to change became a mantra for the choir. They embraced criticism and worked hard to improve their sound. They operated as a prime example of teamwork. Tim told me that after filming finished he wanted the choir to tour other mail centres to inspire the national workforce and encourage more pride in the organisation.

At the hospital the mood was very different. Rather than the direct, and potentially divisive, split between workforce and management I experienced at Severn Trent Water and the Royal Mail, there was a clear hierarchical structure. Everyone knows their place in a hospital and they seem happy to stay there since it is a pretty well-oiled machine. The porters recognise that they are relatively low down the pecking order and the surgeons know they are at the top.

I spoke off camera to a pharmaceutical porter called Aaron who told me that through being in the choir he had a new appreciation of how much pressure those further up the chain were under. Eddie, a tough-talking vascular surgeon, always entered rehearsals looking slightly flustered and had probably just come from cutting some poor soul apart with a very sharp scalpel. Sitting together in the choir humanised them both. Eddie, in particular, approached the music technically, much as he would approach a patient. He was not one for the touchy-feely stuff, and admitted that for him slicing into a patient was 'like making a cup of tea ... and it has to be.' In Eddie's world there is little room for emotional engagement: you do your job as well as you can, you tell other people what you need and then you get out. Job done. It's about saving lives.

As someone who has been in a hospital room when the staff have had to deliver bad news to loved ones I instinctively lurched when he said this. With every fibre of my being I want the hospital to care for me in the holistic sense. But actually Eddie is right. He said, 'People have the wrong idea of what the hospital does. I'm not here to hold your hand, I'm here to save your life.' As cold as it sounds it's true; you don't want a surgeon to be clouded by the emotions of the patients and their families. It was so interesting to hear this from the doctor's side. Eddie was under immense pressure to achieve the impossible and practically resurrect people. Why should I demand an emotional empathy as well?

When it comes to singing and representing your workplace through a choir it's a different matter. Eddie and others resisted what they considered to be the mawkish sentimentality of the song I chose for them, singing with precision but a total lack of emotional engagement. They had trained themselves out of feeling. This was where the more 'lowly' members of the choir came into their own: Derek the food porter, Sarah the young physio and Natalie, a speech and language therapy assistant, all sang with the heart I was looking for. I just had to inspire the same emotion in the rest of the choir.

Natalie was particularly interesting because she was a part of the hospital's work in the community following the birth of her daughter, who had various complications in her early months, which resulted in her being profoundly deaf. Natalie's whole reason for being at the hospital was because she wanted to help other parents who, like her, were adjusting to life with a deaf child. She personified empathy.

I wanted 'Everybody Hurts' not to be 'sentimental' as Eddie had charged but rather a warm, outgoing message from the hospital to its patients. The words 'Hold on, hold on' repeated at the end of the song seemed to me perfect for this group of people dedicated to helping others. Where singing had given the

Military Wives Choir a voice, I wanted the hospital choir to be a front door for the organisation, one that made people understand that they would receive an excellent level of care.

The choir were suspicious. I think they thought I was deliberately trying to make them cry for the purposes of television. Their suspicions were unfounded – I was trying to get them to perform expressively, but I challenge people and *that* makes them cry. Singing an emotional song should be moving for the listener, not necessarily for the singer … but you have to feel *something*. We had a good old tussle over this song.

In the end, the hospital choir produced a beautiful sound and a convincing performance. In each location people seemed astonished by what these singers had achieved in such a short space of time. The Manchester Airport choir blasted their way through 'Movin' On Up' by Primal Scream to squeals of delight from an extremely partisan crowd. The water company rocked out their version of 'Proud Mary', showing great potential in their rendering of the close harmony. Bristol's Royal Mail choir was bopping to the refrain 'Return to Sender'.

Confidence was high. But I had a little surprise up my sleeve that would jolt everybody and sharpen up their performance. There was somebody unexpected in the audience.

Singing with a Swing

Ralph Allwood MBE is a conductor, choir trainer and for 25 years was Eton's Precentor, a wonderful Latin title for the director of the chapel choir at the school. At the Royal Mail in Bristol, dressed in tweeds and smart tie, he stood out a mile in a roomful of posties. Ralph was to be one of three judges at the semi-final and finals of the *Sing While You Work* contest, but he'd come along incognito, though clearly not undercover, to check up on the choir's progress.

Revealing the presence of the judge to the choir filled me with a sense of glee. Although at first, when I told them who he was, they were ashen-faced, they were nonetheless hungry to find out what he thought. Ralph entered the choir room to nervous applause. He grinned back with his winning schoolboy charm and immediately congratulated them warmly. Relief. Not just for them, for me too. I'd seen Ralph conduct and knew that he'd seen it all before, so I was also nervous. Ralph gave the Bristol choir some praise and then, reading the room, said, 'But you want the good stuff, don't you? You want to know how to improve.' Everyone nodded and murmured in agreement.

Before he let rip with his salvos of criticism it struck me that here was a group of singers who only weeks before had been terrified of singing, but were now eagerly waiting for a top choral expert to lay into them, even looking forward to it. It's amazing what a performance can do for confidence. They were so buoyed up by the success of performing to their colleagues, friends and families that they knew they could take it.

Of course Ralph has a way of sugaring the pill. All good conductors of amateur choirs know this to be vital: you can destroy morale with a single unkind word. Visiting all four choirs, Ralph and his fellow judge Manvinder Rattan (the musical director of the John Lewis Partnership) delivered a range of improvements that they wanted to see. The key points related to the impact of the sound, breathing more effectively, connecting with the audience and creating a good blended sound.

Almost immediately the four choirs set to work. One or two were dismayed to discover that they had new songs to learn. These songs were to be show numbers: 'Sing, Sing, Sing', 'Accentuate the Positive', 'The Rhythm of Life' and 'If They Could See Me Now'. The idea behind this choice was that all the choirs needed to get away from focusing solely on the sound and start selling their songs to the audience. During the first performances, all four choirs had stared at me as if their very lives depended on it and the judges had noted that for the most part their expressions looked as if their families were being held at gunpoint: not ideal for a performance that is supposed to be entertaining.

I set the Manchester Airport choir some homework: to get out and sing to their colleagues, practising in front of each other and concentrating on making eye contact. When I returned for the next rehearsal the results were startling. The entire choir had come to life – Lisa from the sopranos had choreographed movements that verged on dance moves. The altos leapt in on their first phrase, with smouldering intensity, eying up the audience and making a certain conductor feel a little hot under the collar ...

The spirit of jazz was infecting the workplaces of the UK. But at the hospital some serious choral rehearsal was underway. The choir spent hours getting their vowel sounds to match perfectly so that they could achieve the desired blend requested by Manvinder Rattan. This may sound overly technical but is actually fairly basic: if, for example, the choir has to sing an 'oo' vowel there could conceivably be 30 regional variations of the pronunciation of 'oo'. It's the choirmaster's job to encourage unity – it doesn't particularly matter which 'oo' you sing, Yorkshire, Cardiff or London, as long as everyone does the same. When the same vowel flows across the whole choir the effect is stunning – the sound becomes one. All 30 voices blend and become indistinguishable from each other.

The second technical consideration bothering me was the question of volume. My goodness, did they all shout. There is a general problem with singing that people tend to mistake 'intensity' for 'volume' – instead of investing energy in making the words crystal clear there's a natural tendency just to bellow and hope for the best. At Bristol this was reaching epidemic proportions.

In movies pirates are often given a Bristolian accent because so many seafaring folk came from that town. With their tendency to crank up the volume, the Royal Mail choir were starting to sound more like Cap'n Blackbeard's Shantymen. With days to go before the semi-final I returned to the Royal Mail to see what they had prepared. What was instantly clear was that they were not workshy: they had practised every single day and they were totally on top of the extremely complicated words from 'Rhythm of Life' and the only marginally less complicated dance moves, which had to accommodate Peter the bass with his walking stick, a soprano with a very bad back and several examples of two-left-footedness. It shouldn't have worked. It should have sounded dreadful. And yet from their first run-through it was electrifying to behold.

They gave it everything. Now it was time for me to contend with the volume issue. I finally persuaded them that singing quietly would make all the difference. There was a moment of epiphany when they eventually began with a tiny sound, mouthing their words like demons possessed by some unearthly spirit. As the song went on, however, they returned to their default position: the shout.

As a choirmaster you often pray for inspiration to St Cecilia, the patron saint of music. I closed my eyes and sent the good saint the mental equivalent of a desperate text message: how could I convert this bunch of piratical posties into a well-drilled choral unit? My prayer was answered: I was prompted to ask the men (as I often do) to imitate opera singers. Instantly the penny – or at least the doubloon – dropped. The sound became rich, pleasant to listen to and genuinely choral. There was stunned silence from the ladies. '*Why* haven't you been making that sound all along?' I implored. I begged them to remember this fantastic sound for the semi-final because there was no question in my mind that they were the underdogs.

The day of the semi-final arrived and I pulled up in a black cab to Colston Hall, a 2,000-seat concert venue in the heart of the city of Bristol. By the end of the day one of the four choirs would be eliminated. The two male judges were joined by gospel and soul legend Ruby Turner as the coachloads of singers began arriving.

Lewisham Hospital choir had a difficult journey. They had set off at 7am and arrived shortly after 1pm. I could have cycled there quicker. But hospital staff must be used to long hours and hardship: I didn't hear one murmur of complaint. They simply smiled and got on with it. The NHS spirit at work. After a perfunctory rehearsal in the hall for each choir, it was time to perform. Showtime – and time for a showdown.

Coda: Make This Moment Last for Ever

Just when everything looked like we might have reached the pinnacle of the Military Wives experience, I received another message from Gary Barlow at the very beginning of 2012: 'Can I grab 30 mins with you sometime to talk about the Diamond Jubilee?'

I had little difficulty finding the necessary half an hour, and arrived at Gary's West London house very excited but utterly parched. Gary welcomed me warmly and popped the kettle on. Suffice to say, it's a nice house. We exchanged pleasantries and sat at his kitchen table to establish what he wanted. He told me that he'd teamed up with Andrew Lloyd Webber to create a song for Her Majesty the Queen's Diamond Jubilee concert in June. Gary was going to travel the world finding and recording musicians for the track and he wanted the Military Wives Choir to be the main artist. We would also be performing at the Jubilee concert outside Buckingham Palace in front of the Queen and the Royal Family, a crowded Mall and a TV audience of millions both in the UK and around the Commonwealth.

Gary said he had become aware of my work a few years before, but when he heard and saw 'Wherever You Are', 'All of a sudden I thought, "Ooh ..." I'd been asked about the Jubilee and felt it could be a very interesting angle, because of the nature of it, being servicemen's wives, the British stamp on it all.'

I was stunned that our little project had come to this. A week or two later I found myself face to face with Gary again as he sang me the track that they'd penned for us. It's a situation that many women (and a fair few men) would probably kill to be in: a private performance from Take That's GB himself. The pressure was immense as he scrutinised my face for the slightest reaction. Would I like it? Could the Military Wives sing it? I had been determined to tell him the truth, whatever it was. Thank goodness I liked it on first listen.

Gary is used to playing songs to people, but I felt that this was something different, more of a personal project than some of his records may have been. 'I don't want to sound over-confident,' he remembers, 'but I knew it was a bloody good song. I'd have been surprised and shocked if you'd have turned round and gone, "Nah, I can't hear it."' I was privileged to be played the song so early in the process. 'You were the first person other than me and Andrew to hear the song. As soon as you smiled on the third play of the chorus I could see how it was going to work, how it was going to fit in. An exciting moment.' An exciting moment indeed and the first of many to come.

Gary booked Studio One at Abbey Road to record the choir. The pressure was mounting. I was now faced with something of a dilemma – should I invite only the 'originals' from Chivenor, Plymouth and Catterick, or should I attempt to represent the burgeoning national choirs?

I weighed up the decision with Nicky Clarke. There was much to be gained from inviting select members from across the ten choirs that existed at the time. Unlike the preparation for 'Wherever You Are', which had been intense, I was unavailable to rehearse the choir since I was now filming *Sing While You Work*. Choosing the best singers from across all the choirs seemed to me to be the only way to guarantee the best possible performance. This was a record for the Queen, after all. It had to be good and it had to be right first time. I also wanted the effect of being involved in such an amazing concert to spread around the new choirs – so that those involved could return to their own choirs more confident, more experienced and having the authority gained from representing the MWC on the national stage. It was the best way to proceed.

Of course holding auditions meant that inevitably some women did not get that opportunity. It was especially difficult for some members of the Chivenor choir. It reminded me of the moment when we spread the choir from Chivenor to Plymouth; the women had reacted badly to the thought that they might lose the choir that had begun to mean so much to them. I took this objection seriously but felt that the overall benefit to the MWC outweighed the fact that some women would not be coming.

The night before the recording we gathered together at the Marriott Hotel on Kilburn High Road and I heard this hastily assembled National Military Wives Choir for the first time. It was unbelievable. The sound of those women's voices was utterly beautiful. Auditioning, although difficult, had produced a musical level that was far beyond the achievement of any one choir. The individual choir leaders from all over the country had prepared the singers for their trip to London, and as soon as I heard the results I fell in love with the sound.

From the word go the recording session was remarkable. The women sang with an unbelievable confidence and were immaculately in tune. As I looked around the crowd I could see women from all over the country united under one banner. Many of them had partners in Afghanistan or other parts of the world as we were singing. For them to sing for the Queen was a huge honour and there were many tears of pride shed that day.

Gary had trudged around the world creating the backing track and this was the first time he'd heard the wives sing it. There was an element of risk for him; the investment in making the song and the accompanying documentary was significant: 'It was like working backwards. One of the first things you usually do on a record is get your vocal in and build everything else around it. We were doing it the other way round, adding the vocals last. So when the choir started to sing all of a sudden it was like that shot in *Jaws* when everything comes into focus. It was making sense. I knew then that it was going to work.'

Final preparations were soon underway for the concert itself. I saw Gary early in the week of the single's release to do some publicity at Radio 2. As we headed up in the lift to appear on the Chris Evans show he told me about the stage that had been built around the Victoria Memorial on the Mall. I couldn't wait. The single went in at number 11 in the singles charts (a mild disappointment for us given our track record!).

However, that was before the concert. On the day itself, when I walked out onto the stage I had never experienced anything like the noise that over 200,000 people can make. It was electrifying. I warmed up the audience by teaching them the refrain 'Just SIIIIIIIIIIINNNNGGGG'. They sounded amazing. As I looked around all the faces, I could see were beaming and singing along.

I caught Gary's eye a couple of times during the performance and he looked elated. The women felt that Gary was the main attraction, but for him it was the other way around. Gary remembers: 'Every time I looked at the wives they all waved at me, blowing kisses, and it was like, "No, no, *you're* the stars up here. This is *your* record. I'm playing the piano while you sing: I'm the backline here."'

The Military Wives Choir sang their hearts out. For Gary the occasion was bigger than any of us could comprehend. Gary felt this was more than a simple dedication: 'Although it was for the Queen and we all knew that it was, it was so much bigger than that. Our whole understanding of this record was to bring the nation together with one voice.'

Later in the concert we stood by the side of the stage to sing the National Anthem. Her Majesty the Queen passed close to us and smiled as she went by. On her way back from lighting the beacon (a rather theatrical moment where she used a large diamond to ignite a towering flame, marking the official moment of celebration), the Queen stopped to speak to us. Unfailingly polite, she thanked us for our contribution. Fireworks went off and the band struck up 'Land of Hope and Glory'. I looked down the line and saw many of the women begin to cry.

We had come so far together. Congratulations came thick and fast that night – not just for the Jubilee single, but for everything that had happened to us in the last six months. Sir Elton John embraced me, as did Annie Lennox. Sir Paul McCartney, a hero of mine, said he'd been watching my career with interest. I told him that I'd been watching his and that he'd done very well indeed ... Miranda Hart tried to get me to photograph her with Sir Cliff Richard in the background. It was a surreal evening.

At the end of the evening I stood in Buckingham Palace with my wife Becky and Nicky Clarke. With a glass of champagne we toasted the success of the Military Wives Choir and all the women who had made this dream a reality. At precisely that moment HRH Prince William, the Duke of Cambridge interrupted us to add his congratulations. Prince William told us with gentle humour that many of the men he worked with had wives in a MWC and that they'd all been complaining that they'd been forced to pay for dresses for the performance. Taking a more serious tone he thanked us for everything that the MWC was doing to offer support to more and more women.

We'd done it. The Military Wives had achieved a level of recognition that was unimaginable less than a year before. We'd been to Number 10 Downing Street where the Prime Minister had given us his backing and promised me he would look into reimbursing the VAT on the charity single at Christmas. General Sir David Richards, chief of the defence staff, the most important man in the military, had told me how much he valued the work we'd done. Now we had the Royal seal of approval: the Queen herself wrote to us to say that the choir was a highlight of the Jubilee concert.

In case I'd been in any doubt about Her Majesty's enthusiasm for the Military Wives Choir, one night at the Royal Academy of Arts the Queen presented me with a Diamond Jubilee award for contribution to the arts. To say I was surprised is an understatement. After the Queen had presented me with the most astonishing crystal chalice I have ever clapped eyes on, I stood in a small huddle with Sir Jonathan Ive (Apple's head of design), Bono, Sir Derek Jacobi and Alan Yentob.

The Queen approached and exchanged greetings with Sir Jonathan before addressing the assembled crowd: 'I just love the way this man gets everyone singing.' Her gloved hand waved in my general direction. 'Do you sing, Ma'am?' I enquired. 'I *can* sing,' she retorted. 'I just like the way you get *everyone else* singing.' The faintest of smiles played across her lips: the famous dry wit, and then she was off to meet a thousand other people.

Many people have asked me if the Queen is musical. I have evidence to suggest that she has a good ear. Before the Diamond Jubilee concert I was asked by Lord Lloyd Webber to bring six of the singers from the choir to perform the song with Gary Barlow for the Queen's private birthday party. I jumped at the chance and we found ourselves at Lloyd Webber's country house singing our hearts out to a crowd of royal guests. After our performance the Queen remarked to me that 'the melody of the chorus is quite complex.' She was right. It's not an easy sing, requiring a few vocal leaps.

I suddenly realised that the Queen has probably attended more musical performances than anyone else in the world. She is surrounded by music from the moment she wakes up. Of *course* she has an opinion on it. During the press launch we were unsure how to answer the delicate question of whether the Queen actually liked the song. Andrew Lloyd Webber was asked this live on Chris Evans' show and responded by saying that the Queen rarely passes comment about her personal feelings. Later that day we had word from Buckingham Palace that the Queen did indeed like the song and we could go ahead and tell everyone. We all swelled with pride.

A few weeks later I had an envelope from the Prime Minister's office to tell me that I'd been nominated for an OBE for services to music. The letter is worded to say that your name has been put forward for approval by the Queen, so you have to wait until the day the list is announced for official confirmation. The confirmation came at last and so I'm now officially Dr Gareth Edmund Malone OBE DMus (H.C.) ARAM FRSA pgDip dipABRSM BA(Hons). Isn't that absurd? I think of myself as Gareth.

It is seven years since I was initially contacted by Ana DeMoraes and more than a decade since I got the job with the London Symphony Orchestra. Over that period I have worked with some of the most brilliant people in the country and they have helped me to understand the value of singing with other people. It feels as though the recognition was not just for my personal work but also for choirs in general. There is no doubt in my mind that choirs are now a mainstream activity as they once were in the nineteenth century and as they should be.

Playing a part in that re-imagining of what choirs could be in the twenty-first century has been tremendous fun and a huge honour.

Through all the rehearsals, the pain and the nights working away from home, one thought has sustained me: music belongs to everyone. There are times when we are isolated, depressed or just need the company of others; for me there is no finer way to lift the spirits than by singing. Singing is a gift we all share, and watching all these choirs over the past seven years as they discover this precious ability has inspired me to keep working. I would be nothing without their voices, and to all of them I offer my sincerest thanks.